HUMAN
RESOURCE
MANAGEMENT
ESSENTIAL PERSPECTIVES

6E

HUMAN
RESOURCE
MANAGEMENT
ESSENTIAL PERSPECTIVES

6E

ROBERT L. MATHIS
University of Nebraska at Omaha

JOHN H. JACKSON
University of Wyoming

SOUTH-WESTERN
CENGAGE Learning™

Australia • Brazil • Japan • Korea • Mexico • Singapore • Spain • United Kingdom • United States

SOUTH-WESTERN
CENGAGE Learning™

Human Resource Management: Essential Perspectives, Sixth Edition

Dr. Robert L. Mathis, Dr. John H. Jackson

Vice President of Editorial, Business: Jack W. Calhoun

Vice President/Editor-in-Chief: Karen Schmohe

Senior Acquisition Editor: Michele Rhoades

Senior Developmental Editor: Susanna C. Smart

Senior Editorial Assistant: Ruth Belanger

Marketing Manager: Gretchen Swann

Marketing Coordinator: Leigh T. Smith

Senior Marketing Communications Manager: Jim Overly

Content Project Management: PreMediaGlobal

Media Editor: Rob Ellington

Frontlist Buyer, Manufacturing: Miranda Klapper

Rights Acquisition Specialist: Sam Marshall

Production Service: PreMediaGlobal

Senior Art Director: Tippy McIntosh

Internal Designer: PreMediaGlobal

Cover Designer: Tippy McIntosh

Cover Image: ©Tippy McIntosh

For product information and technology assistance, contact us at **Cengage Learning Customer & Sales Support, 1-800-354-9706**

For permission to use material from this text or product, submit all requests online at **www.cengage.com/permissions** Further permissions questions can be emailed to **permissionrequest@cengage.com**

Library of Congress Control Number: 2011927004

ISBN-13: 978-0-538-48170-0

ISBN-10: 0-538-48170-6

South-Western
5191 Natorp Boulevard
Mason, OH 45040
USA

Cengage Learning is a leading provider of customized learning solutions with office locations around the globe, including Singapore, the United Kingdom, Australia, Mexico, Brazil, and Japan. Locate your local office at: **www.cengage.com/global**

Cengage Learning products are represented in Canada by Nelson Education, Ltd.

To learn more about South-Western, visit **www.cengage.com/ South-Western**

Purchase any of our products at your local college store or at our preferred online store **www.cengagebrain.com**

Printed in the United States of America
1 2 3 4 5 6 7 15 14 13 12 11

Dr. Robert L. Mathis

Dr. Robert L. Mathis is Professor Emeritus of Management at the University of Nebraska at Omaha (UNO). Born and raised in Texas, he received a BBA and MBA from Texas Tech University and a PhD in Management and Organization from the University of Colorado. At UNO he has received the University's "Excellence in Teaching" award.

Dr. Mathis has co-authored several books and published numerous articles covering a variety of topics during his career. Dr. Mathis also has held national offices in the Society for Human Resource Management (SHRM) and served as President of the Human Resource Certification Institute (HRCI). He also is certified as a Senior Professional in Human Resources (SPHR) by HRCI.

He has had extensive consulting experiences with organizations of all sizes and in a variety of areas. Firms assisted have been in the telecommunications, telemarketing, financial, manufacturing, retail, health care, and utility industries. He has extensive specialized consulting experience in establishing or revising compensation plans for small- and medium-sized firms. Internationally, Dr. Mathis has consulting and training experience with organizations in Australia, Lithuania, Romania, Moldova, and Taiwan.

Dr. John H. Jackson

Dr. John H. Jackson is Professor of Management at the University of Wyoming. Born in Alaska, he received his BBA and MBA from Texas Tech University. He worked in the telecommunications industry in human resources management for several years before completing his PhD in Management and Organization at the University of Colorado. During his academic career, Dr. Jackson has authored six other college texts and more than 50 articles and papers, including those appearing in *Academy of Management Review, Journal of Management, Human Resource Management,* and *Human Resources Planning.* He has consulted with a variety of organizations on HR and management development matters and served as an expert witness in a number of HR-related cases. At the University of Wyoming, he has served four terms as department head in the Department of Management and Marketing. Dr. Jackson received the university's highest teaching award and has been recognized for his work with two-way interactive television for MBA students. Two Wyoming governors have appointed him to the Wyoming Business Council and the Workforce Development Council. Dr. Jackson serves as president of Silverwood Ranches, Inc.

The importance of human resource issues for managers and organizations is evident every day. As indicated by frequent headlines and news media reports on downsizing, shortages of qualified workforce, employee discrimination, union activity, and other topics, the management of human resources is growing in importance in the United States and the world. Many individuals are affected by HR issues; consequently, they will benefit by becoming more knowledgeable about HR management and the nature of various activities. Every manager's HR actions can have major consequences for organizations.

This book has been prepared to provide an essential overview of HR management for students, HR practitioners, operating managers, and others in organizations. The positive reception of previous editions of *Human Resource Management: Essential Perspectives* confirmed the need for such a book. Consequently, we are pleased to provide an updated version. In addition, this book presents information in a way that is useful to various industry groups and professional organizations. Finally, this condensed view of HR management also addresses the interest in U.S. practices of HR management in other countries, making it a valuable resource for managers worldwide.

As authors, it is our belief that our book will continue to be a useful and understanding means for those desiring a concise discussion of the important issues and practices in HR management. It is our hope that it will contribute to more effective management of human resources in organizations.

Robert L. Mathis, PhD, SPHR
John H. Jackson, PhD

Brief Contents

Contents

HR's Role and Strategic Nature

HR—MEETING MANAGEMENT CHALLENGES

The role that HR plays in successful organizations is different today and can be a large part of an organization's success. Key issues include:

- Why HR has evolved from primarily an administrative function
- What are appropriate HR roles in Strategy Formulation
- How HR can measure its contributions to organizational success

Many resources affect an organization's performance. The people who are employed there are certainly a major contributor in some situations. Their talents, experience, reliability, expertise, and relationships affect the job they do and whether the organization succeeds or not. This chapter highlights how developing HR Frameworks for people to do their work successfully is important.

HUMAN RESOURCES AS ORGANIZATIONAL CORE COMPETENCY

As a field, human resource management is undergoing significant transformation. **Human resource (HR) management** is designing management systems to ensure that human talent is well used to accomplish organizational goals. Whether employees are in a big company with thousands of jobs or a small nonprofit agency, managing people in an organization is about more than simply administering a pay program, designing training, or avoiding lawsuits. If human resources are to be an important part of successfully competing in the marketplace, a different level of thinking about HR management is necessary.

The development and implementation of specific organizational strategies must be based on the areas of strength in an organization. Referred to as *core competencies*, those strengths are the foundation for creating a competitive advantage for an organization. A **core competency** is a unique capability that creates high value and differentiates an organization from its competition.

HR Functions

HR management can be thought of as seven interlinked functions taking place within organizations as Figure 1-1 shows. Additionally, external forces—legal, economic, technological, global, environmental, cultural/geographic, political, and social—significantly affect how HR functions are designed, managed, and changed. The functions can be grouped as follows:

- **Strategic HR Management:** As part of maintaining organizational competitiveness, *strategic planning for HR effectiveness* can be increased through the use of *HR metrics* and *HR technology*.

FIGURE 1-1 HR Management Functions

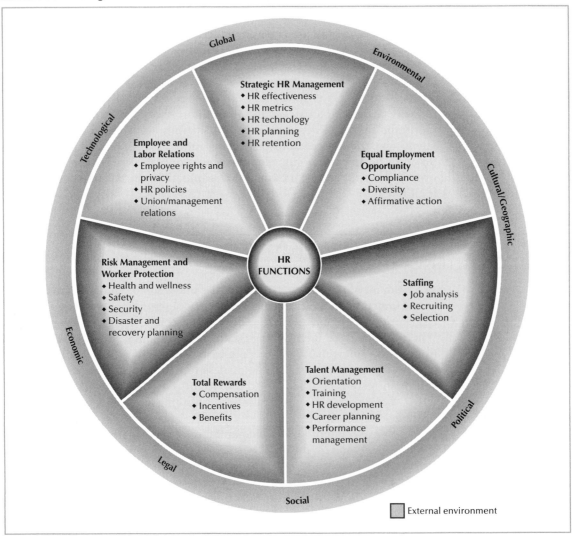

- **Equal Employment Opportunity:** *Compliance* with equal employment opportunity (EEO) laws and regulations affects all other HR activities.
- **Staffing:** The aim of staffing is to provide a sufficient supply of qualified individuals to fill jobs in an organization. *Workers, job design,* and *job analysis* lay the foundation for staffing by identifying what *people* do in their jobs. Through *HR planning,* managers anticipate the future supply and demand for employees and the nature of workforce issues, including the *retention* of employees. These factors are used when *recruiting* applicants for job openings. The *selection* process is concerned with choosing qualified individuals to fill those jobs.
- **Talent Management and Development:** Beginning with the *orientation* of new employees, talent management and development include different types of *training.* Also, *HR development* and *succession planning* of employees and managers is necessary to prepare for future challenges. *Career planning* identifies paths and activities for individual employees as they move within the organization. Assessing how well employees perform their jobs is the focus of *performance management.*
- **Total Rewards:** *Compensation* in the form of *pay, incentives,* and *benefits* rewards people for performing organizational work. To be competitive, employers develop and refine their basic *compensation* systems and may use *variable pay programs* such as incentive rewards. The rapid increase in the cost of *benefits,* especially health care benefits, will continue to be a major issue for most employers.
- **Risk Management and Worker Protection:** Employers must address various workplace risks to ensure protection of workers by meeting legal requirements and being more responsive to concerns for workplace *health* and *safety.* Also, workplace *security* has grown in importance along with *disaster and recovery planning.*
- **Employee and Labor Relations:** The relationship between managers and their employees must be handled legally and effectively. *Employer and employee rights* must be addressed. It is important to develop, communicate, and update *HR policies and procedures* so that managers and employees alike know what is expected. In some organizations, *union/management relations* must be addressed as well.

Organizational Culture and HR

The ability of an organization to use its human capital as a core competency depends in part on the organizational culture that is operating. **Organizational culture** consists of the shared values and beliefs that give members of an organization meaning and provide them with rules for behavior. The culture of an organization is seen in the norms of expected behaviors, values, philosophies, rituals, and symbols used by its employees, and it evolves over a period of time. Only if an organization has a history in which people have shared experiences for years does a culture stabilize. A relatively new firm, such as a business existing for less than 2 years, may not have developed a stabilized culture.

Competitive Advantage of Organizational Culture. Organizational culture should be seen as the "climate" of the organization that employees, managers, customers, and others experience. This culture affects service and quality, organizational productivity, and financial results. One facet of the culture of the organization, as viewed by the people in it, is that culture may affect the attraction and retention of competent employees.[1]

ORGANIZATIONAL PRODUCTIVITY

HR management can play a significant role in organizations by helping to create a culture that emphasizes effectiveness and productivity. In its most basic sense, **productivity** is a measure of the quantity and quality of work done, considering the cost of the resources used. Productivity can be a competitive advantage because when the costs to produce goods and services are lowered by effective processes, lower prices can be charged or more revenue made. Better productivity does not necessarily mean more output; perhaps fewer people (or less money or time) are used to produce the same amount.

One useful way of measuring the productivity of human resources is to consider **unit labor cost,** which is computed by dividing the average cost of workers by their average levels of output. Using unit labor costs, one can see that paying relatively high wages still can result in a firm being economically competitive if high productivity levels are achieved. Low unit labor costs can be a basis for a strategy focusing on human resources. Productivity and unit labor costs can be evaluated at the global, country, organizational, departmental, or individual level as part of various HR measurement metrics.

Productivity at the organizational level ultimately affects profitability and competitiveness in a for-profit organization and total costs in a not-for-profit organization. Perhaps of all the resources used for productivity in organizations, the ones often most closely scrutinized are the human resources. HR management efforts designed to enhance organizational productivity are as follows:

- *Organizational restructuring* involves eliminating layers of management and changing reporting relationships, as well as cutting staff through downsizing, layoffs, and early retirement buyout programs. That has become a concern in a number of industries as economic factors have changed.
- *Redesigning work* often involves having fewer employees who work longer hours and perform multiple job tasks. It may also involve replacing workers with capital equipment or making them more efficient by use of technology or new processes.
- *Aligning HR activities* means making HR efforts consistent with organizational efforts to improve productivity. This alignment includes ensuring that HR functions are not working against productivity.
- *Outsourcing analyses* involve HR in conducting cost-benefit analyses to justify outsourcing. Additional factors may include negotiating with outsourcing vendors, ensuring that contractors domestically and internationally are operating legally and appropriately, and linking organizational employees to the employees of the outsourcing firm.

Customer Service and Quality Linked to HR

Having managers and employees focus on customers contributes significantly to achieving organizational goals and maintaining competitive advantages. In most organizations, service quality is greatly influenced by individual employees who interact with customers. Employee job satisfaction also can be influenced by positive customer satisfaction. Customers often consider continuity of customer service representatives as important when making marketing and sales decisions.

Unfortunately, overall customer satisfaction with sales quality has declined in the United States and other countries. For example, the decline in customer satisfaction has affected many of the U.S. airlines. Even though some airlines have made efforts to improve services, customers continue to be rather skeptical of the improvements in the industry.[2]

Ethics and HR Management

Closely linked with the strategic role of HR is the way managers and HR professionals influence the ethics of people in organizations. How those ethics affect work and lives for individuals may aid in producing more positive work outcomes.

The need for great attention to ethics has grown in the past few years, as evidenced by the corporate scandals at numerous financial and investment firms in the United States and globally. These scandals illustrate that ethical lapses are not just symbolic; they affect numerous firms and employees. The expansion of the Internet has led to more publicity about ethical issues, including ethics in electronic job boards and postings. An increase in ethics issues has been identified by the Ethics Resource Center. One survey of 3,000 U.S. workers found that within a year, 52% had seen one incident of misconduct and 36% had observed two or more ethical violations. The survey also reported that almost 70% of the employers had done ethics training.[3]

The primary determinant of ethical behavior is organizational culture, which is the shared values and beliefs in an organization mentioned earlier. However, when the following four elements of ethics programs exist, ethical behavior is more likely to occur:

- A written code of ethics and standards of conduct
- Training on ethical behavior for all executives, managers, and employees
- Advice to employees on ethical situations they face, often made by HR
- Systems for confidential reporting of ethical misconduct or questionable behavior

Because people in organizations are making ethical decisions on a daily basis, HR management plays a key role as the "keeper and voice" of organizational ethics. All managers, including HR managers, must deal with ethical issues and be sensitive to how they interplay with HR activities. Figure 1-2 identifies some of the most frequent areas of ethical misconduct involving HR activities.

FIGURE 1-2 Examples of HR-Related Ethical Misconduct Activities

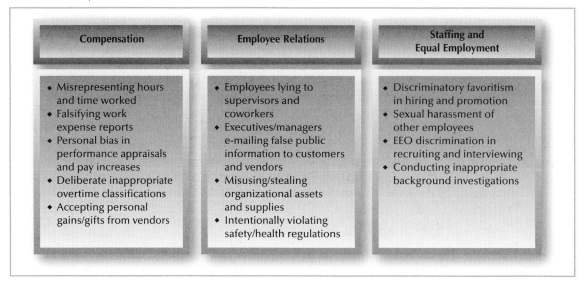

HR MANAGEMENT CHALLENGES

An overriding theme facing managers and organizations is to operate in a "cost-less" mode, which means continually looking for ways to reduce costs of all types—financial, operations, equipment, and labor. Pressures from global competitors have forced many U.S. firms to close facilities, use international outsourcing, adapt their management practices, increase productivity, and decrease labor costs to become more competitive. The growth of information technology, particularly that linked to the Internet, has influenced HR management as it handles the number, location, and required activities of employees.

These shifts have caused some organizations to reduce the number of employees, while at the same time scrambling to attract and retain employees with different capabilities than were previously needed. Responding to organizational cost pressures and restructurings, as well as the other HR challenges, has resulted in the transformation of HR management in organizations.

Economics and Job Changes

The shifts in the U.S. and global economy in the past years have changed the number and types of jobs present in the United States. The last recession affected many industries such as automotive and financial firms. In general, the United States has continued to have private- and public-sector jobs that are service economy in nature.

Further, projections of growth in some jobs and decline in others illustrate the shifts occurring in the U.S. economy. Most of the fastest-growing occupations percentage-wise are related to information technology and health care. The highest growth of jobs by percentage is in occupations that generally require more education and expertise training.

Workforce Availability and Quality Concerns. Various parts of the United States face significant workforce shortages that exist due to an inadequate supply of workers with the skills needed to perform the jobs being added. It may not be that there are too few people—only that there are too few with many of the skills being demanded. For instance, one survey of more than 2,000 employers found that the hardest jobs to fill are engineers, nurses, technicians, teachers, and sales representatives.[4]

Even though many Americans are graduating from high school and college, employers are concerned about the preparation and specific skills of new graduates. That is another reason why international outsourcing has grown. Unless major improvements are made to U.S. educational systems, U.S. employers will be unable to find enough qualified workers for the growing number of skilled jobs of all types. That is why talent management and development has become one of the most important issues emphasized by HR management.

Growth in Contingent Workforce. *Contingent workers* (temporary workers, independent contractors, leased employees, and part-timers) represent about one-fourth of the U.S. workforce. Many employers operate with a core group of regular employees who have critical skills, and then expand and shrink the workforce by using contingent workers.

The number of contingent workers has grown for many reasons. One reason is economics. Temporary workers are used to replace full-time employees, and many contingent workers are paid less and/or receive fewer benefits than regular employees. For instance, omitting contingent workers from health care benefits saves some firms 20% to 40% in labor costs.

Another reason for the increased use of contingent workers is that it may reduce legal liability for some employers. As more and more employment-related lawsuits have been filed, employers have become more wary about adding regular full-time employees. By using contract workers, including those in other countries, employers may reduce a number of legal issues regarding selection, discrimination, benefits, discipline, and termination.

Globalization of HR

The internationalization of business has proceeded at a rapid pace. Many U.S. firms, both large and small, receive a substantial portion of their profits and sales from other countries. Firms such as Coca-Cola, ExxonMobil, Microsoft, and General Electric derive half or more of total sales and profits from outside the United States. The reverse is also true. For example, Toyota, based in Japan, has grown its market share and its number of jobs in the United States and North America. Also, Toyota, Honda, Nissan, and other

Japanese automobile manufacturers, electronics firms, and suppliers have maintained operations in the United States, whereas Chrysler and General Motors have had to reduce major operations.

The globalization of business has shifted from trade and investment to the integration of global operations, management, and strategic alliances, which has significantly affected the management of human resources. Individuals from other countries are employees. There are three types of global workers: expatriate, host-country national, and third-country national.

An **expatriate** is a citizen of one country who is working in a second country and employed by an organization headquartered in the first country. Experienced expatriates can provide a pool of talent that can be tapped as the organization expands its operations more broadly into even more countries.

A **host-country national** is a citizen of one country who is working in that country and employed by an organization headquartered in a second country. Host-country nationals often know the culture, politics, laws, and business customs better than an outsider would.

A **third-country national** is a citizen of one country who is working in a second country and employed by an organization headquartered in a third country. For example, a U.S. citizen working for a British oil company as a manager in Norway is a third-county national. Staffing with third-country nationals shows a truly global approach.

When labor costs in the United States are compared with those in Germany and Korea, the differences are significant, as Figure 1-3 shows. As a result of these differences, many U.S. and European firms are moving jobs to lower-wage countries.

FIGURE 1-3 Hourly Compensation Costs for Manufacturing Production Workers

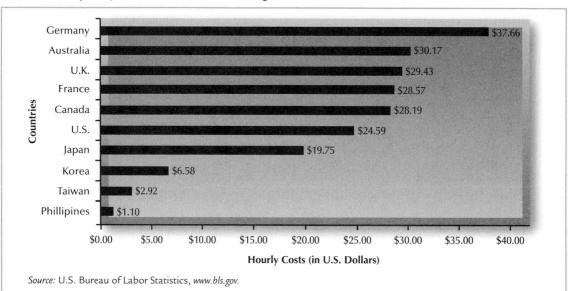

Source: U.S. Bureau of Labor Statistics, *www.bls.gov.*

Workforce Demographics and Diversity

The U.S. workforce has been changing dramatically. It is more diverse racially and ethnically, more women are in it than ever before, and the average age of its members is increasing. As a result of these demographic shifts, HR management in organizations has had to adapt to a more varied labor force both externally and internally. This growing diversity and aging of the workforce has raised employer concerns and means that HR is having to devote more time and effort to ensuring that nondiscriminatory policies and practices are followed.

HR Technology

Greater use of technology has led to organizational use of a *human resource management system (HRMS)*, which is an integrated system providing information used by HR management in decision making. This terminology emphasizes that making HR decisions, not just building databases and using technology, is the primary reason for compiling data in an information system.

The rapid expansion of HR technology serves two major purposes in organizations. One relates to administrative and operational efficiency, and the other to effectiveness. The most basic example is the automation of payroll and benefits activities. Beyond such basic applications, the use of Web-based information systems has allowed the HR unit in organizations to become more administratively efficient and communicate more quickly to employees.

The use of HR technology is also related to strategic HR planning. Having accessible data enables managerial decision making to be based to a greater degree on information rather than relying on managerial perceptions and intuition.

MANAGING HR IN ORGANIZATIONS

In a real sense, *every* manager in an organization is an HR manager. Sales managers, head nurses, drafting supervisors, college deans, and accounting supervisors all engage in HR management, and their effectiveness depends in part on the success of organizational HR systems. However, it is unrealistic to expect a nursing supervisor or an engineering manager to know about the nuances of equal employment regulations or how to design and administer a compensation and benefits system. For that reason, many organizations have people in an HR department who specialize in these activities, but HR in smaller organizations may be somewhat different.

In the United States and worldwide, small businesses employ more than 50% of all private-sector employees and generate new jobs each year.[5] In surveys over several years by the U.S. Small Business Association (SBA), the issues identified as significant concerns in small organizations were consistent: having sufficient numbers of qualified workers, the rapidly increasing costs of benefits, rising taxes, and compliance with government regulations. Notice these concerns have an HR focus, especially when governmental compliance with wage/hour, safety, equal employment, and other regulations are considered.

However, not every small organization is able to maintain an HR department. In a company with an owner and only three employees, the owner usually takes care of HR issues. As an organization grows, often a clerical employee is added to handle payroll, benefits, and required HR recordkeeping. If new employees are hired, supervisors and managers usually do the recruiting, selecting, and training. These HR activities reduce the time that supervisors and managers have to focus on operations, sales and marketing, accounting, and other business areas. Thus, for both small and large employers, numerous HR activities are being outsourced to specialized vendors. Typically, at around 100 employees, an organization will need to designate a person to specialize in HR management.

HR Management Roles

Several roles can be fulfilled by HR management. The nature and extent of these roles depend on both what upper management wants HR management to do and what competencies the HR staff have demonstrated. Three roles are typically identified for HR.

- *Administrative:* Focusing on clerical administration and recordkeeping, including essential legal paperwork and policy implementation.
- *Operational and employee advocate:* Managing most HR activities in line with the strategies and operations that have been identified by management and serving as employee "champion" for employee issues and concerns.
- *Strategic:* Helping to define the strategy relative to human capital and its contribution to organizational results.

HR Management Competencies and Careers

As HR management becomes more complex, greater demands are placed on individuals who make HR their career specialty. The transformation of HR toward being more strategic has implications for the competencies needed by HR professionals. Views of HR have changed over the years as the needed competencies and the results have changed. HR professionals at all levels need the following:

- Strategic knowledge and impact means
- Legal, administrative, and operational capabilities
- Technology knowledge and usage abilities

Senior HR leaders may need additional capabilities and competencies such as: (a) more business, strategic, HR, and organizational knowledge; (b) ability to lead changes; and (c) ethical behavior and results orientation/ performance. For a listing of some of the knowledge resources available in HR and their Internet addresses, see Appendix A.

HR and Strategy

The **strategy** an organization follows is its proposition for how to compete successfully and thereby survive and grow. Several different approaches to strategy formation exist. Many organizations have a relatively formal process for developing a written strategy encompassing a 5-year period with objectives and goals for each unit.

Strategic decisions relate to using resources in such a way that the organization can outperform its competitors. Organizations seek to achieve and maintain a competitive advantage in the marketplace by delivering high-quality products and services to their customers in a way that competitors cannot duplicate. Strategies might include revising existing products, acquiring new businesses, or developing new products or services using existing capabilities. Other strategic approaches might be to maintain a secure position with a single stable product (like WD-40) or to emphasize a constant stream of new products (like Apple). These are all viable strategies for different businesses, but the strategies chosen will determine the number, nature, and capabilities of people needed in the organization. Further, the people already in the organization may limit the strategies that might be successful.[6]

Regardless of which specific strategies are adopted for guiding an organization, having the right people in the right place at the right time will be critical to make the overall strategies work. If a strategy requires worker skills that are currently not available in the company, it will require time to find and hire people with those skills. Strategic HR management entails providing input into organizational strategic planning and developing specific HR initiatives to help achieve the organizational goals.

Although HR administrative and legally mandated tasks are important, strategic HR means adding value by improving the performance of the business. Some businesses are highly dependent on human capital for a competitive advantage; others are less so.

STRATEGIC PLANNING

Strategic planning is the process of defining an organizational strategy, or direction, and making decisions on allocating the resources of the organization (capital and people) to pursue this strategy. Successful organizations engage in this core business process on an ongoing basis. The plan serves as the roadmap that gives the organization direction and aligns resources. The process involves several sequential steps that focus on the future of the organization.

Figure 1-4 shows the strategic planning process for the organization. The planning process begins with an assessment of the current state of the business and the environmental forces that may be important during the planning cycle. Analysis of the strengths, weaknesses, opportunities, and threats (SWOT) is a typical starting point because it allows managers to consider both internal and external conditions.

FIGURE 1-4 Strategic Planning Process

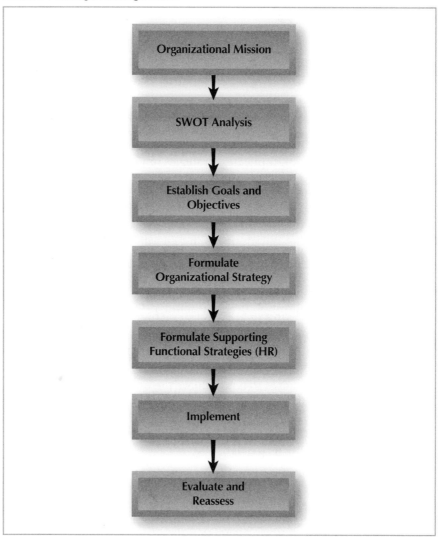

HR as Organizational Contributor

In organizations where there are identifiable core competencies related to people, HR practices can play a significant strategic role in organizational effectiveness. Effective management of talent provides managers with high-quality human resources to carry out the organizational strategies.

A wide array of data from both academics and consulting firms shows that HR practices really do make a significant difference to business outcomes. Some recognized HR best practices include:[7]

- *Incentive compensation:* Pay-for-performance systems that tie employee rewards directly to successful performance of job responsibilities

- *Training:* Talent development programs to ensure that all employees have the proper knowledge, skills, and abilities to perform their jobs and to grow with the organization
- *Employee participation:* Soliciting and using employee ideas and suggestions to give employees a sense of importance and value to the organization
- *Selectivity:* Setting stringent hiring standards to maintain a high level of quality when bringing employees into the organization
- *Flexible work arrangements:* Providing alternative work schedules to help employees balance their personal and professional lives

HR Effectiveness and Financial Performance

There are many different ways of measuring the financial contributions of HR and many challenges associated with doing so. Return on investment (ROI) is a common measure used by financial professionals to assess the value of an investment. For example, if a firm invests $20,000 for a supervisory training program, what does it gain in lower worker compensation costs, lower legal costs, higher employee productivity, and lower employee turnover? The benefits of HR programs are not always immediately visible, which is what makes measuring HR's impact such a challenge. However, efforts should be made to financially assess HR practices.

Strategy and Competition

Before the managers in an organization begin strategic determination, they study and assess the dynamics of the environment in which they operate to better understand how these conditions might affect their plans. This process of **environmental scanning** helps to pinpoint strengths, weaknesses, opportunities, and threats that the organization will face.

The quality and quantity of talent, the organizational culture, and the talent pipeline and leadership bench strength must be considered as well. The strengths and weaknesses of the organization represent factors within the organization that either create or destroy value. When assessing the internal environment, managers evaluate the quantity and quality of human resources, HR practices, and the organizational culture.

The strength of the talent pipeline is particularly important as the organization plans its future. Fulfilling strategic objectives is impossible without sufficient skills and talent. Leadership development and succession planning programs ensure that high-quality talent will be available to carry out the strategy. Effective development programs can reduce the high failure rate of people in leadership positions. Selecting individuals with the right talents and teaching them leadership skills can improve the quality of leaders and promote strategic success. **Succession planning** is the process of identifying a plan for the orderly replacement of key employees. The succession plan is the blueprint for managing the internal talent pipeline. Managers identify individuals who can fulfill new roles in the future and include them in the succession plan. This internal pool of talent is the reserve needed to meet the objectives in the strategic plan.

Competitors exist in both the product and labor markets. Competition in the product market determines the potential for the organization. If the organization is in a highly competitive industry (such as consumer electronics), strategies for growth rely heavily on innovation and driving down product costs. Competition in the labor market establishes the pricing for high-quality talent and determines the availability of workers. A detailed competitive analysis in both product and labor markets provides important information to managers regarding the possibility of meeting strategic objectives.

GLOBAL COMPETITIVENESS AND HR STRATEGY

The globalization of business has meant that more organizations now operate across borders with ties to foreign operations, international suppliers, vendors, employees, and other business partners. A global presence can range from importing and exporting to operating as a **multinational corporation (MNC)**. An MNC, sometimes called a "transnational corporation," is a corporation that has facilities and other assets in at least one country other than its home country. Because human resources are considered assets, the definition of MNC covers a large number of companies.

Having a global HR mindset means looking at HR issues from an international perspective, using ideas and resources throughout the world, and ensuring openness to other cultures and ideas. To effectively compete on an international scale, the organization needs expertise to administer all HR activities in a wide range of nations. Policies and practices should be established to address the unique demands for operating in a global context. For example, the organization may decide to standardize talent development and succession planning but permit local managers to establish compensation and labor relations policies. An ideal international approach strikes a balance between home-country and host-country policies that utilizes the best practices within the organization.

Globally-operating organizations must be aware of widely varying HR legal/regulatory systems due to politics, economic differences, and other factors. Emerging economies, in particular, pose major challenges to smooth operations and reliable conditions.

Offshoring

Competitive pressure to lower costs has resulted in many jobs being moved overseas in recent years. **Offshoring** is the relocation by a company of a business process or operation from one country to another. Firms offshore the production of goods as well as the delivery of services to lower-wage countries. Call centers in India are an example of business service offshoring to countries with well-educated, English-speaking workers. Product and software development projects are increasingly being offshored due to the loss of science and engineering talent in the United States. Predictions are that offshoring will increase in the future, and few firms have plans to return offshored jobs to the home country.

Global Staffing

Staffing for global operations includes a wide variety of alternatives. The optimal solution is to combine the expertise of local employees with the organization-specific knowledge of employees from the home country (head-quarters). Some countries require that the organization employ a certain percentage of workers from the host country.

Leadership development is especially important for MNCs. It is becoming more important for individuals in top management positions to have international experience so that they understand the worldwide marketplace. Effective selection and development processes are needed to ensure that the right individuals are chosen for these roles. Leading across cultures requires specific skills, and organizations should provide formal training along with expatriate assignments to develop leaders who can achieve results in this demanding environment.

HR'S ROLE IN MERGERS AND ACQUISITIONS

The overall purpose of a merger or acquisition is to generate shareholder value by creating a more competitive, cost-efficient company by combining two existing companies. Strategic HRM can contribute to the success of mergers and acquisitions (M&As). Research has clearly shown that the majority of M&As fail to deliver on the expected financial, marketing, or product gains, with only about one-third of companies reporting that they achieved their goals.[8] A significant number of failed ventures can trace their roots to HR issues that were not properly addressed such as loss of key staff, culture clashes, and poor communication. To maximize the chances of a successful integration, HR should be involved before, during, and after the deal is completed.

To determine whether or not the two organizations should combine, a rigorous process of due diligence is conducted. **Due diligence** is a comprehensive assessment of all aspects of the business being acquired. Financial, sales and marketing, operations, and human resource staffs are all involved before the final decision is made to merge or acquire the company.

After the deal has been closed, the focus of HR activity switches to the orderly transition of basic HR processes such as payroll and benefits migration. The immediate concerns are often about basic services needed to run the operations. Frequent communication, employee hotlines, and guidance for managers all contribute to employee retention and loyalty during the chaotic early days of the transition. Early in the transition, managers focus on identifying key talent and establishing initiatives to retain these critical employees. Retention bonuses, special assignments, and enhanced severance can be used to keep key talent in place during the integration stage.

To realize the expected benefits of a merger, the months following the initial integration are critical. Culture changes started in the early days must be maintained. Practical issues regarding talent management and development along with combining compensation systems will solidify the new, united organization. Failure to effectively blend the workforces and move beyond the "us-and-them" mentality can lead to inferior business results, a loss of shareholder value, and the failure of the merger. Continued change efforts are needed to bring all employees to the "one organization" mentality.

STRATEGIES FOR MANAGING TALENT SUPPLY IMBALANCES

Organizations need to plan for both the quantity and quality of the workforce. Having sufficient workers with the right qualifications is essential to achieve the strategic plan. If the firm employs too many people for its needs, a talent surplus exists; if too few, a talent shortage. Because of the rapidly changing conditions, the organization may face a surplus in some parts of the business while facing a shortage in others.

Managing a Talent Surplus

A talent surplus can be managed within a strategic HR plan in a number of ways. The reasons for the surplus will guide the ultimate steps taken by the organization. If the workforce has the right qualifications but the sales revenue has fallen, the primary strategies would involve retaining workers while cutting costs. However, if the workforce is not appropriately trained for the jobs needed, the organization may lay off those employees who cannot perform the work. Managers may use various strategies in a progressive fashion to defer workforce reductions until absolutely necessary.

Reduction in Work Hours or Compensation. In order to retain qualified employees, managers may institute reduced work hours on a temporary basis. Selected groups of employees may have their workweek reduced or all employees can be asked to take a day or week off without pay.

Across-the-board pay cuts can reduce labor costs while retaining skilled employees. It is important that pay cuts start at the very top of the organization so that employees do not bear all of the hardship. Uniform pay cuts can be felt as a shared sacrifice for the survival of the firm. Organizations may also reduce employee benefits, such as eliminating matching 401K contributions or raising employee health insurance premiums.

Attrition and Hiring Freezes. Attrition occurs when individuals quit, die, or retire and are not replaced. By use of attrition, no one is cut out of a job, but those who remain must handle the same workload with fewer people. Unless turnover is high, attrition will eliminate only a relatively small number of employees in the short run, but it can be a viable alternative over a longer period of time. Therefore, employers may combine attrition with a freeze on hiring. Employees usually understand this approach better than they do other downsizing methods.

Voluntary Separation Programs. Organizations can reduce the workforce while also minimizing legal risks if employees volunteer to leave. Often firms entice employees to volunteer by offering them additional severance, training, and benefits payments. Early retirement buyouts are widely used to encourage more senior workers to leave organizations early. These programs are viewed as a way to accomplish workforce reductions without resorting to layoffs.

Workforce Downsizing.   It has been given many names, including downsizing, rightsizing, and reduction in force (RIF), but it almost always means cutting employees. Layoffs on a broad scale have occurred with frightening regularity in recent years. Trimming underperforming units or employees as part of a plan that is based on sound organizational strategies may make sense. After a decade of many examples and studies, it is clear that downsizing has worked for some firms. However, it does not increase revenues; it is a short-term cost-cutting measure that can result in a long-term lack of talent. When companies cannibalize the human resources needed to change, restructure, or innovate, disruption follows for some time. Also, downsizing can hurt productivity by leaving "surviving" employees overburdened and demoralized.

Legal Considerations for Workforce Reductions

HR must be involved during workforce adjustments to ensure that the organization does not violate any of the nondiscrimination or other laws governing workforce reductions. Selection criteria for determining which employees will be laid off must comply with Title VII of the Civil Rights Act as well as the Age Discrimination in Employment Act and the Americans with Disabilities Act. A careful analysis and disparate impact review should be conducted before final decisions are made.

Under the federal Consolidated Omnibus Budget Reconciliation Act (COBRA), displaced workers can retain their group medical coverage for up to 18 months for themselves, and for up to 36 months for their dependents, if they pay the premiums themselves. Federal stimulus programs included enhanced COBRA coverage for displaced workers.

Employers must also comply with the Older Workers Benefit Protection Act (OWBPA) when implementing RIFs. The OWBPA requires employers to disclose the ages of both terminated and retained employees in layoff situations, and a waiver of rights to sue for age discrimination must meet certain requirements.

To provide employees with adequate notice of plant closings or mass layoffs, a federal law was passed, the Worker Adjustment and Retraining Notification (WARN) Act. This law requires private or commercial organizations that employ 100 or more full-time workers who have worked more than 6 months in the previous year to give a 60-day notice before implementing a layoff or facility closing that involves more than 50 people.

Managing a Talent Shortage

Managing a shortage of employees seems simple enough—simply hire more people. However, as mentioned earlier, there can be mismatches between the qualifications needed by employers and the skills possessed by workers. Companies can use a number of alternative tactics to manage a talent shortage:

- Use overtime
- Outsource work
- Implement alternate work arrangements
- Bring back recent retirees
- Use contingent workers
- Reduce turnover

The existing workers can work overtime to produce goods or services. This strategy can work on a short-term basis but is not a solution for a longer-term talent shortage. Workers may appreciate the extra hours and pay for awhile, but eventually fatigue sets in and productivity and quality may drop and injuries and absenteeism may increase. Reducing turnover of qualified employees should be an ongoing effort to maintain a talented workforce. Special attention may be required in times of talent shortages to hold on to skilled employees.

Alternate work arrangements, nontraditional schedules that provide flexibility to employees, include job sharing and telecommuting. These are creative solutions to attract and retain skilled employees who want flexibility. Employees are given more freedom in determining when and how they will perform their jobs. These arrangements are not costly to the organization but do require management support and planning to be effective. Retirees may be rehired on a part-time or temporary basis to fill talent gaps. The advantage is that these individuals are already trained and can be productive immediately. Care must be taken not to interfere with pension payments or other benefits tied to retirement.

The use of contingent employees, which are noncore employees who work at an organization on a temporary or as-needed basis, can provide short-term help. Professional employer organizations can lease employees to the firm, which is often a good solution for technical talent. Independent contractors can be hired on an as-needed basis to fill talent shortages. The use of independent contractors must be managed closely to ensure compliance with wage and hour, safety, and employee benefit statutes. When using contingent workers, special efforts are needed to assimilate them into the workforce and avoid an "us-and-them" mentality. Contingent workers fill an important need and managers can maximize their contributions through good employee relations practices.

Outsourcing involves transferring the management and/or routine performance of a business function to an external service provider. Organizations in the United States outsource a wide variety of noncore functions to reduce costs or to obtain skills and expertise not available in the organization.

TECHNOLOGY CHALLENGES

Technological advances have a major impact on organizations. New methods for communicating, processing information, and manufacturing have led to economic development around the globe. However, the improvements created by technology often mean that people and organizations must change in order to fully benefit from these advances.

Jobs have undergone major changes as a result of technology advances. In many cases, monotonous, repetitive operations have evolved into complex knowledge work that requires a new skill set. Work that previously was done by hand has been replaced by robotics and automation. Tool and die makers, once prized for their intricate, precision hand work, are now utilizing computer-aided design (CAD) and computer numerically controlled (CNC) software to complete their tasks. The skills needed in this work setting are very different from those of the past; communication, collaboration, technical ability, and adaptability are necessary for success in the future.

Technology has increased employee expectations regarding the speed and frequency of communication from managers. Employees are no longer content to wait for the monthly company newsletter or find out the latest news through formal channels. Company intranet portals can be a prime source of information for employees and should be used to inform employees about important events within the organization and the industry.

Facebook, LinkedIn, and other social networking sites allow employees to remain in constant contact with people inside and outside of the organization. Instant messages and cell-phone texting allow for real-time communication. The line between employees' personal and professional lives becomes blurred as these virtual communities are frequently accessed from the worksite. Potential litigation and damage to the organizational reputation and brand pose risks to the organization if access and content are not properly monitored.

However, monitoring employee actions and performance is much easier and less expensive due to technological advances. Transponders in semi-trailer trucks can record speed, mileage, and other operating data to evaluate driver performance. Video surveillance to reduce employee misconduct such as theft or cheating, or to track productivity is simple to implement. Computer use is routinely monitored.

The majority of organizations have e-mail use policies in place and monitor employee e-mail use. In general, the courts have supported employer monitoring, and there are few legal restrictions on employer action. Concerns about productivity and employee performance must be balanced with concerns for privacy and positive employee relations. Monitoring can lead to a lack of trust and may discourage creativity and the free exchange of ideas between employees.

MEASURING EFFECTIVENESS OF HR

A long-standing myth perpetuates the notion that one cannot really measure the value of HR practices. That myth has hurt HR's credibility because it suggests that either HR efforts do not add value or they are too far removed from business results to matter. That notion is, of course, untrue. HR, like all other functions, must be evaluated by considering the results of its actions and the value it adds to the organization. Unfortunately, the perceptions of managers and employees in many organizations are mixed because HR has not always measured and documented its contributions or communicated those results to executives, managers, and employees. Further, accounting practices treat expenditures on human capital and talent development as expenses rather than capital investments. This encourages a consumption attitude rather than a long-term investment strategy.

People-related costs are typically the largest controllable expense in organizations. Effective management of these costs can make the difference in the survival of the organization. Collecting and analyzing HR information can pinpoint waste and improper allocation of human resources. It is important that managers understand financial and operational measures that drive the business and relate HR decisions to key performance indicators (KPIs).

HR Metrics

HR metrics are specific measures tied to HR performance indicators. Metrics are typically used to assess the HR function and results within the organization over time. A metric can be developed using costs, quantity, quality, timeliness, and other designated goals. Metrics can be developed to track both HR's efficiency and effectiveness. A pioneer in developing HR measurements, Jac Fitz-Enz, has identified a wide range of HR metrics. A number of key HR metrics are shown in Figure 1-5.

Unlike financial reporting, there is no standard for the implementation and reporting of HR measures. Managers choose what and how to report to employees, investors, and other interested parties. This lack of consistency in HR reporting makes it difficult to evaluate an organization and to compare HR practices across organizations.[9]

Benchmarking is the process of comparing metrics of the business processes and outcomes to an industry standard or best practice. In other words, the organization compares itself to "best-in-class" organizations that demonstrate excellence for a specific process. Benchmarking is focused on external practices that the organization can use to improve its own processes and practices. When implementing benchmarking, managers should be careful to find organizations with similar contexts, cultures, operations, and size. Practices that would work effectively in an organization of 500 employees might not transfer very well to an organization with 5,000 employees.

HUMAN CAPITAL EFFECTIVENESS MEASURES

To fulfill its role as a strategic business partner, HR must quantify things that traditional accounting does not account for. Human resources may provide for both the biggest value and the biggest cost to organizations. Many of the HR metrics reflect people-related costs. Measuring the value is more challenging but equally important. Assessing the value of human resources demonstrates the importance of implementing effective HR practices to maintain a high-quality, engaged workforce.

FIGURE 1-5 Key HR Metrics

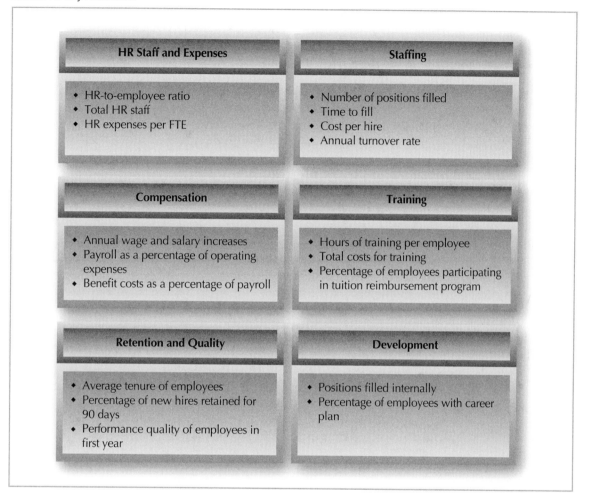

Human capital refers to the collective value of the intellectual capital (competencies, knowledge, and skills) of the employees in the organization. This capital is the constantly renewable source of creativity and innovativeness in the organization but is not reflected in its financial statements.

Revenue per employee is a basic measure of human capital effectiveness. The formula is Revenue/Head Count (full-time employee equivalents). It is a measure of employee productivity and shows the sales revenue generated by each full-time employee. This measure is commonly used in government reporting (see Bureau of Labor Statistics, BLS) as well as by organizations to track productivity over time. If revenues increase but employee head count remains constant, productivity would increase.

A widely used financial measure that can be applied to measure the contribution and cost of HR activities is **return on investment (ROI)**, which is a calculation showing the value of investments in human resources. It can also be used to show how long it will take for the activities to pay for themselves. The following formula can be used to calculate the potential ROI for a new HR activity:

$$\text{ROI} = \frac{C}{A + B}$$

where:

A = Operating costs for a new or enhanced system for the time period
B = One-time cost of acquisition and implementation
C = Value of gains from productivity improvements for the time period

ROI is stressed because it is used in most other functions in an organization and is the "language" used by financial staff and top management. It allows managers to choose among various investment opportunities to determine the best use of funds.

Human capital value added (HCVA) is an adjusted operating profitability figure calculated by subtracting all operating expenses *except* for labor expenses from revenue and dividing by the total full-time head count. It shows the operating profit per full-time employee. Because labor is required to generate revenues, employment costs are added back into operating expense. The formula for HCVA is:

$$\frac{\text{Revenue} - \text{Operating Expense} - (\text{Compensation} + \text{Benefit Costs})}{\text{Full-Time Head Count}}$$

Human capital return on investment (HCROI) directly shows the amount of profit derived from investments in labor, the leverage on labor cost. The formula for HCROI uses the same adjusted operating profitability figure as for HCVA, but it is divided by the human capital cost:

$$\frac{\text{Revenue} - \text{Operating Expense} - (\text{Compensation} + \text{Benefit Costs})}{(\text{Compensation} + \text{Benefits Costs})}$$

Human economic value added (HEVA) shows the wealth created per employee. It shows how much more valuable the organization has become due to the investment in human capital. Wealth is the net operating profit of a firm after the cost of capital is deducted. Cost of capital is the minimum rate of return demanded by shareholders. When a company is making more than the cost of capital, it is creating wealth for shareholders. An HEVA approach requires that all policies, procedures, measures, and methods use cost of capital as a benchmark against which their return is judged. Human resource decisions can be subjected to the same analysis. The formula for HEVA is:

$$\frac{\text{Net Profit after Taxes} - \text{Cost of Capital}}{\text{Full-Time Head Count}}$$

Many financial measures can be tracked and reported to show the contribution human resources make to organizational results. Without such measures, it would be difficult to know what is going on in the organization, identify performance gaps, and provide feedback. Managers should require the same level of rigor in measuring HR practices as they do for other functions in the organization.[10]

Regardless of the time and effort placed on HR measurement and HR metrics, the most important consideration is that HR effectiveness and efficiency must be measured regularly for managers to know how HR is contributing to organizational success.

HR Audit

One general means for assessing HR is through an HR audit, which is similar to a financial audit. An **HR audit** is a formal research effort to assess the current state of HR practices in an organization. This audit is used to evaluate how well activities in each of the HR areas (staffing, compensation, health and safety, etc.) have been performed, so that management can identify areas for improvement. An HR audit often helps smaller organizations without a formal HR professional to identify issues associated with legal compliance, administrative processes and recordkeeping, employee retention, and other areas.

NOTES

1. Charles Rothrock and David Gregory, "How Corporate Culture Affects Organizational Value," *SHRM White Paper*, April 1, 2006, *www.shrm.org*.
2. Jenna McGregor, "When Service Means Survival," *BusinessWeek*, March 2, 2009, 26–33.
3. Ethics Resource Center, *www.ethics.org*.
4. "The Hardest Jobs to Fill in America," *Forbes*, June 4, 2009, *www.Forbes.com*.
5. *Small Business by the Numbers* and other reports from the U.S. Small Business Administration, *www.sba.gov*.
6. ". . . and HR Planning Is Less Formal," *Personnel Today*, February 27, 2007, 1–3; Sumita Ketkar and P. K. Sett, "HR Flexibility and Firm Performance: Analysis of a Multi-Level Causal Model," *International Journal of Human Resource Management*, 20 (2009), 1009–1038.
7. James Combs, Yongmei Liu, et al., "How Much Do High Performance Work Practices Matter? A Meta-Analysis of Their Effects on Organizational

Performance," *Personnel Psychology*, 59 (2006), 501–528; Jason Shaw, Brian Dineen, et al., "Employee-Organization Exchange Relationships, HRM Practices, and Quit Rates of Good and Poor Performers," *Academy of Management Journal*, 52 (2009), 1016–1033.
8. David Wentworth, "M&A Bounces Back: What Have We Learned?" *Institute for Corporate Productivity (i4cp) TrendWatcher*, No. 478, October 2, 2009; Harry Barkema and Mario Schijven, "Toward Unlocking the Full Potential of Acquisitions: The Role of Organizational Restructuring," *Academy of Management Journal*, 51 (2008), 696–722.
9. John Dooney, "SHRM Symposium on Human Capital Analytics," Society for Human Resource Management, 2007, *www.shrm.org*.
10. "Human Capital Strategy: Human Capital Measurement," November 30, 2007, *www.humancapitalstrategy.blogspot.com*.

INTERNET RESOURCES

Ethics & Policy Integration Centre—The Ethics & Policy Integration Centre is an online resource for ethical and policy issues. Visit the website at *www.ethicaledge.com.*

HRN Management Group—Information on strategic issues for HR, including news and success stories for key HR decision makers, is available by linking to the HRN Management Group website at *www.hronline.com.*

Society for Human Resource Management— The Society for Human Resource Management is the largest association devoted to Human Resource Management. Some of the most essential and comprehensive resources available for Human Resource professionals are contained within the SHRM website at *www.shrm.org.*

U.S. Department of Labor, Bureau of Labor Statistics—This website contains data on workforce composition and trends from the U.S. Department of Labor, Bureau of Labor Statistics. Visit the site at *www.stats.bls.gov.*

SUGGESTED READINGS

Rebecca M.J. Wells, "Outstanding Customer Satisfaction: The Key to a Talented Workforce?" *Academy of Management Perspectives*, August 2007, 87–89.

"Occupational Employment Projections to 2016," *Monthly Labor Review*, November 2007, *www.bls.gov.*

David Ulrich, Wayne Brockbank, et al., *HR Competencies: Mastery of the Intersection of People and Business* (Alexandria, VA: SHRM, 2008).

William Smith and Filiz Tabak, "Monitoring Employee Emails: Is There Any Room for Privacy?" *Academy of Management Perspectives*, November 2009, 33–48.

Equal Employment Opportunity and Diversity

HR—MEETING MANAGEMENT CHALLENGES

Equal employment opportunity and diversity of the workforce represent major issues for HR in most organizations. To explain why, this chapter considers:

- The legal underpinnings of EEO
- The controversy surrounding affirmative action
- Sources of increasing diversity

EEO remains one of an organization's challenges because of the amount of litigation associated with it. Yet the diversity in the workforce will increase in the years ahead, making it necessary to manage this part of the human resources function effectively.

EQUAL EMPLOYMENT OPPORTUNITY (EEO)

In the United States, using race, gender, disability, age, religion, and certain other characteristics as the basis for choosing among people at work is generally illegal. Doing so can also be quite expensive, as fines and back wages can be awarded as well as sizable lawsuit settlements. Inequality in the treatment of people with different backgrounds has been an issue for many years, but it was the Civil Rights Act of 1964 that started a legislative movement toward leveling the playing field in employment. Initially focus was on race, gender, and religion, but these characteristics were soon followed by age, pregnancy, and individuals with disabilities. Since then numerous Executive Orders, regulations, and interpretations by courts have affected the employer/employee relationship. Perhaps nothing has had the impact of Equal Employment Opportunity (EEO) on HR during the same period of time.

At the core of equal employment is the concept of discrimination. The word *discrimination* simply means "recognizing differences among items or people." For example, employers must discriminate (choose) among applicants for a job on the basis of job requirements and candidates' qualifications. However, when discrimination is based on race, gender, or some other factors, it is illegal and employers face problems. The following bases for protection have been identified by various federal, state, and/or local laws:

- Race, ethnic origin, color (including multiracial/ethnic backgrounds)
- Sex/gender (including pregnant women and also men in certain situations)
- Age (individuals over age 40)
- Individuals with disabilities (physical or mental)
- Military experience (military status employees and Vietnam-era veterans)
- Religion (special beliefs and practices)
- Marital status (some states)
- Sexual orientation (some states and cities)

These categories are composed of individuals who are members of a **protected category** under EEO laws and regulations.

Disparate Treatment

The first type of illegal discrimination occurs with employment-related situations in which either: (1) different standards are used to judge individuals, or (2) the same standard is used, but it is not related to the individuals' jobs. **Disparate treatment** occurs when members of one group are treated differently from others. For example, if female applicants must take a special skills test not given to male applicants, then disparate treatment may be occurring.[1]

Disparate Impact

Disparate impact occurs when members of a protected category are substantially underrepresented as a result of employment decisions that work to their disadvantage. The landmark case that established the importance of disparate impact as a legal foundation of EEO law is *Griggs v. Duke Power*, 1401 U.S. 424 (1971). The decision by the U.S. Supreme Court established two major points:

1. It is not enough to show a lack of discriminatory intent if the employment tool results in a disparate impact that discriminates against one group more than another or continues a past pattern of discrimination.
2. The employer has the burden of proving that an employment requirement is directly job related as a "business necessity." Consequently, the intelligence test and high school diploma requirements of Duke Power were ruled not to be related to the job.

This and a number of other decisions make it clear that employers must be able to document through statistical analyses that disparate treatment and disparate impact have not occurred.[2] Knowing how to perform these analyses is important in order for employers to follow appropriate equal employment guidelines.

FIGURE 2-1 EEO Concepts

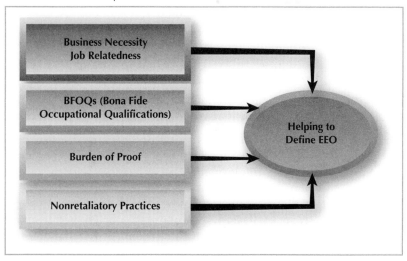

EQUAL EMPLOYMENT OPPORTUNITY CONCEPTS

Several basic EEO concepts have resulted from court decisions, laws, and regulatory actions. Four of these (see Figure 2-1) help clarify key EEO ideas.

Business Necessity and Job Relatedness. A **business necessity** is a practice necessary for safe and efficient organizational operations. Business necessity has been the subject of numerous court decisions. Educational requirements often are based on business necessity. However, an employer who requires a minimum level of education, such as a high school diploma, must be able to defend the requirement as essential to the performance of the job (job related), which may be difficult. For instance, equating a degree or diploma with the possession of math or reading abilities is considered questionable.

Bona Fide Occupational Qualification (BFOQ). Employers may discriminate on the basis of sex, religion, or national origin if the characteristic can be justified as a "bona fide occupational qualification reasonably necessary to the normal operation of the particular business or enterprise." Thus, a **bona fide occupational qualification (BFOQ)** is a characteristic providing a legitimate reason why an employer can exclude persons on otherwise illegal bases of consideration.

What constitutes a BFOQ has been subject to different interpretations in various courts. Legal uses of BFOQs have been found for hiring Asians to wait on customers in a Chinese restaurant or Catholics to serve in certain religious-based positions in Catholic churches.

Burden of Proof.   Another legal issue that arises when discrimination is alleged is the determination of who has the **burden of proof,** which is what individuals who file suit against employers must prove to establish that illegal discrimination has occurred.

Based on the evolution of court decisions, current laws, and regulations the plaintiff charging discrimination must:

- be a *protected-category member,* and
- prove that *disparate impact* or *disparate treatment* existed.

Once a court rules that a preliminary case has been made, the burden of proof shifts to the employer. The employer then must show that the bases for making employment-related decisions were specifically job related and consistent with considerations of business necessity.

Nonretaliation.   Employers are prohibited from retaliating against individuals who file discrimination charges. **Retaliation** occurs when employers take punitive actions against individuals who exercise their legal rights. For example, an employee who had reported harassment by a supervisor was fired, but the Supreme Court found that it is unlawful to discriminate against someone who has "made a charge, testified, assisted, or participated in any manner in an investigation, proceeding, or hearing."

To avoid charges of retaliation, the following actions are recommended for employers:

- Train supervisors on what retaliation is and what is not appropriate.
- Conduct a thorough internal investigation of any claims and document the results.
- Take appropriate action when any retaliation occurs.

RACE/ETHNIC/NATIONAL ORIGIN

The focus now shifts to equal employment laws and necessary considerations for managing HR in light of these laws. For a listing of all the major EEO laws and regulations, see Appendix B.

Civil Rights Act of 1964, Title VII

Although the very first civil rights act was passed in 1866, it was not until passage of the Civil Rights Act of 1964 that the keystone of antidiscrimination employment legislation was put into place. The Equal Employment Opportunity Commission (EEOC) was established to enforce the provisions of Title VII, the portion of the act that deals with employment.

Title VII of the Civil Rights Act states that it is illegal for an employer to:

1. *fail or refuse to hire or discharge any individual, or otherwise discriminate against any individual with respect to his compensation, terms, conditions, or privileges of employment because of such individual's race, color, religion, sex, or national origin, or*

2. *limit, segregate, or classify his employees or applicants for employment in any way that would deprive or tend to deprive any individual of employment opportunities or otherwise adversely affect his status as an employee because of such individual's race, color, religion, sex, or national origin.*

Title VII, as amended by the Equal Employment Opportunity Act of 1972, covers most employers in the United States. Any organization meeting one of the criteria in the following list is subject to rules and regulations that specific government agencies have established to administer the act:

- All private employers of 15 or more persons who are employed 20 or more weeks a year
- All educational institutions, public and private
- State and local governments
- Public and private employment agencies
- Labor unions with 15 or more members
- Joint labor/management committees for apprenticeships and training

Executive Orders 11246, 11375, and 11478

Numerous executive orders require that employers holding federal government contracts not discriminate on the basis of race, color, religion, national origin, or sex. An *Executive Order* is issued by the president of the United States to provide direction to government departments on a specific area. The Office of Federal Contract Compliance Programs (OFCCP) in the U.S. Department of Labor has responsibility for enforcing nondiscrimination in government contracts.

Executive Orders 11246, 11375, and 11478 are major federal EEO efforts for government contractors; many states have similar requirements for firms with state government contracts.

Civil Rights Act of 1991

The Civil Rights Act of 1991 requires employers to show that an employment practice is *job related for the position* and is consistent with *business necessity.* The act clarifies that the plaintiffs bringing the discrimination charges must identify the particular employer practice being challenged and must show only that protected-category status played *some role in their treatment.* One key provision of the 1991 act relates to how U.S. laws on EEO are applied globally.

Race and National Origin Issues

The original purpose of the Civil Rights Act of 1964 was to address race and national origin discrimination. This concern continues to be important today, and employers must be aware of potential HR issues that are based on race, national origin, and citizenship in order to take appropriate actions.

Employment discrimination can occur in numerous ways, from refusal to hire someone because of the person's race/ethnicity to the questions asked in a selection interview. For example, a trucking company settled a discrimination lawsuit by African American employees who were denied job assignments and promotions because of racial bias. In addition to paying a fine, the firm must report to the EEOC on promotions from part-time to full-time for dock worker jobs.

Sometimes racial discriminations can be more subtle. For example, some firms have tapped professional and social networking sites to fill open positions. However, networking sites exclude many people. According to one study, only 5% of LinkedIn users are black and 2% are Hispanic. This lack of access to these sites can easily be viewed as racial discrimination.[3]

Under federal law, discriminating against people because of skin color is just as illegal as discriminating because of race. For example, one might be guilty of color discrimination but not racial discrimination if one hired light-skinned African Americans over dark-skinned people.

Racial/Ethnic Harassment.   The area of racial/ethnic harassment is such a concern that the EEOC has issued guidelines on it. It is recommended that employers adopt policies against harassment of any type, including ethnic jokes, vulgar epithets, racial slurs, and physical actions. The consequences of not enforcing these policies are seen in a case involving a small business employer that subjected Latinos to physical and verbal abuse. Hispanic males at the firm were subjected to derogatory jokes, verbal abuse, physical harm, and other humiliating experiences. Settling the case was expensive for the employer.

Contrast that case with another that shows the advantage of taking quick remedial action. An employee filed a lawsuit against an airline because coworkers told racist jokes and hung nooses in his workplace. The airline was able to show that each time any employee, including the plaintiff, reported problems, management conducted an investigation and took action against the offending employees. The court ruled for the employer in this case because the situation was managed properly.

Affirmative Action

Through **affirmative action,** employers are urged to hire groups of people based on their race, age, gender, or national origin to make up for historical discrimination. It is a requirement for federal government contractors to document the inclusion of women and racial minorities in the workforce. As part of those government regulations, covered employers must submit plans describing their attempts to narrow the gaps between the composition of their workforces and the composition of labor markets where they obtain employees. However, affirmative action has been the subject of numerous court cases and an ongoing political and social debate both in the United States and globally.

For example, a recent Supreme Court ruling held that race should *not* be used to the detriment of individuals who passed an examination and were qualified for promotions. In this case, the city of New Haven, Connecticut, threw out the results of a test for promotion where more white firefighters

FIGURE 2-2 The Debate about Affirmative Action

Arguments: Why Affirmative Action Is Needed

- Affirmative action is needed to overcome past injustices or eliminate the effects of those injustices.
- Affirmative action creates more equality for all persons, even if temporary injustice to some individuals may result.
- Raising the employment level of protected-class members will benefit U.S. society in the long run.
- Properly used, affirmative action does not discriminate against males or whites.
- Goals indicate progress is needed, not quotas.

Arguments: Why Affirmative Action Is Not Needed

- Affirmative action penalizes individuals (males and whites) even though they have not been guilty of practicing discrimination.
- It is no longer needed as an African American has been elected President.
- Affirmative action results in greater polarization and separatism along gender and racial lines.
- Affirmative action stigmatizes those it is designed to help.
- Goals become quotas and force employers to "play by the numbers."

passed than blacks or Hispanics. The city claimed it had to junk the tests because they would lead to an avalanche of lawsuits by black candidates who had not passed. The court said fear of litigation was no reason to rely on race to throw out the results.[4]

Supporters offer many reasons why affirmative action is important, while opponents argue firmly against it. Individuals can examine the points of both sides in the debate and compare them with their personal views of affirmative action. The authors of this text believe that whether one supports or opposes affirmative action, it is important to understand why its supporters believe that it is needed and why its opponents believe it should be discontinued. The reasons given most frequently by both sides are highlighted in Figure 2-2.

Managing Affirmative Action Requirements

Federal, state, and local regulations require many government contractors to compile affirmative action plans to report on the composition of their workforces. An **affirmative action plan (AAP)** is a formal document that an employer compiles annually for submission to enforcement agencies. Generally, contractors with at least 50 employees and $50,000 in government contracts annually must submit these plans. Courts have noted that any employer *may* have a *voluntary* AAP, although employers *must* have such a plan if they are government contractors. Some courts have ordered employers that are not government contractors to submit required AAPs because of past discriminatory practices and violations of laws.

The contents of an AAP and the policies flowing from it must be available for review by managers and supervisors within the organization. Plans vary in length; some are long and require extensive staff time to prepare.

Affirmative Action Plan Metrics.   A crucial but time-consuming part of an AAP is the analyses. The **availability analysis** identifies the number of protected-class members available to work in the appropriate labor markets for given jobs. This analysis can be developed with data from a state labor department, the U.S. Census Bureau, and other sources. The **utilization analysis** identifies the number of protected-class members employed in the organization and the types of jobs they hold.

Once all the data have been analyzed and compared, then *underutilization* statistics must be calculated by comparing the availability analysis with the utilization analysis. It is useful to think of this stage as a comparison of whether the internal workforce is a "representative sampling" of the available external labor force from which employees are hired.

Using the underutilization data, *goals* and *timetables* for reducing underutilization of protected-class individuals must then be identified. Actions that will be taken to recruit, hire, promote, and train more protected-class individuals are described. The AAP must be updated and reviewed each year to reflect changes in the utilization and availability of protected-category members. If the AAP is audited, the employer must be prepared to provide additional details and documentation.

SEX/GENDER DISCRIMINATION LAWS AND REGULATIONS

A number of laws and regulations address discrimination based on sex or gender. Historically, women experienced employment discrimination in a variety of ways. The inclusion of sex as a basis for protected-class status in Title VII of the 1964 Civil Rights Act has led to various areas of legal protection for women.

Pregnancy Discrimination

The Pregnancy Discrimination Act (PDA) of 1978 requires that any employer with 15 or more employees treat maternity leave the same as other personal or medical leaves. Closely related to the PDA is the Family and Medical Leave Act (FMLA) of 1993, which requires that individuals be given up to 12 weeks of family leave without pay and also requires that those taking family leave be allowed to return to jobs. The FMLA applies to both men and women.

Courts have generally ruled that the PDA requires employers to treat pregnant employees the same as nonpregnant employees with similar abilities or inabilities. Employers have been found to have acted properly when terminating a pregnant employee for excessive absenteeism due to pregnancy-related illnesses, because the employee was not treated differently from other employees with absenteeism problems.

Equal Pay and Pay Equity

The Equal Pay Act of 1963 requires employers to pay similar wage rates for similar work without regard to gender. A *common core of tasks* must be similar, but tasks performed only intermittently or infrequently do not make jobs different enough to justify significantly different wages. Differences in pay between men and women in the same jobs may be allowed because of:

1. Differences in seniority
2. Differences in performance
3. Differences in quality and/or quantity of production
4. Factors other than sex, such as skill, effort, and working conditions

Ledbetter v. Goodyear Tire & Rubber Co. was a significant U.S. Supreme Court decision on pay discrimination. Ledbetter, a female manager with Goodyear in Alabama, claimed that she was subjected to pay discrimination because she received lower pay during her career back to 1979, even though she did not file suit until 1998.[5] The decision examined this view and stated that the rights of workers to sue for previous years of paid discrimination are limited. However, in 2009 Congress passed the Lilly Ledbetter Fair Pay Act that canceled the Supreme Court ruling. The new law effectively eliminates the statute of limitations for employees to file pay discrimination claims.

Pay equity is the idea that pay for jobs requiring comparable levels of knowledge, skill, and ability should be similar, even if actual duties differ significantly. This theory has also been called *comparable worth* in earlier cases. Some state laws have mandated pay equity for public-sector employees. However, U.S. federal courts generally have ruled that the existence of pay differences between the different jobs held by women and men is not sufficient to prove that illegal discrimination has occurred.

A major reason for the development of the pay equity idea is the continuing gap between the earnings of women and men. For instance, in 1980, the average annual pay of full-time female workers was 60% of that of full-time male workers. By 2008, the reported rate of about 80% showed some progress but a continuing disparity. See Figure 2-3.

Sexual Harassment

The Equal Employment Opportunity Commission has issued guidelines designed to curtail sexual harassment. **Sexual harassment** refers to actions that are sexually directed, are unwanted, and subject the worker to adverse employment conditions or create a hostile work environment. Sexual

FIGURE 2-3 Female Annual Earnings as Percentage of Male Earnings

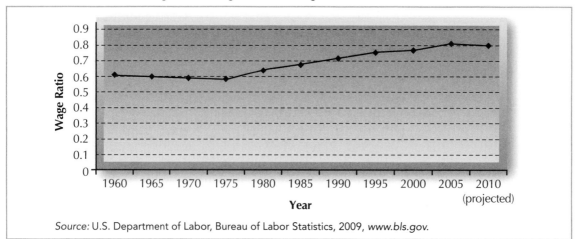

Source: U.S. Department of Labor, Bureau of Labor Statistics, 2009, *www.bls.gov.*

harassment can occur between a boss and a subordinate, among coworkers, and when nonemployees have business contacts with employees.

Most of the sexual harassment charges filed involve harassment of women by men. However, some sexual harassment cases have been filed by men against women managers and supervisors, and some have been filed by both men and women for same-sex harassment.

Managing Sex/Gender Issues

The influx of women into the workforce has had major social, economic, and organizational consequences. The percentage of women in the total U.S. civilian workforce has increased dramatically since 1950, to almost 50% today.

This growth in the number of women in the workforce has led to more sex/gender issues related to jobs and careers. A significant issue is related to biology (women bear children) and to tradition (women have a primary role in raising children). A major result of the increasing share of women in the workforce is that more women with children are working. According to the U.S. Bureau of Labor Statistics, about three-fourths of women aged 25–54 are in the workforce. Further, about half of all women currently working are single, separated, divorced, widowed, or otherwise single heads of households. Consequently, they are "primary" income earners, not co-income providers, and must balance family and work responsibilities. This responsibility may affect managers' perceptions of family/work conflict that may lead to promotability issues for women.

To guard against pay inequities that are considered illegal under the Equal Pay Act, employers should follow these guidelines:

- Include all benefits and other items that are part of remuneration to calculate total compensation for the most accurate overall picture.

- Make sure people know how the pay practices work.
- Base pay on the value of jobs and individual performance.
- Benchmark against local and national markets so that pay structures are competitive.
- Conduct frequent audits to ensure there are no gender-based inequities and that pay is fair internally.

The right to reassign women from hazardous jobs to ones that may be lower paying but less hazardous because of health-related concerns is another gender-related issue encountered by employers. Fears about higher health insurance costs and possible lawsuits involving such problems as birth defects caused by damage sustained during pregnancy have led some employers to institute reproductive and fetal protection policies. However, the U.S. Supreme Court has ruled that such policies are illegal. Also, having different job conditions for men and women is usually held to be discriminatory.

Jobs that pay well but are nontraditional jobs for women include: architects, computer programmers, software engineers, detectives, chefs, engineers, computer repair, construction, building inspectors, machinists, aircraft pilots, and firefighters.

Individuals with Differing Sexual Orientations

As if demographic diversity did not place enough pressure on managers and organizations, individuals in the workforce today have widely varying lifestyles that can have work-related consequences. Legislative efforts have been made to protect individuals with differing lifestyles or sexual orientations from employment discrimination, though at present only a few cities and states have passed such laws.

One visible issue that some employers have had to address is that of individuals who have had or are undergoing sex-change surgery and therapy. Federal court cases and the EEOC have ruled that sex discrimination under Title VII applies to a person's gender at birth. Thus, it does not apply to the new gender of those who have had gender-altering operations. Sexual orientation or sex-change issues that arise at work include the reactions of coworkers and managers and ensuring that such individuals are evaluated fairly and not discriminated against in work assignments, raises, training, or promotions.

Nepotism

Many employers have policies that restrict or prohibit **nepotism**, the practice of allowing relatives to work for the same employer. Other firms require only that relatives not work directly for or with each other or not be placed in positions where collusion or conflict could occur. The policies most frequently cover spouses, brothers, sisters, mothers, fathers, sons, and daughters. Generally, employer antinepotism policies have been upheld by courts, in spite of the concern that they tend to discriminate against women more than men (because women tend to be denied employment or to leave employers more often as a result of marriage to other employees).

Consensual Relationships and Romance at Work

When work-based friendships lead to romance and off-the-job sexual relationships, managers and employers face a dilemma: Should they "monitor" these relationships to protect the firm from potential legal complaints, thereby "meddling" in employees' private, off-the-job lives? Or do they simply ignore these relationships and the potential problems they present? These concerns are significant.

Most executives and HR professionals (as well as employees) agree that workplace romances are risky because they have great potential for causing conflict. They strongly agree that romance must not take place between a supervisor and a subordinate because potential sexual harassment issues could arise. Some employers have addressed the issue of workplace romances by establishing policies dealing with them.

Different actions may be appropriate if a relationship is clearly consensual than if it is forced by a supervisor–subordinate relationship. One consideration is the observation that consensual workplace romances can create hostile work environments for others in organizations.

Dealing with Sexual Harassment

Sexual harassment is a significant concern in many organizations and can occur in a variety of workplace relationships. As shown in Figure 2-4, individuals in many different roles can be sexual harassers. For example, third parties

FIGURE 2-4 Potential Sexual Harassers

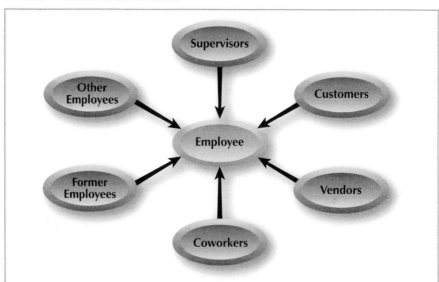

who are neither employers nor employees have been found to be harassers. Both customer service representatives and food servers have won sexual harassment complaints because their employers refused to protect them from regular sexual harassment by aggressive customers.

Most frequently, sexual harassment occurs when a male in a supervisory or managerial position harasses women within his "power structure." However, as noted earlier, women managers have been found guilty of sexually harassing male employees, and same-sex harassment also has occurred. Court decisions have held that a person's sexual orientation neither provides nor precludes a claim of sexual harassment under Title VII. It is enough that the harasser engaged in pervasive and unwelcome conduct of a sexual nature.

Types of Sexual Harassment

Two basic types of sexual harassment have been defined by EEOC regulations and a large number of court cases. The two types are different in nature and defined as follows:

1. **Quid pro quo** is harassment in which employment outcomes are linked to the individual granting sexual favors.

2. **Hostile environment** harassment exists when an individual's work performance or psychological well-being is unreasonably affected by intimidating or offensive working conditions.

In quid pro quo harassment, an employee may be promised a promotion, a special raise, or a desirable work assignment, but only if the employee grants some sexual favors to the supervisor. The second type, hostile environment harassment, may include actions such as commenting on appearance or attire, telling jokes that are suggestive or sexual in nature, allowing revealing photos and posters to be on display, or making continual requests to get together after work that can lead to the creation of a hostile work environment. Rude and discourteous behavior often is linked to sexual harassment.

As computer and Internet technology has spread, the number of electronic sexual harassment cases has grown. Sexual harassment is increasingly occurring via e-mails and Internet access systems. Cyber sexual harassment may occur when an employee forwards an e-mail joke with sexual content or accesses pornographic websites at work and then shares content with other employees. Cyber stalking, in which a person continually e-mails an employee requesting dates and sending personal messages, is growing as instant messaging expands.

Many employers have policies addressing the inappropriate use of e-mail, company computer systems, and electronic technology usage. Serious situations have led to employee terminations. Once a company disciplined more than 200 employees and fired 50 of them for having e-mailed pornographic images and other inappropriate materials using the company information system.

Many employers have equipped their computer systems with scanners that screen for inappropriate words and images. Offending employees receive warnings and/or disciplinary actions associated with "flagged" items.

Employer Responses to Sexual Harassment

Employers must be proactive to prevent sexual and other types of harassment. If the workplace culture fosters harassment, and if policies and practices do not inhibit harassment, an employer is wise to reevaluate and solve the problem before lawsuits follow.

Only if the employer can produce evidence of taking reasonable care to prohibit sexual harassment does the employer have the possibility of avoiding liability through an affirmative defense. Critical components of ensuring such reasonable care include the following:

- Establish a sexual harassment policy.
- Communicate the policy regularly.
- Train employees and managers on avoiding sexual harassment.
- Investigate and take action when complaints are voiced.

Harassment Likelihood

Research suggests that some people are more likely to be sexually harassed than others. For example, one study found that supervisors or women with more workplace authority are more likely to be harassed. Further research suggests that the likelihood of men to sexually harass, and the tolerance for sexual harassment by women vary across countries. Fundamental differences regarding power between men and women and a cultural support of sexual harassment lead to very different sexual harassment situations from country to country. According to this research, Canada, Denmark, Germany, The Netherlands, Sweden, and the United States are likely to have relatively *less* sexual harassment than countries like East Africa, Hong Kong, Indonesia, Malaysia, Mexico, Turkey, and Yugoslavia.[6]

AMERICANS WITH DISABILITIES ACT (ADA)

Organizations with 15 or more employees are covered by the provisions of the ADA, which are enforced by the EEOC. The act applies to private employers, employment agencies, and labor unions. State government employees are not covered by the ADA, which means that they cannot sue in federal courts for redress and damages. However, they may still bring suits under state laws in state courts.

Discrimination is prohibited against individuals with disabilities who can perform the **essential job functions**—the fundamental job duties—of the employment positions that those individuals hold or desire. These functions do not include marginal functions of the position.

For a qualified person with a disability, an employer must make a **reasonable accommodation**, which is a modification to a job or work environment that gives that individual an equal employment opportunity to perform. EEOC guidelines encourage employers and individuals to work together to determine what are appropriate reasonable accommodations, rather than employers alone making those judgments.

Reasonable accommodation is restricted to actions that do not place an undue hardship on an employer. An **undue hardship** is a significant difficulty or expense imposed on an employer in making an accommodation for individuals with disabilities. The ADA offers only general guidelines in determining when an accommodation becomes unreasonable and will place undue hardship on an employer.

Who Is Disabled?

As defined by the ADA, a **disabled person** is someone who has a physical or mental impairment that substantially limits that person in some major life activities, who has a record of such an impairment, or who is regarded as having such an impairment. Figure 2-5 shows the most frequent disabilities identified in ADA charges.

Mental Disabilities. A growing area of concern to employers under the ADA is individuals with mental disabilities. A mental illness is often more difficult to diagnose than a physical disability. Employers must be careful when considering "emotional" or "mental health" factors such as depression in employment-related decisions. They must not stereotype individuals with mental impairments or disabilities but must instead base their evaluations on sound medical information.

FIGURE 2-5 Most Frequent ADA Disabilities Cited

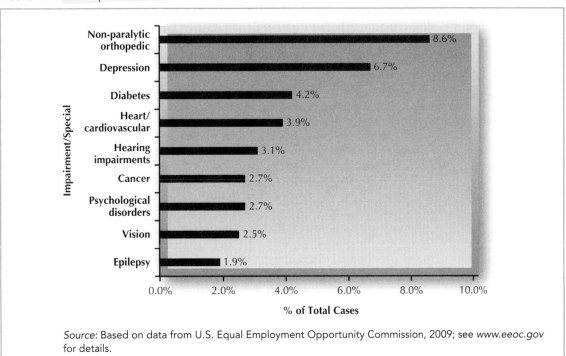

Source: Based on data from U.S. Equal Employment Opportunity Commission, 2009; see *www.eeoc.gov* for details.

Amendments to ADA (ADAAA).   Congress passed amendments to the ADA, effective in 2009, that overruled several key cases and regulations. The effect was to *expand* the definition of disabled individuals to include anyone with a physical or mental impairment that substantially limits one or more major life activities without regard for the ameliorative effects of mitigating measures such as medication, prosthetics, hearing aids, and so on. Major life activities include, among others, walking, seeing, breathing, working, sleeping, concentrating, thinking, and communicating.

Genetic Bias Regulations

Related to medical disabilities is the emerging area of workplace genetic bias. As medical research has revealed the human genome, medical tests have been developed that can identify an individual's genetic markers for various diseases. Whether these tests should be used and how they are used can raise ethical issues.

Employers that use genetic screening tests do so for two primary reasons. Some use genetic testing to make workers aware of genetic problems that may exist so that medical treatments can begin. Others use genetic testing to terminate employees who may make extensive use of health insurance benefits and thus raise the benefits costs and utilization rates of the employer. A major company had to publicly apologize to employees for secretly testing to determine if they were genetically predisposed to carpal tunnel syndrome.

Genetic Information Nondiscrimination Act (GINA).   Congress passed GINA to limit the use of information by health insurance plans. Employers are prohibited from collecting genetic information or making employment decisions based on genetic decisions. "Genetic information" includes genetic tests of the employee or family members and family medical history. It does not apply to "water cooler talk," or the inadvertent acquisition of information.

Managing Disabilities in the Workforce

At the heart of managing individuals with disabilities is for employers to make reasonable accommodations in several areas. First, architectural barriers should not prohibit disabled individuals' access to work areas or restrooms. Second, appropriate work tasks must be assigned. Satisfying this requirement may mean modifying jobs, work area layouts, or work schedules or providing special equipment.

Key to making reasonable accommodations is identifying the essential job functions and then determining which accommodations are reasonable so that the individual can perform the core job duties. Fortunately for employers, most accommodations needed are relatively inexpensive.

Recruiting and Selecting Individuals with Disabilities.   Numerous employers have specifically targeted the recruitment and selection of individuals with disabilities. However, questions asked in the employment process should be job related.

One common selection test is a physical abilities test, which can be challenged as discriminatory based on the ADA. Such physical tests must be specifically job related, and not general. For example, having all applicants lift 50-pound weights, even though only some warehouse workers will have to lift that much, could be illegal. Also, rather than testing with barbells or other artificial weights, the employer should use the actual 50-pound boxes lifted in performing the specific jobs.

Employees Who Develop Disabilities.   For many employers, the impact of the ADA has been the greatest when handling employees who develop disabilities, not dealing with applicants who already have disabilities. As the workforce ages, it is likely that more employees will develop disabilities. For instance, a warehouse worker who suffers a serious leg injury while motorcycling away from work may request reasonable accommodation.

Employers must develop responses for handling accommodation requests from individuals who have been satisfactory employees without disabilities, but who now must be considered for accommodations if they are to be able to continue working. Handled inappropriately, these individuals are likely to file either ADA complaints with the EEOC or private lawsuits.

Employees sometimes can be shifted to other jobs where their disabilities do not affect them as much. For instance, the warehouse firm might be able to move the injured repair worker to a purchasing inventory job inside so that climbing and lifting are unnecessary. But the problem for employers is what to do with the next worker who develops problems if an alternative job is not available. Even if the accommodations are just for one employee, the reactions of coworkers must be considered.

Individuals with Mental Disabilities.   More ADA complaints are being filed by individuals who have or claim to have mental disabilities. The cases that have been filed have ranged from individuals with a medical history of paranoid schizophrenia or clinical depression to individuals who claim that job stress has affected their marriage or sex life. Regardless of the type of employees' claims, it is important that employers respond properly by obtaining medical verifications for claims of mental illnesses and considering accommodation requests for mental disabilities in the same manner as accommodation requests for physical disabilities.

Individuals with Life-Threatening Illnesses.   The U.S. Supreme Court has determined that individuals with life-threatening illnesses are covered by the ADA. Individuals with leukemia, cancer, or AIDS are all considered as having disabilities, and employers must respond to them appropriately or face charges of discrimination. Numerous individuals with life-threatening illnesses may intend to continue working, particularly if their illness is forecast to be multiyear in nature.

An additional requirement of the ADA is that all medical information be maintained in files separated from the general personnel files. The medical files must have identified security procedures, and limited access procedures must be identified.

Management Focus on ADAAA Adaptation.   After the changes made by ADAAA, less effort should be placed on determining whether an individual is indeed disabled—the individual probably is disabled. Rather, management should:

- Define essential functions in advance.
- Handle all requests for accommodation properly.
- Interact with the employee with good faith and documentation.
- Know and follow the reasonable accommodation rules.

OTHER AREAS OF POTENTIAL DISCRIMINATION

The populations of most developed countries—including Australia, Japan, most European countries, and the United States—are aging. These changes mean that as older workers with a lifetime of experiences and skills retire, HR faces significant challenges in replacing them with workers having the capabilities and work ethic that characterize many mature workers in the United States. Employment discrimination against individuals age 40 and older is prohibited by the Age Discrimination in Employment Act (ADEA).

Age Discrimination in Employment Act (ADEA)

The Age Discrimination in Employment Act (ADEA) of 1967, amended in 1978 and 1986, prohibits discrimination in terms, conditions, or privileges of employment against all individuals age 40 years or older working for employers having 20 or more workers. However, the U.S. Supreme Court has ruled that state employees may not sue state government employers in federal courts because the ADEA is a federal law. The impact of the ADEA is increasing as the U.S. workforce has been aging. Consequently, the number of age discrimination cases has been increasing, according to EEOC reports.

Older Workers Benefit Protection Act (OWBPA)

This law is an amendment to the ADEA and is aimed at protecting employees when they sign liability waivers for age discrimination in exchange for severance packages. To comply with the act, employees must be given complete accurate information on the available benefits. For example, an early retirement package that includes a waiver stating the employee will not sue for age discrimination if the employee takes the money for early retirement must include a written, clearly understood agreement to that effect.

The impact of the OWBPA is becoming more evident. Industries such as manufacturing and others offer early retirement buyouts to cut their workforces. For instance, Ford and General Motors offered large buyouts of which thousands of workers have taken advantage.

To counter significant staffing difficulties, some employers recruit older people to return to the workforce through the use of part-time and other scheduling options. During the past decade, the number of older workers holding part-time jobs has increased. It is likely that the number of older workers interested in working part-time will continue to grow.

A strategy used by employers to retain the talents of older workers is **phased retirement,** whereby employees gradually reduce their workloads and pay levels. This option is growing in use as a way to allow older workers with significant knowledge and experience to have more personal flexibility, while the organizations retain them for their valuable capabilities. Some firms also rehire their retirees as part-time workers, independent contractors, or consultants. Some provisions in the Pension Protection Act of 2006 allow pension distributions for employees who are reducing their work hours.

Religion and Spirituality in the Workplace

Title VII of the Civil Rights Act identifies discrimination on the basis of religion as illegal. The increasing religious diversity in the workforce has put greater emphasis on religious considerations in workplaces. However, religious schools and institutions can use religion as a bona fide occupational qualification for employment practices on a limited scale. Also, employers must make *reasonable accommodation* efforts regarding an employee's religious beliefs according to the U.S. Supreme Court.

Employers increasingly are having to balance the rights of employees with differing religious beliefs. One way to do that is to make reasonable accommodation for employees' religious beliefs when assigning and scheduling work, because many religions have differing days of worship and holidays. For example, some firms have established "holiday swapping pools," whereby Christian employees can work during Passover or Ramadan or Chinese New Year, and employees from other religions can work on Christmas. Other firms allow employees a set number of days off for holidays, without specifying the holidays in company personnel policies.

Immigration Reform and Control Acts (IRCA)

The United States has always had a significant number of immigrants who come to work in this country. The increasing number of immigrants who have entered illegally has led to extensive political, social, and employment-related debates. The existence of more foreign-born workers means that employers must comply with the provisions of the Immigration Reform and Control Acts (IRCA). Employers are required to obtain and inspect I-9 forms, and verify documents such as birth certificates, passports, visas, and work permits. They can be fined if they knowingly hire illegal aliens. E-verify is a federal government source that can be used for this verification. Federal contractors must use it to verify employees legal status.

Military Status and USERRA

The employment rights of military veterans and reservists have been addressed in several laws. The two most important laws are the Vietnam Era

Veterans Readjustment Assistance Act of 1974 and the Uniformed Services Employment and Reemployment Rights Act (USERRA) of 1994. Under the latter, employees are required to notify their employers of military service obligations. Employers must give employees serving in the military leaves of absence protections under the USERRA.

With the use of reserves and National Guard troops abroad, the provisions of USERRA have had more impact on employers. This act does not require employers to pay employees while they are on military leave, but many firms provide some compensation, often a differential. Many requirements regarding benefits, disabilities, and reemployment are covered in the act as well.

Sexual Orientation

Recent battles in a number of states and communities illustrate the depth of emotions that accompany discussions of "gay rights." Some states and cities have passed laws prohibiting discrimination based on sexual orientation or lifestyle. Even the issue of benefits coverage for "domestic partners," whether heterosexual or homosexual, has been the subject of state and city legislation. No federal laws of a similar nature have been passed. Whether gays and lesbians have any special rights under the equal protection amendment to the U.S. Constitution has not been decided by the U.S. Supreme Court.

Appearance and Weight Discrimination

Several EEO cases have been filed concerning the physical appearance of employees. Court decisions consistently have allowed employers to set dress codes as long as they are applied uniformly. For example, establishing a dress code for women but not for men has been ruled discriminatory. Also, employers should be cautious when enforcing dress standards for women employees who are members of certain religions that prescribe appropriate and inappropriate dress and appearance standards. Some individuals have brought cases of employment discrimination based on height or weight. The crucial factor that employers must consider is that any weight or height requirements must be related to the job, such as when excess weight would hamper an individual's job performance.

WORKFORCE COMPOSITION AND DIVERSITY

The existing U.S. workforce is changing, and projections indicate that more shifting will occur in the next few years.[7] To analyze the composition of workers and jobs in the United States, the U.S. Bureau of Labor Statistics (BLS) undertakes studies to identify current and future projected compositions. Because of economic shifts and their effects in different industries, some types of workers are scarce but in high demand, while others are available in excessive numbers.

A worker-related shift results from the U.S. workforce becoming more diverse. **Diversity** reflects the differences in human characteristics in an organization. The tangible indicators of diversity that employers must consider include the following:

- Race/ethnicity
- National origin/immigration
- Age/generational differences
- Gender—men and women
- Marital and family status
- Sexual orientation
- Disabilities
- Religion

Figure 2-6 shows various approaches to dealing with diversity.

The "business case" for diversity must be linked to key business goals and strategies and organizational results.[8] The business case for diversity includes the following:

- Diversity allows new talent and ideas from employees of different backgrounds, which can enhance organizational performance.
- Diversity helps recruiting and retention because protected-class individuals often prefer to work in organizations with coworkers of various demographics.
- Diversity allows for an increase of market share because customers can be attracted to purchase products and services with varied demographic marketing activities.
- Diversity can lead to lower costs because there may be fewer discrimination lawsuits.

FIGURE 2-6 Various Approaches to Diversity and Their Results

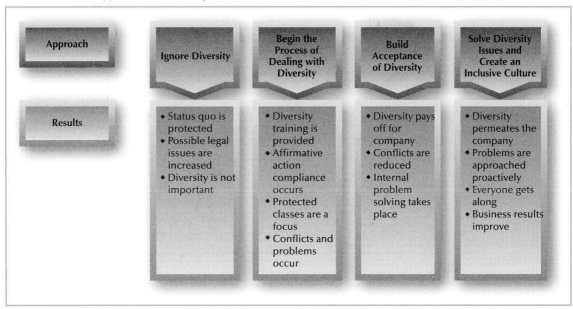

One concern with diversity programs is that they may be perceived as benefiting only certain groups of persons and not others. Diversity actions must be well thought out and address both the positive and negative aspects of such programs, given the workforce composition of many organizations.

Race and Ethnicity

Significant race and ethnic shifts in the U.S. population will occur in the next several decades. By the year 2050, racial/ethnic groups currently in the minority will likely make up more than 50% of the U.S. population. The Census Bureau says whites represent 67% of the population currently, but will be at approximately 48% in 2050. The Hispanic population will increase dramatically, to about 39% of the overall population, and will exceed the African American population. The Asian population will triple to about 9% by 2050.[9]

Another racial/ethnic factor is the growth in the number of immigrants to the United States and other developed countries. The United States has always had a significant number of immigrants who have come to work in this country. The increasing number of immigrants entering illegally has led to extensive political, social, and employment-related issues. In the United States, one concern is the large number of illegal immigrants hired to fill certain jobs at low cost, despite availability of unemployed U.S. workers.

Generational Differences

Much has been written about the expectations of individuals in different age groups and generations. For employers, these varied expectations present challenges, especially given economic, global, technology, and other changes in the workplace. Some common age/generational groups are labeled as follows:

- Matures (born before 1946)
- Baby boomers (born 1946–1964)
- Generation Xers (born 1965–1980)
- Generation Yers (millenials) (born 1981–2000)

As the economy and industries have changed, the aging of the U.S. workforce has become a significant concern. Workers over age 55 are delaying retirement more often, working more years, and/or looking for part-time work or phased retirement. Economic conditions are the predominant reasons why these workers are bypassing the "normal" retirement age of 65. As older and more experienced employees retire in the future, employers will face increasing gaps as they try to replace the experience and capabilities of baby boomers.

Generational differences in expectations are likely to add to challenges and conflicts in organizations. For instance, many baby boomers and matures are concerned about security and experience, while younger people have different concerns. Generation Yers are often seen as the "why" generation; they expect to be rewarded quickly, use more technology, and often ask more questions about why managers and organizations make the decisions they do.

Consider the dynamics of a mature manager directing Generation X and Y individuals, or Generation X managers supervising older, more experienced baby boomers as well as generation Y employees. However, stereotyping these individuals by generations may not reflect how actual individuals view their jobs and produce organizational results.

Gender Diversity

Women are becoming a greater percentage of workers in the U.S. workforce; they comprise more than 46% of the total employed individuals. However, men average more work time daily than do women.[10] Interestingly, as the economic and labor market has been shifting, the job fields dominated by men have been hit harder than those consisting mostly of women. Male workers are more heavily represented in manufacturing, farming, and other "male-dominated" industries, so male employees have been impacted more severely by the market shifts than women employees with their higher rates of participation in industries such as health care and education.

From this follows some of the gender issues that occur in organizations. First, women overall have lower average pay than men due to the nature of their jobs and work hours. Second, in most industries and countries, women make up a much smaller percentage of senior executives and managers in many organizations and occupations. Over the past decade more women have become managers, but women comprise less of senior level executive and board members than their numbers would suggest. Some of the wage gap between men and women is due to the greater family/home responsibilities that females have to meet.

Both women and men also are increasingly facing the need to aid older family members, as matures and baby boomers encounter health disabilities and other problems.

DIVERSITY TRAINING

Traditional diversity training has a number of different goals. One prevalent goal is to minimize discrimination and harassment lawsuits. Other goals focus on improving acceptance and understanding of people with different backgrounds, experiences, capabilities, and lifestyles.

Components of Traditional Diversity Training

Approaches to diversity training vary, but often include at least three components. *Legal awareness* is the first and most common component. Here, the training focuses on the legal implications of discrimination. A limited approach to diversity training stops with these legal "do's and don'ts."

By introducing *cultural awareness*, trainers hope to build greater understanding of the differences among people. Cultural awareness training helps all participants to see and accept the differences in people with widely varying cultural backgrounds.

The third component of diversity training—*sensitivity training*—is more difficult. The aim here is to "sensitize" people to the differences among them and how their words and behaviors are seen by others. Some diversity training includes exercises containing examples of harassment and other behaviors.

Mixed Results for Diversity Training

The effects of diversity training are viewed as mixed by both organizations and participants. A limited number of studies have been done on the effectiveness of diversity training. There is some concern that the programs may be interesting or entertaining, but may not produce longer-term changes in people's attitudes and behaviors toward others with characteristics different from their own.

Some argue that traditional diversity training more often than not has failed, pointing out that it does not reduce discrimination and harassment complaints. Rather than reducing conflict, in a number of situations diversity training has heightened hostility and conflicts. In some firms, it has produced divisive effects, and has not taught the behaviors needed for employees to work well together in a diverse workplace.[11]

This last point, focusing on behaviors, seems to hold the most promise for making diversity training more effective. For instance, dealing with cultural diversity as part of training efforts for sales representatives and managers has produced positive results. Teaching appropriate behaviors and skills in relationships with others is more likely to produce satisfactory results than focusing just on attitudes and beliefs among diverse employees.

The negative consequences of diversity training may manifest themselves broadly in a backlash against all diversity efforts. This backlash takes two main forms. First, and somewhat surprisingly, the individuals in protected groups, such as women and members of racial minorities, sometimes see the diversity efforts as inadequate and nothing but "corporate public relations." Thus, it appears that by establishing diversity programs, employers can raise the expectation levels of protected-group individuals, but the programs may not *be* meeting the expectations.

On the other side, a number of individuals who are not in protected groups, primarily white males, believe that the emphasis on diversity sets them up as scapegoats for societal problems. Sometimes white males show hostility and anger at diversity efforts. Diversity programs are widely perceived as benefiting only women and racial minorities and taking away opportunities for men and nonminorities. This resentment and hostility is usually directed at affirmative action programs that employers have instituted.[12]

Trainers emphasize that the key to avoiding backlash in diversity efforts is to stress that people can believe whatever they wish, but at work their values are less important than their *behaviors*. Dealing with diversity is not about what people can and cannot *say*; it is about being *respectful* to others.

NOTES

1. Margaret M. Pinkham, "Employers Should Take Care When Making Decisions about Caregivers," *Employee Relations Law Journal*, Summer 2008, 35–40.
2. Anne Lindberg, "Disparate Impact or Disparate Treatment: Either Way Leads to Court," *Trend Watcher*, July 10, 2009, 1–5.
3. Fay Hansen, "Discriminatory Twist in Networking Sites Puts Recruiters in Peril," *Work Force Management*, September 2009, 1–5.
4. C. Tuna, N. Koppel, and M. Sanserino, "Job-Test Ruling Cheers Employers," *The Wall Street Journal*, July 1, 2009, B1; Adam Liptak, "Justices Find Bias Against Whites," *The Denver Post*, June 30, 2009, 1A.
5. Allen Smith, "Pay Bias Figures Prominently in New Supreme Court Forum," *HR News*, September 26, 2009, *www.shrm.org/hrnews*.
6. Harsh Luther and Uipan Luther, "A Theoretical Framework Explaining Cross-Cultural Sexual Harassment: Integrating Hofsteds and Schwartz," *Journal of Labor Research*, Winter 2007, 169–188.
7. "Employment Projections" *U.S. Bureau of Labor Statistics, www.bls.gov*.
8. Bill Leonard, "Diversity Initiatives Must Grow from Key Business Goals," *SHRMOnLine*, April 29, 2009, *www.shrm.org/hrdisciplines*; Ellen F. Curtis and Janice L. Dreachslin, "Integrative Literature Review: Diverse Management Interventions and Organizational Performance," *Human Resource Development Review*, 7 (2008), 107–134.
9. "An Older and More Diverse Nation by Mid-Century," *U.S. Census Bureau News*, August 14, 2008, *www.census.gov*.
10. *American Time Use Survey*, U.S. Department of Labor, 2008, *www.bls.gov/tus/#news*.
11. Susan Awbrey, "The Dynamics of Vertical and Horizontal Diversity in Organization and Society," *Human Resource Development Review*, 6 (2007), 7–32.
12. Carol Kulik, et al., "The Rich Get Richer: Predicting Participation in Voluntary Diversity Training," *Journal of Organizational Behavior*, Volume 28 (2007), 753–769.

INTERNET RESOURCES

Equal Employment Opportunity Commission— This website provides information on the EEOC. It includes details on employment discrimination facts, enforcement statistics, and technical assistance programs. Visit the site at *www.eeoc.gov*.

The Affirmative Action and Diversity Project— A resource for opinions surrounding the issues of affirmative action and its cultural and economic aspects can be found at *http://aad.english.ucsb.edu*.

Administration on Aging— This government website provides information on aging and age discrimination from government agencies, associations, and organizations. Visit the site at *www.aoa.gov*.

American Institute for Managing Diversity— The nation's leading nonprofit think tank dedicated to promoting and furthering the field of diversity management can be found at *www.aimd.org*.

SUGGESTED READINGS

"Discrimination Charges on the Rise," *Benefit News.com Employee Benefit News*, September 15, 2007, 82; Sam Hananei, "Federal Job Discrimination Complaints Hit Record," *Yahoo! News*, March 11, 2009, 1–2.

Andrew Slobodien and Katie O'Brien, "The ADA Amendments Act of 2008 and How It Will Change the Workplace," *Employee Relations Law Journal*, Winter 2008, 32–39.

Eileen Kelly, "Accommodating Religious Expression in the Workplace," *Employer Responsibility and Rights Journal*, 20 (2008), 45–56.

Frank Giancola, "The Generation Gap: More Myth than Reality," *Human Resource Planning*, 29 (2006), 32; Susan A. Murphy, *Leading a Multigenerational Workforce* (Washington, DC: AARP, 2007).

Individuals/HR Planning/Job Analysis

HR—MEETING MANAGEMENT CHALLENGES

Understanding how and why employees react to their jobs is a part of Human Resources, as is planning for the number of employees that will be needed. Job analysis helps identify what people are doing in their job and provides a way to initiate job descriptions. Issues include:

- Understanding jobs and the people who do them
- How HR can deal with turnover and retention
- Identifying skills that jobs require and the tasks involved

The common theme of the interaction between people and their jobs is covered in this chapter. Designing systems to keep or retain more people makes sense. Planning to avoid "surprises" in the number of employees that will be needed is basic to good HR management. And finally job analysis keeps the system current and jobs under appropriate scrutiny as things change.

INDIVIDUAL ORGANIZATIONAL RELATIONS

Relationships between individuals and their employers can vary widely from favorable to unfavorable. The individual's performance is a major part of whether the employer wants the individual to stay or go. Competent employees who are satisfied with their employers, who know what is expected, and who have less turnover potential are assets to the organization. But just as individuals in an organization can be a competitive advantage, they can also be a liability. When few employees are satisfied with their jobs, when people are constantly leaving, and when the employees who do remain work ineffectively, the organization faces a *competitive disadvantage* from its employees.

Psychological Contract

A concept that has been useful in discussing individuals' relationships with their employers is that of a **psychological contract**, which refers to the unwritten expectations employees and employers have about the nature of their work relationships. The psychological contract can create either a positive or negative relationship between an employer and an individual. It is best on trust and commitment that leads to meeting both the employer's and employee's expectations and needs.

Unwritten psychological contracts between employers and employees encompass expectations about both tangible items (e.g., wages, benefits, employee productivity, and attendance) and intangible items (e.g., loyalty, fair treatment, and job security). Employers may attempt to detail their expectations through handbooks and policy manuals, but those materials are only part of the total "contractual" relationship.

Traditionally, employees expected to exchange their efforts and capabilities for secure jobs that offered competitive pay, a solid range of benefits, and career progression within an organization, among other factors. But as some organizations have changed in economic terms, they have had to address various organizational crises by downsizing and eliminating workers who had given long and loyal service. Consequently, in these firms, remaining employees may question whether they should remain loyal to and stay with their employers. The psychological contract has changed.

A psychological contract may include these expectations:

Employers Provide

- Competitive compensation and benefits
- Flexibility to balance work and home life
- Career development opportunities

Employees Contribute

- Continuous skill improvement and increased productivity
- Reasonable time with the organization
- Extra efforts and results when needed

Individual Employee Performance and Motivation

The idea of a psychological contract between the individual employee and the organization helps clarify why people might stay or leave a job. But for an employer to *want* to keep an employee, that person must be performing well.

The three major factors that affect how a given individual performs are illustrated in Figure 3-1. They are: (1) individual ability to do the work, (2) effort expended, and (3) organizational support. The relationship of those factors is widely acknowledged in management literature as follows:

$$\text{Performance } (P) = \text{Ability } (A) \times \text{Effort } (E) \times \text{Support } (S)$$

Individual performance is enhanced to the degree that all three components are present with an individual employee, and diminished if any of these factors is reduced or absent. For instance, if several production workers have the abilities to do their jobs and work hard, but the organization provides outmoded equipment or the management style of supervisors causes negative reactions by the workers, the lack of organizational support may reduce individual performance.

FIGURE 3-1 Components of Individual Performance

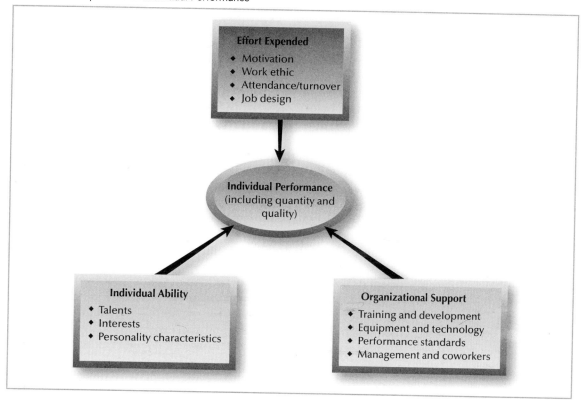

An example of how this performance equation can work in a positive way is seen in the link between individual motivation and organizational support in the form of coworkers. The motivation of poor-performing employees can sometimes be improved when these employees work more intensely with a group of better-performing workers. The link between individual motivation and organizational support has important HR management implications.

The desire within a person causing that person to act is called **motivation**. People usually act to reach a goal, which means that motivation is a goal-directed drive that seldom occurs in a void. The words *need, want, desire,* and *drive* are all similar to *motive,* from which the word *motivation* is derived. Approaches to understanding motivation vary because different theorists have developed their own views and models. Each approach has contributed to the understanding of human motivation, and details on different approaches can be found in various organizational behavior textbooks.

Motivation is complex and individualized, and managerial strategies and tactics must be broad-based to address the motivation concerns of individuals at work. Factors that can inhibit motivation and work performance include a worker's capacities and determination to get work done regardless of difficulties. For instance, with a poor-performing employee, managers must determine whether inadequate individual behavior is due to employee deficiencies, inconsistent reward policies, or low desire for the rewards offered.

Job Satisfaction

In its most basic sense, **job satisfaction** is a positive emotional state resulting from evaluating one's job experiences. Job *dissatisfaction* occurs when one's expectations are not met. For example, if an employee expects clean and safe working conditions, that employee is likely to be dissatisfied if the workplace is dirty and dangerous.

Dimensions of job satisfaction frequently mentioned include worker relationships, pay and benefits, performance recognition, and communications with managers and executives. Sometimes job satisfaction is called *morale*. Frequently cited reasons for decline in morale include more demanding and stressful work, fewer relationships with management, and less confidence in compensation and other rewards.[1]

The degree to which employees believe in and accept organizational goals and want to remain with the organization is called **organizational commitment**. Job satisfaction influences organizational commitment, which in turn affects employee retention and turnover.

A related idea is *employee engagement,* which is the extent to which an employee feels linked to organizational success. Surveys have shown that levels of employee engagement range from 15% to 45% for highly engaged workers, and 5% to 20% for disengaged ones.[2]

Engaged employees may be seen as "loyal" employees who are more than just satisfied with their jobs; they are pleased with the relationships with their employers. In changing labor markets, employers find that turnover of key people occurs more frequently when employee loyalty is low.

EMPLOYEE TURNOVER

Turnover occurs when employees leave an organization and have to be replaced. Many organizations have found that turnover is a costly problem. For instance, health care firms experienced over 30% turnover annually in one state. Just in registered nurse jobs, the turnover cost in the state was more than $125 million per year, with individual nurse turnover costs being $32,000 per person.[3]

The extent to which employers face high turnover rates and costs varies by organization and industry. For higher-level executives and professionals, turnover costs can run as much as two times the departing employees' annual salaries, and rates often are linked to executive job expectations and needed skills changes. In many service industries, the turnover rates and costs are frequently very high. In the retail industry, turnover in some companies averages more than 100% a year for part-time workers and around 75% a year for full-time workers. In the U.S. supermarkets, fast-food restaurants, and other retail service industry firms spend billions of dollars each year to deal with worker turnover.

Types of Employee Turnover

Turnover is classified in a number of ways. One classification uses the following categories, although the two types are not mutually exclusive:

- **Involuntary Turnover**

  Employees are terminated for poor performance or work rule violations

- **Voluntary Turnover**

  Employees leave by choice

Involuntary turnover is triggered at all levels by employers terminating workers due to organizational policies and work rule violations, excessive absenteeism, performance standards that are not met by employees, and other issues. Voluntary turnover too can be caused by many factors, some of which are not employer controlled. Common voluntary turnover causes include job dissatisfaction, pay and benefits levels, supervision, geography, and personal/family reasons. Career opportunities in other firms, when employees receive unsolicited contacts, may lead to turnover for individuals, especially those in highly specialized jobs such as IT. Voluntary turnover may increase with the size of the organization, most likely because larger firms are less effective in preventing turnover and have more employees who are inclined to move.

Another view of turnover classifies it based on whether it is good or bad for the organization:

- **Functional Turnover**

  Lower-performing or disruptive employees leave

- **Dysfunctional Turnover**

  Key individuals and high performers leave at critical times

Not all turnover is negative for organizations; on the contrary, functional turnover represents a positive change. Some workforce losses are desirable, especially if those who leave are lower-performing, less reliable, and/or disruptive individuals. Of course, dysfunctional turnover also occurs. That happens when key individuals leave, often at crucial times. For example, a software project leader who leaves in the middle of a system upgrade in order to take a promotion at another firm could cause the system upgrade timeline to slip due to the difficulty of replacing the employee and could also lead other software specialists in the firm to seek out and accept jobs at competitive firms.

Employees quit for many reasons, only some of which can be controlled by the organization, so another classification uses the following terms to describe types of turnover:

- **Uncontrollable Turnover**

  Employees leave for reasons outside the control of the employer

- **Controllable Turnover**

  Employees leave for reasons that could be influenced by the employer

Some examples of reasons for turnover the employer cannot control include: (1) the employee moves out of the geographic area, (2) the employee decides to stay home with young children or an elder relative, (3) the employee's spouse is transferred, and (4) the employee is a student worker who graduates from college. Even though some turnover is inevitable, employers recognize that reducing turnover saves money, and that they must address the turnover that is controllable. Organizations are better able to keep employees if they deal with the concerns of those employees that might lead to the controllable turnover.

Hiring new workers while laying off others is called **churn**. This practice raises a paradox in which employers complain about not being able to find skilled workers while they are laying off others. As organizations face economic and financial problems that result in layoffs, the remaining employees are more likely to consider jobs at other firms. In this situation, turnover is more likely to occur, and efforts are needed to keep existing employees. HR actions such as information sharing, opportunities for more training/learning, and emphasis on job significance can be helpful in lowering turnover intentions of individuals.

Measuring Employee Turnover

The U.S. Department of Labor estimates that the cost of replacing an employee ranges from one-half to five times the person's annual salary. The turnover rate for an organization can be computed as a monthly or yearly cost. The following formula, in which *separations* means departures from the organization, is widely used:

$$\frac{\text{Number of employee separations during the year}}{\text{Toral number of employees at midyear}} \times 100$$

Common turnover rates range from almost 0% to more than 100% a year and vary among industries. As a part of HR management systems, turnover data can be gathered and analyzed in a number of different ways, including the following categories:

- Job and job level
- Department, unit, and location
- Reason for leaving
- Length of service

- Demographic characteristics
- Education and training
- Knowledge, skills, and abilities
- Performance ratings/levels

Two examples illustrate why detailed analyses of turnover are important. A manufacturing organization had a companywide turnover rate that was not severe, but most of the turnover occurred within one department. That imbalance indicated that some specific actions on training supervisors and revising pay levels were needed to resolve problems in that unit. In a different organization, a global shipping/delivery firm found ways to reduce turnover of sales and service employees. The actions of that firm reduced its turnover, which contributed to an annual savings of more than $18 million in direct and indirect costs. In both of these examples, the targeted turnover rates declined as a result of employer actions taken in response to the turnover analyses that were done.

Areas to be included in calculating detailed turnover costs include the following:

- *Separation costs:* HR staff and supervisory time, pay rates to prevent separations, exit interview time, unemployment expenses, legal fees for separations challenged, accrued vacation expenditures, continued health benefits, and others
- *Vacancy costs:* Temporary help, contract and consulting firm usage, existing employee overtime, and other costs until the person is replaced
- *Replacement costs:* Recruiting and advertising expenses, search fees, HR interviewer and staff time and salaries, employee referral fees, relocation and moving costs, supervisor and managerial time and salaries, employment testing costs, reference checking fees, preemployment medical expenses, relocation costs, and others
- *Training costs:* Paid orientation time, training staff time and pay, costs of training materials, supervisor and manager time and salaries, coworker "coaching" time and pay, and others
- *Hidden/indirect costs:* Costs that are not obvious, such as reduced productivity, decreased customer service, additional unexpected employee turnover, missed project deadlines, and others

RETENTION OF HUMAN RESOURCES

Retaining employees is part of HR staffing and planning efforts. Turnover, as the opposite of retention, often has been seen as a routine HR matter requiring records and reports. However, what was once a bothersome detail has become a substantial HR issue for many employers. Organizations are being forced to study why employees leave and why they stay. Sometimes an individual in the HR area is assigned to specifically focus on retention to ensure that it receives high priority.

Myths and Realities about Retention

Keeping good employees is a challenge that all organizations share and that becomes even more difficult as labor markets change. Unfortunately, some myths have arisen about what it takes to retain employees. Some of the most prevalent myths and realities are as follows:

1. *Money is the main reason people leave.* Money certainly is a vital HR tool, and if people feel they are being paid inadequately, they may be more likely to leave. But if they are paid close to the competitive level they expect, other parts of the job become more important.

2. *Hiring has little to do with retention.* This is not true. Recruiting and selecting the people who fit the jobs and who are less likely to leave in the first place, and then orienting them to the company, can greatly increase retention. It is important to select for retention.

3. *If you train people, you are only training them for another employer.* Developing skills in employees may indeed make them more marketable, but it also tends to improve retention. When an employer provides employees with training and development assistance, job satisfaction may increase and employees are more likely to stay, particularly if they see more future opportunities internally.

4. *Do not be concerned about retention during organizational change.* That is exactly the time to worry about retention. Although some people's jobs may have to be cut because of economic organizational factors, the remaining employees that the company would like to keep may have the most opportunity and reason to leave voluntarily. For example, during a merger or acquisition, most workers are concerned about job security and their employer's future. If they do not feel a part of the new organization early on, many may leave or evaluate alternatives.

5. *If solid performers want to leave, the company cannot hold them.* Employees are best viewed as "free agents," who indeed can leave when they want. The key to keeping solidly performing employees is to create an environment in which they want to stay and grow.

Drivers of Retention

Because both people and jobs are so varied, managers and HR professionals need to realize that individuals may remain or leave their employment for both job-related and personal reasons. For instance, if employees choose to leave an organization for family reasons (e.g., because a spouse is transferring or to raise children), there may be a limited number of actions the employer can take to keep them on the job. However, there are significant actions that an employer can take to retain employees in many other circumstances. Figure 3-2 illustrates some of these "drivers" of retention, or areas in which employers can take action to strengthen the possibility of keeping employees.

Retention Assessment and Metrics

To ensure that appropriate actions are taken to enhance retention, management decisions require data and analyses rather than subjective impressions, anecdotes of selected individual situations, or panic reactions to the loss of key people.

The analysis of turnover data is an attempt to get at the cause of retention problems. Analysis should recognize that turnover is a symptom of other factors that may be causing problems. When the causes are treated, the symptoms can go away.

Some of the first areas to consider when analyzing data for retention include the work, pay/benefits, supervision, and management systems. Common methods of obtaining useful perspectives are employee surveys, exit interviews, and first-year turnover evaluations.

Retention evaluation is part of the broader organizational HR planning and staffing roles. The determination of the correct supply of human

FIGURE 3-2 Drivers of Retention

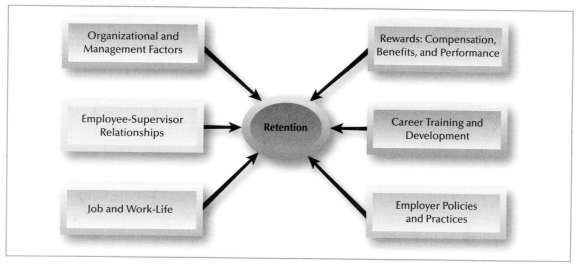

resources in a company is made by Human Resource planning and is covered next.

HUMAN RESOURCE PLANNING

Human resource planning is the process of analyzing and identifying the need for and availability of human resources so that the organization can meet its objectives. The focus of HR planning is to ensure the organization has the *right number of human resources*, with the *right capabilities*, at the *right times*, and in the *right places*. In HR planning, an organization must consider the availability and allocation of people to jobs over long periods of time, not just for the next month or even the next year.

Additionally, as part of the analyses, HR plans can include several approaches. Actions may include shifting employees to other jobs in the organization, laying off employees or otherwise cutting back the number of employees, retraining present employees, and/or increasing the number of employees in certain areas. Factors to consider include the current employees' knowledge, skills, and abilities and the expected vacancies resulting from retirements, promotions, transfers, and discharges. To do this, HR planning requires efforts by HR professionals working with executives and managers.

Organizational Size and HR Planning

The need for HR planning in larger organizations is especially important. For example, in a review, the U.S. government's Corps of Engineers, with a workforce of 35,000, was found to have an outdated strategic HR plan. Also, it had not done an organization-wide needs analysis for current and future workforce.

If adjustments to foreseeable changes were not made, people or even entire divisions could be working at cross-purposes with the rest of the organization.[4]

In a smaller business, even though the owner/manager knows on a daily basis what is happening and what should be done, planning is still important. One difficult area for HR planning in small businesses is family matters and succession. Particular difficulties arise when a growing business is passed from one generation to another, resulting in a mix of family and nonfamily employees.

HR Planning Process

The steps in the HR planning process are shown in Figure 3-3. Notice that the process begins with considering the organizational strategic planning objectives. Then the possible *available workforce* must be evaluated by identifying both the external and internal workforce.

Once those assessments are complete, forecasts must be developed to identify both the demand for and supply of human resources. Management then formulates HR staffing plans and actions to address imbalances, both short-term and long-term. One means of developing and measuring HR planning

FIGURE 3-3 HR Planning Process

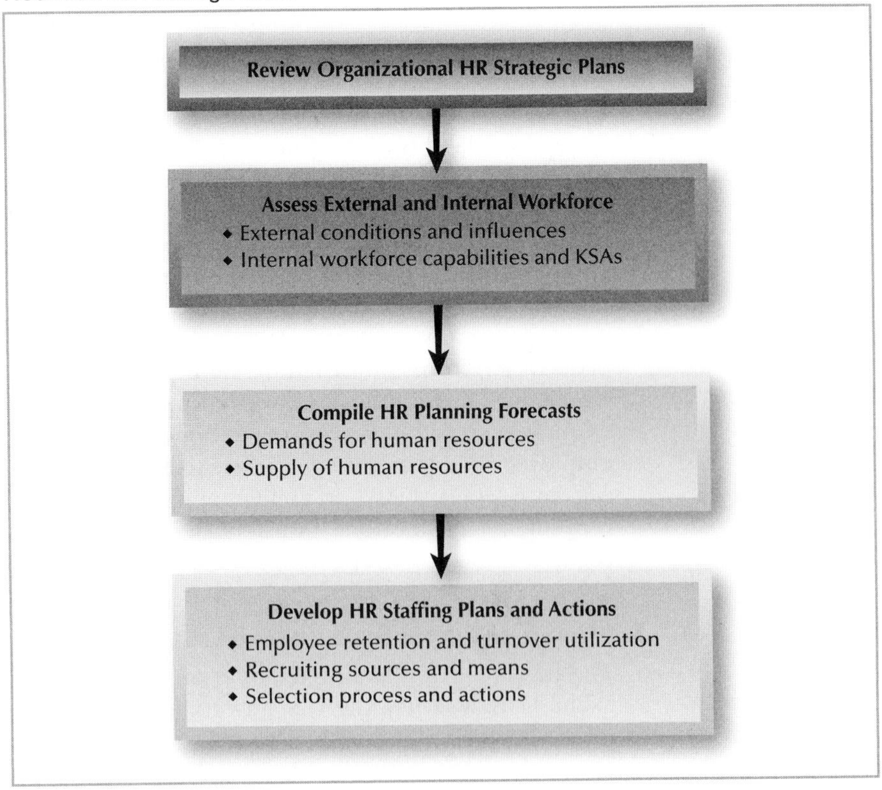

Review Organizational HR Strategic Plans

Assess External and Internal Workforce
- External conditions and influences
- Internal workforce capabilities and KSAs

Compile HR Planning Forecasts
- Demands for human resources
- Supply of human resources

Develop HR Staffing Plans and Actions
- Employee retention and turnover utilization
- Recruiting sources and means
- Selection process and actions

is use of a team of subject matter experts (SMEs) to increase the validity and reliability of the HR planning results. Specific strategies may be developed to fill vacancies or deal with surplus employees. For example, a strategy might be to fill 50% of expected vacancies by training employees in lower-level jobs and promoting them into more advanced anticipated openings.

Finally, HR plans are developed to provide specific direction for employee recruiting, selection, and retention. The most telling evidence of successful HR planning is a consistent alignment of the availabilities and capabilities of human resources with the needs of the organization over shorter or longer periods of time.

Assessing the External Workforce

The first stage of HR planning is to *examine organization objectives and plans*. If a network technology firm plans to double its number of client accounts from 100 to 200 in a 3-year period, that firm also must identify how many and what types of new employees will be needed to staff the expanded services, locations, and facilities. Several common external factors to be considered are highlighted next.

Economic and Governmental Factors

The general cycles of economic recession and economic boom in different businesses affect HR planning. Factors such as interest rates, inflation, and economic decline or growth affect the availability of workers and should figure into organizational and HR plans and objectives. There is a considerable difference between finding qualified applicants in a 4% unemployment market and in a 9% unemployment market. As the unemployment rate rises, the number of qualified people looking for work increases, often making it easier to fill some jobs.

A broad array of government regulations affects the labor supply and therefore HR planning. As a result, HR planning must be done by individuals who understand the legal requirements of various government regulations. In the United States and other countries, tax legislation at local, state, and federal levels affects HR planning. Elimination or expansion of tax benefits for job-training expenses might alter some job-training activities associated with workforce expansions. In summary, an organization must consider a wide variety of government policies, regulations, and laws during the HR planning process.

Competitive Evaluations

When making HR plans, employers must consider a number of geographic and competitive concerns. The *net migration* into a particular region is important. For example, in the past decade, the populations of some U.S. cities in the South, Southwest, and West have grown rapidly and have provided sources of labor. However, areas in the Northeast and Midwest have experienced declining populations.

Direct competitors are another important external force in HR planning. Failure to consider the competitive labor market and to offer pay scales and benefits competitive with those of organizations in the same general industry and geographic location may cost a company dearly in the long run.

Finally, the impact of *international competition* must be considered as part of environmental scanning. Global competition for labor intensifies as global competitors shift jobs and workers around the world, as illustrated by the outsourcing of jobs from the United States to countries with cheaper labor.

Changing Workforce Considerations

As mentioned in the previous chapter, significant changes in the workforce, both in the United States and globally, must be considered when doing external assessments for HR planning. Shifts in the composition of the workforce, combined with the use of different work patterns, have created workplaces and organizations that are notably different from those of a decade ago.

Many organizations face major concerns about having sufficient workers with the necessary capabilities. When scanning the potential and future workforce, it is important to consider a number of variables, including:

- Aging of the workforce
- Growing diversity of workers
- Female workers and work-life balancing concerns
- Availability of contingent workers
- Outsourcing possibilities

ASSESSING THE INTERNAL WORKFORCE

Analyzing the jobs that will need to be done and the capabilities of people who are currently available in the organization to do them is the next part of HR planning. The needs of the organization must be compared against the labor supply available both inside and outside the organization.

The starting point for evaluating internal workforce strengths and weaknesses is an audit of the jobs being done in the organization. A comprehensive analysis of all current jobs provides a basis for forecasting what jobs will need to be done in the future. Much of the data in the audit should be available from existing staffing and organizational databases. The following questions may be some key ones addressed during the internal assessment:

- What jobs exist now and how essential is each job?
- How many individuals are performing each job?
- What are the reporting relationships of jobs?
- What are the vital KSAs needed in the jobs?
- What jobs will be needed to implement future organizational strategies?
- What are the characteristics of those anticipated jobs?

FORECASTING HR SUPPLY AND DEMAND

The information gathered from scanning the external environment and assessing internal strengths and weaknesses is used to predict HR supply and demand in light of organizational objectives and strategies. **Forecasting** uses information from the past and the present to identify expected future conditions. Projections for the future are, of course, subject to error. Fortunately, experienced people usually are able to forecast with enough accuracy to positively affect long-range organizational planning.

The demand for employees can be calculated for an entire organization and/or for individual units in the organization. For example, a forecast might indicate that a firm needs 125 new employees next year, or that it needs 25 new people in sales and customer service, 45 in production, 20 in accounting and information systems, 2 in HR, and 33 in the warehouse. The unit breakdown obviously allows HR planners to better pinpoint the specific skills needed than does the aggregate method.

Once human resources needs have been forecast, then availability of qualified individuals must be identified. Forecasting availability considers both *external* and *internal* supplies. Although the internal supply may be somewhat easier to calculate, it is important to calculate the external supply as accurately as possible.

Estimating internal supply considers the number of external hires and the employees who move from their current jobs into others through promotions, lateral moves, and terminations. It also considers that the internal supply is influenced by training and development programs, transfer and promotion policies, and retirement policies, among other factors. In forecasting the internal supply, data from the replacement charts and succession planning efforts are used to project potential personnel changes, identify possible backup candidates, and keep track of attrition (resignations, retirements, etc.) for each department in an organization. Next we will consider how HR can help design the jobs those employees will do.

JOB DESIGN

Job design refers to organizing tasks, duties, responsibilities, and other elements into a productive unit of work. Identifying the components of a given job is an integral part of job design. Job design receives attention for three major reasons:

- Job design can influence *performance* in certain jobs, especially those where employee motivation can make a substantial difference.
- Job design can affect *job satisfaction*. Because people are more satisfied with certain job elements than others, identifying what makes a "good" job becomes critical. Reduced turnover and absenteeism also can be linked to effective job design.

FIGURE 3-4 Some Characteristics of People and Jobs

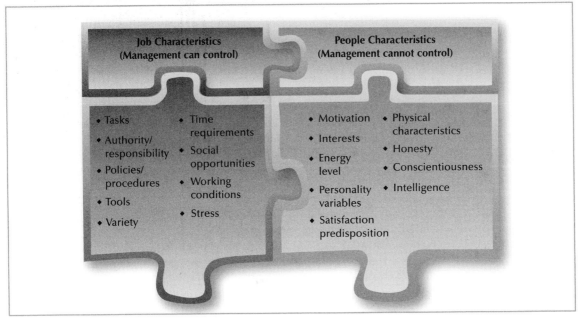

- Job design can impact both *physical* and *mental health*. Problems that may require assistance such as hearing loss, backache, leg pain, stress, high blood pressure, and even heart disease sometimes can be traced directly to job design.

Managers play a significant role in job design because often they are the people who establish jobs and their design components. They must make sure that job expectations are clear, that decision-making responsibilities and the accountability of workers are clarified, and that interactions with other jobs are integrated and appropriate.

The nature and characteristics of both jobs and people should be considered when job design is done. As Figure 3-4 indicates, managers can influence or control job characteristics, but usually not people characteristics.

Person-Job Fit

Not everyone would enjoy being an HR manager, an engineer, a nurse, or a drill-press operator. But some people like and do well at each of these jobs. The **person-job fit** is a simple but important concept of matching characteristics of people with characteristics of jobs. An employer can try to make a "round" person fit a "square" job, but it is hard to successfully reshape people. By redesigning jobs, the person-job fit may sometimes be improved more easily. For example, bank tellers talk to people all day; an individual who would rather not talk to others all day may do better in a job that does not require so much interaction because that part of the bank teller job probably cannot be changed. Different people will consider some jobs "good" and others "bad." As a result, people will fit different kinds of work.

Common Approaches to Job Design

One approach for designing or redesigning jobs is to simplify the job tasks and responsibilities. Job simplification may be appropriate for jobs that are to be staffed with entry-level employees. However, making jobs too simple may result in boring jobs that appeal to few people, causing high turnover. Several other approaches also have been used as part of job design.

Job Enlargement and Job Enrichment. Attempts to alleviate some of the problems encountered in excessive job simplification fall under the general headings of job enlargement and job enrichment. **Job enlargement** involves broadening the scope of a job by expanding the number of different tasks to be performed. **Job enrichment** is increasing the depth of a job by adding responsibility for planning, organizing, controlling, or evaluating the job.

Job Rotation. One technique that can break the monotony of an otherwise simple routine job is **job rotation**, which is the process of shifting a person from job to job. There are several advantages to job rotation with one being that it develops an employee's capabilities for doing several different jobs. Clear policies that identify for employees the nature and expectations of job rotations are more likely to make job rotation work.[5]

Job Sharing. Another alternative used is **job sharing**, in which two employees perform the work of one full-time job. For instance, a hospital allows two radiological technicians to fill one job, and each individual works every other week. Such arrangements are beneficial for employees who may not want or be able to work full-time because of family, school, or other reasons. The keys to successful job sharing are that both "job sharers" must work effectively together and each must be competent in meeting the job requirements.

Using Worker Teams. Typically, a job is thought of as something done by one person. However, where appropriate, jobs may be designed for teams to take advantage of the increased productivity and commitment that can follow such a change. Organizations can assign jobs to teams of employees instead of just individuals. Some firms have gone as far as dropping such terms as *workers* and *employees*, replacing them with *teammates, crew members, associates,* and other titles that emphasize teamwork.

The use of work teams has been a popular form of job redesign in the last decade. Improved productivity, increased employee involvement, greater coworker trust, more widespread employee learning, and greater employee use of knowledge diversity are among the potential benefits.[6] In a transition to work teams, efforts are necessary to define the areas of work, scope of authority, and goals of the teams. Also, teams must recognize and address dissent, conflict, and other problems.

JOBS AND WORK SCHEDULING

Considerations that can affect job design for both employers and employees are how the work is to be done, the time during which work is scheduled, and the location of employees when working. One factor changing how and when work is done is technology, including the creation of telework for some people.

Individuals who may be working at home or at other places illustrate **telework**, which means that employees work via electronic, telecommunications, and Internet means. The use of technology for telework is expected to grow, with almost 70% of private-sector respondents predicting more usage of IT resources in telework.[7] Some employers are allowing employees to *telecommute* one or more days a week. Telecommuting allows employees to work from home when bad weather or widespread health issues (e.g., pandemic flu) prevents them from coming to office facilities.

Alternative Work Schedule

Different types of work schedules have been developed for employees in different occupations and areas. The traditional U.S. work schedule of 8 hours a day, 5 days a week, is in transition. Workers in various occupations may work less or more than 8 hours at a workplace, and may have additional work at home.

The work schedules associated with jobs vary. Some jobs must be performed during "normal" daily work hours and on weekdays, while others require employees to work nights, weekends, and extended hours. Hours worked vary globally as well. There are significant differences in the hours worked in different countries. Given the global nature of many organizations, HR must adjust to different locations because of the international variations. Organizations are using many different work scheduling arrangements, based on industry demands, workforce needs, and other organizational factors. These different types include shift work and the compressed workweek.

Shift Work.   A common work schedule design is *shift work*. Many organizations need 24-hour coverage and therefore may schedule three 8-hour shifts per day. Most of these employers provide some form of additional pay, called a *shift differential*, for working the evening or night shifts. Some types of shift work have been known to cause difficulties for some employees personally, such as weariness, irritability, lack of motivation, and illness.[8] Nevertheless, some employers must have 24-hour, 7-day coverage, so shift work is likely to continue to be an option.

Compressed Workweek.   One type of work schedule design is the **compressed workweek**, in which a full week's work is accomplished in fewer than five 8-hour days. Compression usually results in more work hours each day and fewer workdays each week, such as four 10-hour days, a 3-day week, or 12-hour shifts. One survey in chemical industry plants found that 96% of the workers who shifted to 12-hour schedules did not wish to return to 8-hour schedules.[9] However, 12-hour schedules have led to sleep difficulties, fatigue, and an increased number of injuries.

Flexible Work Schedules. Flexible work schedules allow organizations to make better use of workers by matching work demands to work hours. One type of scheduling is **flextime**, in which employees work a set number of hours a day but vary the starting and ending times. In some industries, flextime allows more employees to be available at peak times when more customers and clients are present. The flexibility has aided in recruiting and retaining key staff members.

Work-Life Balancing

For many employees throughout the world, balancing their work and personal lives is a significant concern. Work-life balance is one of the top concerns in most countries.

Thousands of employees, both in large global firms like IBM and Hewlett-Packard and in many smaller firms, have flexible work schedules and/or use technology to work from locations away from the workplace as a way to help balance work and personal lives. Health care firms frequently allow employees to adjust their work schedules in order to address personal, family, health, and other issues.

JOB ANALYSIS

While job design attempts to develop jobs that fit effectively into the flow of the organizational work, the more narrow focus of job analysis centers on using a formal system to gather data about what people are doing in their jobs. A basic building block of HR management, **job analysis**, is a systematic way of gathering and analyzing information about the content, context, and human requirements of jobs. Most other functions in HR are based on and affected by job analysis.

An overview of job analysis is shown in Figure 3-5. The value of job analysis begins as the information is compiled into *job descriptions* and *job specifications* for use in virtually all HR activities.

Purposes of Job Analysis

Job analysis has grown in importance as the workforce and jobs have changed. To be effective, HR planning, recruiting, and selection all should be based on job requirements and the capabilities of individuals identified by job analysis. In EEO matters, accurate details on job requirements are needed, as the credentials in job descriptions can affect court decisions.[10] Additionally, compensation, training, and employee performance appraisals all should be based on the specific identified needs of the jobs. Job analysis also is useful in identifying job factors and duties that may contribute to workplace health/safety and employee/labor relations issues.

FIGURE 3-5 Job Analysis in Perspective

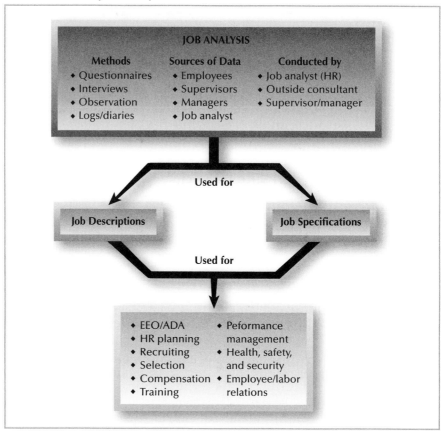

Task-Based Job Analysis

Task-based job analysis is the most common form and focuses on the tasks, duties, and responsibilities performed in a job. A **task** is a distinct, identifiable work activity composed of motions, whereas a **duty** is a larger work segment composed of several tasks that are performed by an individual. Because both tasks and duties describe activities, it is not always easy or necessary to distinguish between the two. For example, if one of the employment supervisor's duties is to interview applicants, one task associated with that duty would be asking job-related questions. **Responsibilities** are obligations to perform certain tasks and duties. Task-based job analysis seeks to identify all the tasks, duties, and responsibilities that are part of a job.

Competency-Based Job Analysis

Unlike the traditional task-based approach to analyzing jobs, the competency approach considers how knowledge and skills are used. **Competencies** are individual capabilities that can be linked to performance by individuals or teams.

The concept of competencies varies widely from organization to organization. The term *technical competencies* is often used to refer to specific knowledge and skills of employees. For example, the following have been identified as *behavioral competencies*:

- Customer focus
- Team orientation
- Technical expertise
- Results orientation
- Communication effectiveness

- Leadership
- Conflict resolution
- Innovation
- Adaptability
- Decisiveness

IMPLEMENTING JOB ANALYSIS

Prior to the job analysis process itself is the planning done to gather data from managers and employees. Probably the most important consideration is to identify the objectives of the job analysis, which might be as simple as updating job descriptions or as comprehensive as revising the compensation programs in the organization. Whatever the purpose identified, the effort needs the support of top management.

Preparing for and Introducing the Job Analysis

Preparation for job analysis includes identification of the jobs to be analyzed. Next reviewing organization charts, existing job descriptions, previous job analysis information, and other resources is part of the planning. This phase also identifies those who will be involved in conducting the job analysis and the methods to be used. A key part is identifying and communicating the process to appropriate managers, affected employees, and others.

Conducting the Job Analysis

If questionnaires are used, it is often helpful to have employees return them to supervisors or managers for review before giving them back to those conducting the job analysis. Questionnaires should be accompanied by a letter explaining the process and instructions for completing and returning them. If interviews are used, they may occur after the return of the questionnaires to clarify more details. Once data from job analyses are compiled, the information should be sorted by job, organizational unit, and job family.

Developing Job Descriptions and Job Specifications

At the fourth stage, the job analysts draft job descriptions and job specifications. Generally, organizations find that having managers and employees write job descriptions is not recommended for several reasons. First, it reduces consistency in format and details, both of which are important given the legal consequences of job descriptions. Second, managers and employees vary in their writing skills so they may write the job descriptions and job specifications to reflect what they do and what their personal qualifications are, not what the job requires. However, completed drafts should be reviewed with managers and supervisors, and then employees, before they are finalized.

Maintaining and Updating Job Descriptions and Job Specifications

Once job descriptions and specifications have been completed and reviewed by all appropriate individuals, a system must be developed for keeping them current and posted on a firm's intranet source. One effective way to ensure that appropriate reviews occur is to use current job descriptions and job specifications as part of other HR activities. For example, each time a vacancy occurs, the job description and specifications should be reviewed and revised as necessary *before* recruiting and selection efforts begin. Similarly, in some organizations, managers and employees review job descriptions during performance appraisal interviews.

Questionnaires

The questionnaire is a widely used method of gathering data on jobs. A survey instrument is developed and given to employees and managers to complete. The typical job questionnaire often covers the areas shown in Figure 3-6.

The questionnaire method offers a major advantage in that information on a large number of jobs can be collected inexpensively in a relatively short period of time. However, the questionnaire method assumes that employees can accurately analyze and communicate information about their jobs. Using interviewing and observation in combination with the questionnaire method allows analysts to clarify and verify the information gathered in questionnaires.

FIGURE 3-6 Typical Areas Covered in a Job Analysis Questionnaire

Duties and Percentage of Time Spent on Each	Contact with Other People
• Regular duties • Special duties performed less frequently	• Internal contacts • External contacts
Supervision	**Physical Dimensions**
• Supervision given to others • Supervision received from others	• Physical demands • Working conditions
Decisions Made	**Jobholder Characteristics**
• Records and reports prepared • Materials and equipment used • Financial/budget responsibilities	• Knowledge • Skills • Abilities • Training needed

Job Analysis and O*Net

A variety of resources related to job analysis are available from the U.S. Department of Labor (DOL). The resources have been developed and used over many years by various entities. *Functional job analysis* uses a competency approach to job analysis. A functional definition of what is done in a job can be generated by examining the three components of *data, people,* and *things.* The levels of these components traditionally have been used to identify and compare important elements of more than 120 jobs in the *Dictionary of Occupational Titles (DOT).* But O*Net is now the main DOL resource available and provides employers with a wide range of useful items.

Although not specifically a job analysis, O*Net is a database compiled by the U.S. Department of Labor to provide basic occupational data that cover more than 800 occupations based on the Standard Occupational Classification (SOC) developed by the government. O*Net also provides extensive links to additional resources on workplace issues.

Legal Aspects of Job Analysis

EEO legal compliance must focus on the jobs that individuals perform. The Uniform Guidelines on Employee Selection Procedures make it clear that HR requirements must be tied to specific job-related factors if employers are to defend their actions as a business necessity. This approach has direct impact on job descriptions and persons with disabilities who may apply for those jobs.

One result of the ADA is increased emphasis by employers on conducting job analyses, as well as developing and maintaining current and accurate job descriptions and job specifications. The ADA requires that organizations identify the *essential job functions,* which are the fundamental duties of a job. These do not include the marginal duties. The three major considerations used in determining essential functions and marginal functions are as follows:

- Percentage of time spent on tasks
- Frequency of tasks done
- Importance of tasks performed

Job analysis also should identify the *physical demands* of jobs. For example, the important physical skills and capabilities used on the job of nursing representative could include being able to hear well enough to aid clients and doctors. However, hearing might be less essential for a heavy equipment operator in a quarry.

Typically, job analysis identifies the percentage of time spent on each duty in a job. This information helps determine whether someone should be classified as exempt or nonexempt under the wage/hour laws.

JOB DESCRIPTIONS AND JOB SPECIFICATIONS

The output from analysis of a job is used to develop a job description and its job specifications. Together, these two documents summarize job analysis information in a readable format and provide the basis for defensible

FIGURE 3-7 Sample Job Description

Identification Section
Position Title: Customer Service Supervisor
Department: Marketing/Customer Service
Reports To: Marketing Director

EEOC Class: O/M
FLSA Status: Exempt

General Summary
Supervises, coordinates, and assigns work of employees to ensure customer
service department goals and customer needs are met.

Essential Job Functions
1. Supervises the work of Customer Service Representatives to enhance performance by coordinating duties, advising on issues or problems, and checking work. (55%)
2. Provides Customer Service training for company employees in all departments. (15%)
3. Creates and reviews reports for service orders for new and existing customers. (10%)
4. Performs employee performance evaluations, training, and discipline. (10%)
5. Follows up with customer complaints and issues and provides resolutions. (10%)
6. Conducts other duties as needed by guided by Marketing Director and executives.

Knowledge, Skills, and Abilities
- Knowledge of company products, services, policies, and procedures.
- Knowledge of marketing and customer programs, data, and results.
- Knowledge of supervisory requirements and practices.
- Skill in completing multiple tasks at once.
- Skill in identifying and resolving customer problems.
- Skill in oral and written communication, including Spanish communications.
- Skill in coaching, training, and performance evaluating employees.
- Skill in operating office and technological equipment and software.
- Ability to communicate professionally with coworkers, customers and vendors.
- Ability to work independently and meet managerial goals.
- Ability to follow oral and written instructions.
- Ability to organize daily activities of self and others and to work as a team player.

Education and Experience
Bachelor's degree in business or marketing, plus 3–5 years of industry experience. Supervisory, marketing, and customer service experience helpful.

Physical Requirements	Percentage of Work Time Spent on Activity			
	0–24%	25–49%	50–74%	75–100%
Seeing: Must be able to see well enough to read reports.				X
Hearing: Must be able to hear well enough to communicate with customers, vendors, and employees.				X
Standing/Walking: Must be able to move about department			X	
Climbing/Stooping/Kneeling: Must be able stoop or kneel to pick up paper products or directories.	X		X	
Lifting/Pulling/Pushing: Must be able to lift up to 50 pounds.	X			
Fingering/Grasping/Feeling: Must be able to type and use technical sources.				X

Working Conditions: Normal working conditions absent extreme factors.

Note: *The statements herein are intended to describe the general nature and level of work being performed, but are not to be seen as a complete list of responsibilities, duties, and skills required of personnel so classified. Also, they do not establish a contract for employment and are subject to change at the discretion of the employer.*

job-related actions. They also identify individual jobs for employees by providing documentation from management.

In most cases, the job description and job specifications are combined into one document that contains several sections. A **job description** identifies the tasks, duties, and responsibilities of a job. It describes what is done, why it is done, where it is done, and, briefly, how it is done.

While the job description describes activities to be done, the **job specifications** list the knowledge, skills, and abilities (KSAs) an individual needs to perform a job satisfactorily. KSAs include education, experience, work skill requirements, personal abilities, and mental and physical requirements. Accurate job specifications identify what KSAs a person needs to do the job, not necessarily the current employee's qualifications.

Performance standards flow directly from a job description and indicate what the job accomplishes and how performance is measured in key areas of the job description. If employees know what is expected and how performance is to be measured, they have a much better chance of performing satisfactorily. Unfortunately, performance standards are often not developed as supplemental items from job descriptions. Even if performance standards have been identified and matched to job descriptions, they must be communicated to employees if the job descriptions are to be effective HR tools. Figure 3-7 shows a job description.

NOTES

1. For a more detailed review of job satisfaction factors, see "2009 Employee Job Satisfaction: Understanding the Factors That Make Work Gratifying," *SHRM Research*, 2009, *www.shrm.org*; Daniel C. Ganseter, "Measurement Challenges for Studying Work-Related Stressors and Strains," *Human Resource Management Review*, 18 (2008), 259–270.

2. Frank Giancola, "Employee Engagement: What You Need to Know," *Workspan*, October 2007, 55–59.

3. "Estimating Turnover Costs," *www.keepemployees.com*.

4. "Corps of Engineers Needs to Update Its Workforce Planning . . .," *Human Capital*, U.S. Government Accountability Office, May 2008, *www.goa.gov*.

5. Margaret Fiester, "Job Rotation, Total Rewards, Measuring Value," *HR Magazine*, August 2008, 33.

6. Ramon Rico, et al., "Team Implicit Coordination Processes," *Academy of Management Review*, 33 (2008), 163–184.

7. Rita Zeidner, "Telework Influencing Technology Investments," *HR Magazine*, July 2008, 22.

8. "Extended Unusual Work Shifts," *U.S. Occupational Safety & Health Administration*, September 7, 2005, *www.osha.gov*.

9. Martin Moore-Ede, et al., "Advantages and Disadvantages of Twelve-Hour Shifts, A Balanced Perspective," 2007, *www.ciridian.com*.

10. *Lamb v. Boeing Co.*, No. 5-18431 (4th Cir., Jan. 11, 2007).

INTERNET RESOURCES

Loyalty Research Center—This research center provides employee loyalty/employee engagement research and consulting services. Visit their site at *www.loyaltyresearch.com.*

Human Resource Planning Society—Information and resources on building a strategic HR plan are available at *www.hrps.org.*

Team Building, Inc.—This website provides information for team building services and team building training products. Visit the site at *www. teambuildinginc.com.*

Job Analysis.net—A resource for conducting a job analysis, including different types of methods, legal issues, questionnaires, and job descriptions, can be found at *www.jobanalysis.net.*

SUGGESTED READINGS

Arne L. Kallenberg, "The Mismatched Worker: When People Don't Fit Their Jobs," *Academy of Management Perspectives,* February 2008, 24–40.

Piers Steel and Cornelius König, "Integrating Theories of Motivation," *Academy of Management Review,* 31 (2006), 889–913.

Terrance M. McMenamin, "A Time to Work: Recent Trends in Shift Work and Flexible Schedules," *Monthly Labor Review,* December 2007, 3–14.

For details, go to the website listed in the boxed feature, as well as *www.dol.gov* and *www.onetcenter.org.* The value of O*Net is identified in various publications, including Max Maller, *The Manager's Guide to HR,* Chapter 1 (Alexandria, VA: SHRM, 2009).

Staffing: Recruiting and Selection

HR—MEETING MANAGEMENT CHALLENGES

Finding and choosing the right people for a job remains one of the most important HR issues. Considerations include:

- How best to locate good candidates
- Selecting good employees is more than just interviewing
- Poor background investigation can get you sued

Keeping a flow of good employees coming into the organization is a challenge. Recruiting and selection will always be needed as a certain amount of turnover will always occur. The key to success is approaching the recruiting and selection properly.

STAFFING

The staffing process used by an employer, based on HR planning and retention as key components, includes successful recruiting and selection efforts.

Recruiting is the process of generating a pool of qualified applicants for organizational jobs. If the number of available candidates equals the number of people to be hired, no real selection is required—the organization must either leave some openings unfilled or take all the candidates. One survey of employers in slow labor markets found that almost half of the hiring managers cited less qualified applicants as the biggest recruiting and hiring challenge.[1] It is important to view recruiting broadly as a key part of staffing, and not just as a collection of administrative and operational activities.

RECRUITING

Although recruiting can be expensive, an offsetting concept that must be considered is the *cost of unfilled jobs*. For example, consider a company in which three operations-related jobs are vacant. Assume these three vacancies cost the company $300 for each business day the jobs remain vacant. If the jobs are not filled for four months, the cost of this failure to recruit in a timely fashion will be about $26,000.

Although cost is certainly an issue, and some employers are quite concerned about cost per hire as well as the cost of vacancies, *quality* might be an important trade-off. For example, if an organizational strategy focuses on quality as a competitive advantage, a company might choose to hire only from the top 15% of candidates for critical jobs, and from the top 30% of candidates for all other positions. Though this approach may raise the cost per hire, it will improve workforce quality.

Labor Markets

Because recruiting takes place in different labor markets that can vary a great deal, learning some basics about labor markets aids in understanding recruiting. **Labor markets** are the external supply pool from which employers attract employees. To understand where recruiting takes place, one can think of the sources of employees as a funnel, in which the broad scope of labor markets narrows progressively to the point of selection and job offers, as Figure 4-1 shows. Of course, if the selected candidates reject the offers, then HR staff members must move back up the funnel to the applicant pool for other candidates, and in extreme cases may need to reopen the recruiting process.

When the unemployment rate is high in a given market, many people are looking for jobs. When the unemployment rate is low, there are fewer applicants. Unemployment rates vary with business cycles and present very different challenges for recruiting at different times. For instance, in some U.S. states, when many automobile plants closed and workers were laid off, manufacturers in other industries and even retailers experienced a significant increase in their numbers of job applicants, making recruiting easier and larger applicant pools a fact.

Different Labor Markets

The supply of workers in various labor markets differs substantially and affects staffing. Organizations recruit in a number of different labor markets, including industry-specific markets and occupational, educational and technical, and geographic markets.

FIGURE 4-1 Labor Market Components

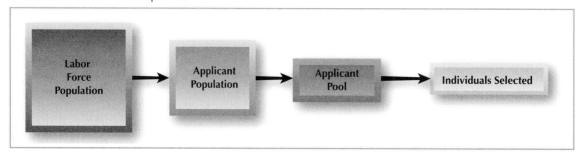

Labor markets can be classified by industry and occupation. For example, the biggest increases in U.S. jobs until the year 2016 are going to be in the positions of registered nurses, retail sales and customer service representatives, home health aides, and post-secondary teachers.[2] These data illustrate that recruiting will be more difficult in filling these jobs during the next few years. Trucking and welding jobs are also expected to present significant recruiting difficulties.

Another way to look at labor markets is by considering the educational and technical qualifications that define the people being recruited. Employers may need individuals with specific licenses, certifications, or educational backgrounds. An example of a tight labor market is that of business professors with PhDs, who are forecast to be in short supply in the next few years due to the retirement of baby boomers from faculty positions. Other examples of shortages in specific labor markets include certified auto mechanics, heating and air-conditioning technicians, and network-certified computer specialists.

A common way to classify labor markets is based on geographic location. Markets can be local, area or regional, national, or international. Local and area labor markets vary significantly in terms of workforce availability and quality, and changes in a geographic labor market may force changes in recruiting efforts. For instance, if a new major employer locates in a regional labor market, other existing area employers may see a decline in their numbers of applicants.

Employers in the United States are tapping global labor markets when necessary and expanding export work to overseas labor markets when doing so is advantageous. Firms in different industries are expanding in India, China, Indonesia, Romania, Poland, and other countries.

STRATEGIC RECRUITING DECISIONS

Recruiting efforts may be viewed as either continuous or intensive. *Continuous* efforts to recruit offer the advantage of keeping the employer in the recruiting market. For example, with college recruiting, some organizations may find it advantageous to have a recruiter on a given campus each year. Employers that visit a campus only occasionally are less likely to build a following at that school over time.

Intensive recruiting may take the form of a vigorous recruiting campaign aimed at hiring a given number of employees, usually within a short period of time.

Employment "Branding" and Image

The "employment brand" or image of an organization is the view of it held by both employees and outsiders. Organizations that are seen as desirable employers are better able to attract qualified applicants than are those with poor reputations. For example, one firm had good pay and benefits, but its work demands were seen as excessive, and frequent downsizings had resulted in some terminations and transfers. The result was high turnover and fewer applicants interested in employment at the company. That firm had a poor brand or image as an employer.

Organization-Based versus Outsourced Recruiting

A basic decision is whether the recruiting will be done by the employer or outsourced to someone else. This decision need not be focused on an "either-or" situation entirely. In most organizations, HR staff members handle many of the recruiting efforts. However, because recruiting can be a time-consuming process and HR staff and other managers in organizations have many other responsibilities, outsourcing is a way to decrease the number of staff needed for recruiting and free some of their time for other responsibilities.

Professional Employer Organizations and Employee Leasing

A specific type of outsourcing uses professional employer organizations (PEOs) and employee leasing. The employee leasing process is simple: An employer signs an agreement with the PEO, after which the staff is hired by the leasing firm and leased back to the company for a fee. In turn, the leasing firm writes the paychecks, pays taxes, prepares and implements HR policies, and keeps all the required records for the employer.

One advantage of leasing companies for employees is that they may receive better benefits than they otherwise would get in many of the small businesses that use leasing firms. But all this service comes at a cost to employers. Leasing companies often charge employers between 4% and 6% of employees' monthly salaries. Thus, while leasing may save employers money on benefits and HR administration, it also may increase total payroll costs.

Regular versus Flexible Staffing

Another strategic decision affects whether recruiting will be done to fill staffing needs with regular full-time or part-time employees. Decisions as to which should be recruited hinge on whether to seek regular employees or to use more flexible approaches, which might include temporaries or independent contractors. A number of employers have decided that the cost of keeping a regular workforce has become excessive and is growing worse due to economic, competitive, and governmental considerations. However, not just money is at issue. The large number of employment regulations also constrains the employment relationship, making many employers reluctant to hire new regular full-time employees.

Temporary Workers.   Employers who use temporary employees can hire their own temporary staff members or contract with agencies supplying temporary workers on a rate-per-day or rate-per-week basis. Originally developed to provide clerical and office workers to employers, temporary workers in professional, technical, and even managerial jobs are becoming more common. The importance of using temporary workers is illustrated through the use of computer technology by an educational publisher. The publisher utilized an automated employment, recruiting, and screening system to obtain sufficient temporary workers for its firm. That employer obtained sufficient qualified workers which resulted in a return on its hiring investment of $6 for every $1 of cost.[3]

Independent Contractors.   Some firms employ independent contractors as workers who perform specific services on a contract basis. These workers must be truly independent as determined by regulations used by the U.S. Internal Revenue Service and the U.S. Department of Labor. Independent contractors are used in a number of areas, including building maintenance, security, advertising, and others. One major reason for the use of independent contractors is that some employers experience significant savings because benefits are not provided to those individuals.

EEO and Recruiting Efforts

Recruiting as a key employment-related activity is subject to various considerations, especially equal employment laws and regulations. As part of legal compliance in the recruiting process, organizations must work to reduce external disparate impact, or underrepresentation of protected-class members compared to the labor markets utilized by the employer. If disparate impact exists, then the employer may need to make special efforts to persuade protected-class individuals to apply for jobs. For employers with affirmative action plans (AAPs), special ways to reduce disparate impact can be identified as goals listed in those plans. Also, many employers that emphasize internal recruiting should take actions to obtain protected-class applicants externally if disparate impact exists in the current workforce.

 ## Realistic Job Previews

Providing a balanced view of the advantages, demands, expectations, and challenges in an organization or a job may help attract employees with more realistic expectations and reduce the number of employees who quit a few months after being hired because the "reality" they discover does not match what they expected. Thus, recruiting efforts can benefit from *realistic job previews.*

Recruiting Source Choices: Internal versus External

Most employers combine the use of internal and external recruiting sources. Both promoting from within the organization (internal recruitment) and hiring from outside the organization (external recruitment) come with advantages and disadvantages.

Organizations that face rapidly changing competitive environments and conditions may need to place a heavier emphasis on external sources in addition to developing internal sources. A possible strategy might be to promote from within if a qualified applicant exists and to go to external sources if not.

However, for organizations existing in environments that change slowly, emphasis on promotion from within may be more suitable. Once the various recruiting policy decisions have been addressed, the actual recruiting methods can be identified and used for both internal and external recruiting.

INTERNET RECRUITING

Numerous Internet job boards, such as Monster and Yahoo! HotJobs, provide places for employers to post jobs or search for candidates. Job boards offer access to numerous candidates. Some Internet locations allow recruiters to search one website, such as MyJobHunter.com, to obtain search links to many other major job sites. Applicants can also use these websites to do one match and then send résumés to all jobs in which they are interested. However, a number of the individuals accessing these sites are "job lookers" who are not serious about changing jobs, but are checking out compensation levels and job availability in their areas of interest. Despite such concerns, HR recruiters find general job boards useful for generating applicant responses.

Many professional associations have employment sections at their websites. As illustration, for HR jobs, see the Society for Human Resource Management site, *www.shrm.org*, or WorldatWork, *www.worldatwork.org*. The SHRM organization has established a Job Posting Center that numerous recruiters and employers can use to post a wide range of industry openings. A number of private corporations maintain specialized career or industry websites to focus on IT, telecommunications, engineering, medicine, and other areas.

Despite the popularity of job boards and association job sites, many employers have learned that their own websites can be most effective and efficient when recruiting candidates. The most successful of these websites are created by experienced firms and take extensive actions to guide job seekers to the employer. Employers include employment and career information on their websites under headings such as "Employment" or "Careers." This is the place where recruiting (both internal and external) is often conducted. On many of these sites, job seekers are encouraged to e-mail résumés or complete online applications.

Recruiting and Internet Social Networking

The Internet has led to social networking of individuals on blogs, twitters, and a range of websites. Many people initially use the social media more than job board sites.[4] Internet connections often include people who work together as well as past personal contacts and friends.

The informal use of the Web presents some interesting recruiting advantages and disadvantages for both employers and employees. Social networking sites allow job seekers to connect with employees of potential hirers. For instance, some sites include posts on what it is like to work for a boss, and job hunters can contact the posters and ask questions. An example is LinkedIn, which has a job-search engine that allows people to search for contacts who work for employers with posted job openings.

Legal Issues in Internet Recruiting

With Internet recruiting expanding, new and different concerns have arisen. Several of these issues have ethical and moral as well as legal implications. The following examples illustrate some of these concerns:

handwritten margin note: importance of getting potential employees into our building?

- When companies use screening software to avoid looking at the thousands of résumés they receive, are rejections really based on the qualifications needed for the job?
- How can a person's protected-category and other information be collected and analyzed for reports?
- Are too many individuals in protected categories being excluded from the later phases of the Internet recruiting process?
- Which applicants really want jobs? If someone has accessed a job board and sent an e-mail asking an employer about a job opening, does the person actually want to be an applicant?
- What are the implications of Internet recruiting in terms of confidentiality and privacy?

Employment lawyers are issuing warnings to employers about remarks and other characteristics posted on LinkedIn, Facebook, and Twitter. According to one survey of employers, about three-fourths of hiring managers in various-sized companies checked persons' credentials on LinkedIn, about half used Facebook, and approximately one-fourth used Twitter.[5] Some of the concerns raised have included postings of confidential details about an employee's termination, racial/ethnic background, or gender and the making of discriminatory comments. All of these actions could lead to wrongful termination or discrimination lawsuits. Thus, because Internet usage has both advantages and disadvantages for recruiting, legal advice should be obtained, and HR employment-related policies, training, and enforcement should include such advice.

Advantages of Internet Recruiting

Employers have found a number of advantages to using Internet recruiting. A primary one is that many employers have saved money using Internet recruiting versus other recruiting methods such as newspaper advertising, employment agencies, and search firms, all of which can cost substantially more.

Another major advantage is that a very large pool of applicants can be generated using Internet recruiting. Individuals may view an employer more positively and obtain more useful information, which can result in more individual applications.

Internet recruiting also can save time. Applicants can respond quickly to job postings by sending electronic responses, rather than using "snail mail."

A good website and useful Internet resources also can help recruiters reach "passive" job seekers—those who have a good job and are not really looking to change jobs but who might consider it if a better opportunity were presented. These individuals often do not list themselves on job boards, but they might visit a company website for other reasons and check out the careers or employment section.

Disadvantages of Internet Recruiting

The positive things associated with Internet recruiting come with a number of disadvantages. Because of broader exposure, Internet recruiting often creates additional work for HR staff members and others internally. More online job postings must be sent; many more résumés must be reviewed; more e-mails, blogs, and twitters need to be dealt with; and expensive specialized software may be needed to track the increased number of applicants resulting from Internet recruiting efforts.

As noted, many individuals who access Internet recruiting sources are browsers who may submit résumés just to see what happens, but they are not actively looking for new jobs.

EXTERNAL RECRUITING

Even when the overall unemployment rate increases, some jobs and/or employers still face recruiting challenges. Regardless of the methods used, external recruiting involves some common advantages and disadvantages. Some of the prominent traditional and evolving recruiting methods are highlighted next.

Media Sources

Media sources such as newspapers, magazines, television, radio, and billboards typically have been widely used in external recruiting. Some firms have sent direct mail using purchased lists of individuals in certain fields or industries. Internet usage has led to media sources being available online, including postings, ads, videos, webinars, and many other expanding media services. In some cities and towns, newspaper ads are still very prominent, though they may trigger job searchers to go to an Internet source for more details.

Competitive Recruiting Sources

Other sources for recruiting include professional and trade associations, trade publications, and competitors. Many professional societies and trade associations publish newsletters or magazines and have websites containing job ads. Such sources may be useful for recruiting the specialized professionals needed in an industry.

Some employers have extended recruiting to customers. Retailers such as Wal-Mart and Best Buy have had aggressive programs to recruit customers to become employees in stores. While in the store, customers at these firms can pick up applications, apply online using kiosks, and even schedule interviews with managers or HR staff members. Other firms have included employment announcements when sending out customer bills or newsletters.

Employment Agencies

Employment agencies, both public and private, are a recruiting source. Every state in the United States has its own state-sponsored employment agency. These agencies operate branch offices in cities throughout the states and do not charge fees to applicants or employers. They also have websites that potential applicants can use without having to go to the offices.

Private employment agencies operate in most cities. For a fee collected from either the employee or the employer, these agencies do some preliminary screening and put employers in touch with applicants. Private employment agencies differ considerably in the levels of service, costs, policies, and types of applicants they provide.

Labor Unions

Labor unions may be a useful source of certain types of workers. For example, in electrical and construction industries, unions traditionally have supplied workers to employers. A labor pool is generally available through a union, and workers can be dispatched from the hiring hall to particular jobs to meet the needs of employers.

In some instances, labor unions can control or influence recruiting and staffing activity. An organization with a strong union may have less flexibility than a nonunion company in deciding who will be hired and where those people will be placed. Unions can benefit employers through apprenticeship and cooperative staffing programs, as they do in the building and printing industries.

Job Fairs

Employers in various labor markets needing to fill a large number of jobs quickly have used job fairs and special recruiting events. Job fairs have been held by economic development entities, employer and HR associations, and other community groups to help bring employers and potential job candidates together. For instance, the SHRM chapter in a midwestern metropolitan area annually sponsors a job fair at which 75 to 100 employers can meet applicants. Publicity in the city draws several hundred potential recruits for different types of jobs.

Educational Institutions and Recruiting

College and university students are a significant external source of entry-level professional and technical employees. Most universities maintain career placement offices in which employers and applicants can meet. A number of considerations affect an employer's selection of colleges and universities at which to conduct interviews.

Because college/university recruiting can be expensive and require significant time and effort, employers need to determine whether both current and future jobs require persons with college degrees in specific fields. A number of factors determine success in college recruiting. Some employers actively build continuing relationships with individual faculty members and career staff at designated colleges and universities. Maintaining a presence on campus by providing guest speakers to classes and student groups increases the contacts for an employer. Employers with a continuing presence and support on a campus are more likely to see positive college recruiting results.

High schools and vocational/technical schools may be valuable sources of new employees for some organizations. Many schools have a centralized guidance or placement office. Participating in career days and giving company tours to school groups are ways of maintaining good contact with school sources. Cooperative programs, in which students work part-time and receive some school credits, also may be useful in generating qualified future applicants for full-time positions.

INTERNAL RECRUITING

Filling openings internally may add motivation for employees to stay and grow in the organization rather than pursuing career opportunities elsewhere. The most common internal recruiting methods include: organizational databases, job postings, promotions and transfers, current-employee referrals, and re-recruiting of former employees and applicants. Some of the common advantages and disadvantages of internal recruiting are highlighted in Figure 4-2.

FIGURE 4-2 Advantages and Disadvantages of Internal Recruiting

ADVANTAGES	DISADVANTAGES
• The morale of a promotee is usually high. • The firm can better assess a candidate's abilities due to prior work actions. • Recruiting costs are lower for some jobs. • The process is a motivator for good performances by employees. • The process can aid succession planning, future promotions, and career development. • The firm may have to hire only at the entry level and then move employees up based on experience and performance.	• "Inbreeding" of employees may result in a less diverse workforce, as well as a lack of new ideas. • Those persons not promoted may experience morale problems. • Employees may engage in "political" infighting for promotions. • A development program often is needed to transfer employees into supervisory and management jobs. • Some managers may resist having employees promoted into their departments.

Internal Databases and Recruiting

HR information systems allow HR staff to maintain background and knowledge, skills, and abilities (KSA) information on existing employees. As openings arise, HR can access databases by entering job requirements and then get a listing of current employees meeting those requirements. Employment software can sort employee data by occupational fields, education, areas of career interests, previous work histories, and other variables. For instance, if a firm has an opening for someone with an MBA and marketing experience, the key words *MBA* and *marketing* can be entered in a search field, and the program displays a list of all current employees with these two items identified in their employee profiles.

The advantage of such databases is that they can be linked to other HR activities. Opportunities for career development and advancement are a major reason why individuals stay at or leave their employers. With employee databases, internal opportunities for individuals can be identified. Employee profiles are continually updated to include such items as additional training and education completed, special projects handled, and career plans and desires noted during performance appraisals and career mentoring discussions.

RECRUITING EVALUATION

To determine how effective various recruiting sources and methods have been, it is important to evaluate recruiting efforts. But in a survey, a majority of HR executives identified that their firms were not getting sufficient metrics on the quality of hires and how well the new hires fit into the organizations.[6]

To evaluate recruiting, organizations can see how their recruiting efforts compare with past patterns and with the recruiting performance of other organizations. Measures of recruiting effectiveness can be used to see whether sufficient numbers of targeted population groups are being attracted.

Information about job performance, absenteeism, cost of training, and turnover by recruiting source also helps adjust future recruiting efforts. For example, some companies find that recruiting at certain colleges or universities furnishes stable, high performers, whereas recruiting at other schools provides employees who are more prone to leave the organization. General metrics for evaluating recruiting include quantity and quality of applicants.

Quantity of Applicants

Because the goal of a good recruiting program is to generate a large pool of applicants from which to choose, quantity is a natural place to begin evaluation. The basic measure here considers whether the quantity of recruits is sufficient to fill job vacancies. A related question is: Does recruiting at this source provide enough qualified applicants with an appropriate mix of protected-category individuals?

Quality of Applicants

In addition to quantity, a key issue is whether or not the qualifications of the applicant pool are sufficient to fill the job openings. Do the applicants meet job specifications, and do they perform the jobs well after hire? What is the failure rate for new hires for each recruiter? Measures that can be used include items such as performance appraisal scores, months until promotion, production quantity, and sales volume for each hire.

Recruiting Satisfaction

The satisfaction of two groups is useful in evaluating recruiting. Certainly the views of managers with openings to fill are important, because they are "customers" in a very real sense. But the applicants (those hired and those not hired) also are an important part of the process and can provide useful input.

Managers can respond to questions about the quality of the applicant pool, the recruiter's service, the timeliness of the process, and any problems that they see. Applicants might provide input on how they were treated, their perceptions of the company, and the length of the recruiting process and other aspects.

Time Required to Fill Openings

Looking at the length of time it takes to fill openings is a common means of evaluating recruiting efforts. If openings are not filled quickly with qualified candidates, the work and productivity of the organization are likely to suffer. If it takes 45 days to fill vacant positions, managers who need those employees will be unhappy. As noted earlier, unfilled positions have an associated cost.

Evaluating the Cost of Recruiting

Different formulas can be used to evaluate recruiting costs. The calculation most often used to measure such costs is to divide total recruiting expenses for the year by the number of hires for the year:

$$\frac{\text{Recruiting expenses}}{\text{Number of recruits hired}}$$

The problem with this approach is accurately identifying what details should be included in the recruiting expenses. Should expenses for testing, background checks, relocations, or signing bonuses be included, or are they more properly excluded?

INCREASING RECRUITING EFFECTIVENESS

Evaluation of recruiting should be used to make recruiting activities more effective. Some common activities can help effectiveness are:

- *Résumé mining*—a software approach to getting the best résumés for a fit from a big database

- *Applicant tracking*—an approach that takes an applicant all the way from a job listing to performance appraisal results
- *Employer career website*—a convenient recruiting place on an employer's website where applicants can see what jobs are available and apply
- *Internal mobility*—a system that tracks prospects in the company and matches them with jobs as they come open
- *Realistic job previews*—a process that persons can use to get details on the employer and the jobs
- *Responsive recruitment*—whereby applicants receive timely responses

Another key way to increase recruiting effectiveness rests with the recruiters themselves. Those involved in the recruiting process can either turn off recruits or create excitement. For instance, recruiters who emphasize positive aspects about the jobs and their employers can enhance recruiting effectiveness. Thus, it is important that recruiters communicate well with applicants and treat them fairly and professionally.

SELECTION AND PLACEMENT

Some would argue that picking the right people for the jobs that need to be done is the most important part of human resource management. Certainly for a business that depends on good people and good performance for the organization to succeed, its importance is very high. For an organization that is failing, improvement may need to come from many different sources, but it is difficult to imagine appropriate changes coming without some new competent people to carry out those changes. In athletic organizations that are not doing well, it is the selection of new coaches and players that creates improvements, if any are to come, and the continued selection of good athletes and coaches that allows ongoing success.

Selection is the process of choosing individuals with the correct qualifications needed to fill jobs in an organization. Without these qualified employees, an organization is far less likely to succeed. A useful perspective on selection and placement comes from two HR observations that underscore the importance of effective staffing:

- *"Hire hard, manage easy."* The investment of time and effort in selecting the right people for jobs will make managing them as employees much less difficult because many problems are eliminated.
- *"Good training will not make up for bad selection."* When people without the appropriate aptitudes are selected, employers will have difficulty training them to do those jobs that they do not fit.

Placement

The ultimate purpose of selection is **placement**, or fitting a person to the right job. Placement of human resources should be seen primarily as a matching process. How well an employee is matched to a job can affect the amount and quality of the employee's work, as well as the training and operating costs required to prepare the individual for work life. Further, employee morale is an issue because good fit encourages individuals to be positive about their jobs and what they accomplish.[7]

Selection and placement activities typically focus on applicants' knowledge, skills, and abilities (KSAs), but they should also focus on the degree to which job candidates generally match the situations experienced both on the job and in the company. Psychologists label this *person-environment fit*. In HR it is usually called **person/job fit**. Fit is related not only to satisfaction with work but also to commitment to a company and to quitting intentions.

Lack of fit between KSAs and job requirements can be classified as a "mismatch." A mismatch results from poor pairing of a person's needs, interests, abilities, personality, and expectations with characteristics of the job, rewards, and the organization in which the job is located. Five mismatch situations are:[8]

- Skills/job qualifications
- Geography/job location
- Time/amount of work
- Earnings/expectations
- Work/family

Criteria, Predictors, and Job Performance

Regardless of whether an employer uses specific KSAs or a more general approach, effective selection of employees involves using selection criteria and predictors of these criteria. At the heart of an effective selection system must be the knowledge of what constitutes good job performance. When one knows what good performance looks like on a particular job, the next step is to identify what it takes for the employee to achieve successful performance. These are called selection criteria. A **selection criterion** is a characteristic that a person must possess to successfully perform work. Figure 4-3 shows that ability, motivation, intelligence, conscientiousness, appropriate risk, and permanence might be selection criteria for many jobs. Selection criteria that might be more specific to managerial jobs include "leading and deciding," "supporting and cooperating," "organizing and executing," and "enterprising and performing."

To determine whether candidates might possess certain selection criteria (such as ability and motivation), employers try to identify **predictors of selection criteria** that are measurable or visible indicators of those positive characteristics (or criteria). For example, as Figure 4-3 indicates, three good predictors of "permanence" might be individual interests, salary requirements, and tenure on previous jobs. If a candidate possesses appropriate amounts of any or all of these predictors, it might be assumed that the person would stay on the job longer than someone without those predictors.

The information gathered about an applicant through predictors should focus on the likelihood that the individual will execute the job competently once hired. Predictors can be identified through many formats such as application forms, tests, interviews, education requirements, and years of experience, but such factors should be used only if they are found to be valid predictors of specific job performance. Using invalid predictors can result in selecting the "wrong" candidate and rejecting the "right" one.

FIGURE 4-3 Job Performance, Selection Criteria, and Predictors

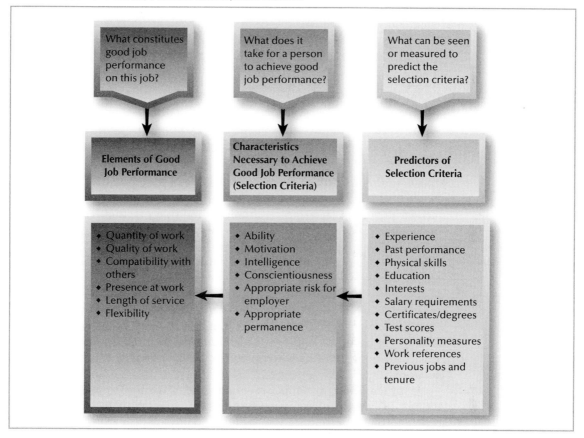

Combining Predictors

If an employer chooses to use only one predictor, such as a pencil-and-paper test, to select the individuals to be hired, the decision becomes straightforward. If the test is valid and encompasses a major dimension of a job, and an applicant does well on the test, then that person should be given a job offer. When an employer uses several predictors such as "three years of experience," "possesses a college degree," and "acceptable aptitude test score," job applicants are evaluated on all of these requirements and the multiple predictors must be combined in some way. Two approaches for combining predictors are:

- *Multiple hurdles:* A minimum cutoff is set on each predictor, and each minimum level must be "passed." For example, to be hired, a candidate for a sales representative job must achieve a minimum education level, a certain score on a sales aptitude test, and a minimum score on a structured interview.

- *Compensatory approach:* Scores from individual predictors are added and combined into an overall score, thereby allowing a higher score on one predictor to offset, or compensate for, a lower score on another. The combined index takes into consideration performance on all predictors. For example, when admitting students into graduate business programs, a higher overall score on an admissions test might offset a lower undergraduate grade point average.

THE SELECTION PROCESS

Most organizations take a series of consistent steps to process and select applicants for jobs. Company size, job characteristics, the number of people needed, the use of electronic technology, and other factors cause variations on the basic process. Selection can take place in a day or over a much longer period of time, and certain phases of the process may be omitted or the order changed, depending on the employer. If the applicant is processed in one day, the employer usually checks references after selection. Figure 4-4 shows steps in a typical selection process.

Individuals wanting employment can indicate interest in a number of ways. Traditionally, individuals have submitted résumés by mail or fax, or applied in person at an employer's location. But with the growth in Internet recruiting, many individuals complete applications online or submit résumés electronically.

Many employers conduct preemployment screening to determine if applicants meet the minimum qualifications for open jobs before they have the applicants fill out an application. When a job posting generates 1,000 or more applications, which is not unusual with large companies or in difficult economic times, responding to each would be a full-time job. Electronic screening can speed up the process. This may take several forms: disqualification questions; screening questions to get at KSAs and experience; valid assessment tests; and background, drug, and financial screening. Some of the assessments might include auditions for the job that are based on simulations of specific job-related tasks.

Some employers do not use preemployment screening prior to having applicants fill out an application form. Instead, the first step is to have every interested individual complete an application first. These completed application forms then become the basis for prescreening information.

Application forms, which are used universally, can take on different formats. Properly prepared, the application form serves four purposes:

1. It is a record of the applicant's desire to obtain a position.
2. It provides the interviewer with a profile of the applicant that can be used during the interview.
3. It is a basic employee record for applicants who are hired.
4. It can be used for research on the effectiveness of the selection process.

FIGURE 4-4 Selection Process Flowchart

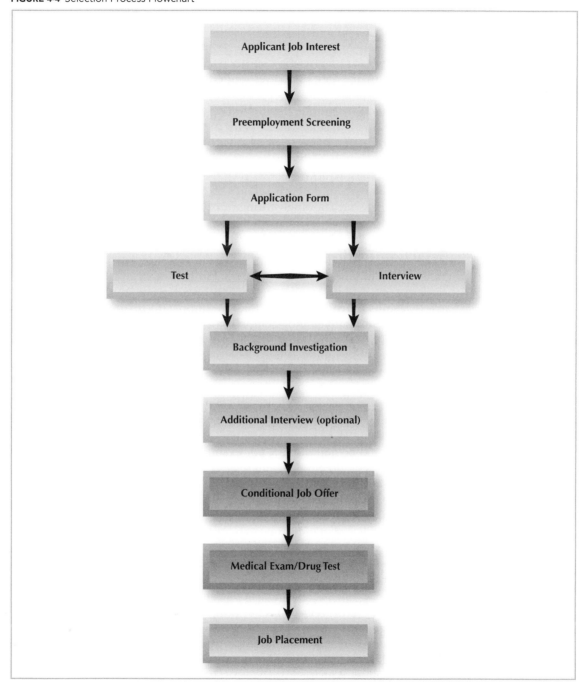

Appendix C shows a sample application form, and Appendix D shows commonly asked illegal inquires. Businesses are required to review and record identity documents, such as Social Security cards, passports, and visas, and to determine if they appear to be genuine. It is illegal to knowingly hire employees who are not in the country legally. The consequences for offending businesses are high; penalties range from $375 to $16,000 per incident and 6 months in prison. If HR personnel know they are working with fraudulent documents, corporate liability exists, and seizure of assets and criminal liability for top management can occur.

A government program called E-Verify is run by the Department of Homeland Security to help with this process. The use of E-Verify is mandatory for government contractors or subcontractors.

An employer should have a policy to comply with immigration requirements and to avoid knowingly hiring or retaining illegal workers. I-9s should be completed, updated, and audited.

Selection Testing

Many different kinds of tests can be used to help select qualified employees. Literacy tests, skill-based tests, personality tests, and honesty tests are used to assess various individual factors that are important for the work to be performed. These useful employment tests allow companies to predict which applicants will be the most successful before being hired.

However, selection tests must be evaluated extensively before being utilized as a recruiting tool. The development of the test items should be linked to a thorough job analysis. Also, initial testing of the items should include an evaluation by knowledge experts, and statistical and validity assessments of the items should be conducted. Furthermore, adequate security of the testing instruments should be coordinated, and the monetary value of these tests to the firm should be determined. For example, Gerber Products Company was found to be using preemployment selection tests for entry-level positions that did not have sufficient evidence of validity. The tests were negatively impacting minority applicants. Gerber paid 1,912 minority and female applicants $900,000 in back pay and interest.[9]

Tests that assess an individual's ability to perform in a specific manner are grouped as ability tests. These are sometimes further differentiated into *aptitude tests* and *achievement tests*. **Cognitive ability tests** measure an individual's thinking, memory, reasoning, verbal, and mathematical abilities. Tests such as these can be used to determine applicants' basic knowledge of terminology and concepts, word fluency, spatial orientation, comprehension and retention span, general and mental ability, and conceptual reasoning. The Wonderlic Personnel Test and the General Aptitude Test Battery (GATB) are two widely used tests of this type. Managers need to ensure that these tests assess cognitive abilities that are job related.

Physical ability tests measure an individual's abilities such as strength, endurance, and muscular movement. At an electric utility, line workers regularly must lift and carry equipment, climb ladders, and perform other physical tasks; therefore, testing of applicants' mobility, strength, and other physical.

Different skill-based tests can be used, including **psychomotor tests**, which measure a person's dexterity, hand–eye coordination, arm–hand steadiness, and other factors. Tests such as the MacQuarie Test for Mechanical Ability can measure manual dexterity for assembly-line workers and others using psychomotor skills regularly.

Many organizations use situational tests, or **work sample tests**, which require an applicant to perform a simulated task that is a specified part of the target job. Requiring an applicant for an administrative assistant's job to type a business letter as quickly as possible would be one such test.

Situational judgment tests are designed to measure a person's judgment in work settings. The candidate is given a situation and a list of possible solutions to the problem. The candidate then has to make judgments about how to deal with the situation. Situational judgment tests are a form of job simulation.

Personality Tests

Personality is a unique blend of individual characteristics that can affect how people interact with their work environment. Many organizations use various personality tests that assess the degree to which candidates' attributes match specific job criteria. For instance, a sporting goods chain offers job applicants a Web-based test. The test evaluates their personal tendencies, and test scores are used to categorize individuals for the hiring decision. Many types of personality tests are available, including the Minnesota Multiphasic Personality Inventory (MMPI) and the Myers-Briggs test.

Personality testing for selection flourished during the 1950s and large companies—such as Sears, Standard Oil, and Procter and Gamble—used such testing extensively. But in the 1960s researchers concluded that personality is not a good predictor for selection, and the use of these tests dropped drastically. In the 1990s, interest in research on personality as a selection tool resurfaced and vendors began selling personality-oriented selection tests. But a seminal research article appearing in *Personnel Psychology* concluded that personality explains so little about actual job outcomes that we should think very carefully about using it *at all* for employment decisions.[10]

Honesty/Integrity Tests

Companies are utilizing different tests to assess the honesty and integrity of applicants and employees. Employers use these tests as a screening mechanism to prevent the hiring of unethical employees, to reduce the frequency of lying and theft on the job, and to communicate to applicants and employees alike that dishonesty will not be tolerated. Honesty/integrity tests can be valid as broad screening devices for organizations if used properly.

However, these instruments have limitations. For instance, socially desirable responding is a key concern; some questions can be considered overly invasive, insulting, and not job related; sometimes "false positives" are generated (or an honest person is scored as "dishonest"); and test scores might be affected by individual demographic factors such as gender and race.

Polygraphs.   The polygraph, more generally and incorrectly referred to as the "lie detector," is a mechanical device that measures a person's galvanic skin response, heart rate, and breathing rate. As a result of concerns about polygraph validity, Congress passed the Employee Polygraph Protection Act, which prohibits the use of polygraphs for preemployment screening purposes by most employers. The act does allow employers to use polygraphs as part of internal investigations of thefts or losses. But in those situations, the polygraph test should be taken voluntarily, and the employee should be allowed to end the test at any time.

SELECTION INTERVIEWING

Selection interviewing of job applicants is done both to obtain additional information and to clarify information gathered throughout the selection process. Interviews are commonly conducted at two levels: first, as an initial screening interview to determine if the person has met minimum qualifications, and then later, as an in-depth interview with HR staff members and/or operating managers to determine if the person will fit into the designated work area. Before the in-depth interview, information from all available sources is pooled so that the interviewers can reconcile conflicting information that may have emerged from tests, application forms, and references.

Interviewing for selection is imperfect and should be focused on gathering valid information that has not been gained in other ways. Because selection interviewing is imperfect, the focus must be on techniques that minimize errors and provide the best information.

Structured Interviews

A **structured interview** uses a set of standardized questions asked of all applicants so that comparisons can be made more easily. This type of interview allows an interviewer to prepare job-related questions in advance and then complete a standardized interviewee evaluation form that provides documentation indicating why one applicant was selected over another.

The structured interview is useful in the initial screening process because many applicants can be effectively evaluated and compared. However, the structured interview does not have to be rigid. The predetermined questions should be asked in a logical manner but should not be read word for word. The applicants should be allowed adequate opportunity to explain their answers, and interviewers should probe with additional questions until they fully understand the responses. This process can make the structured interview more reliable and valid than other interview approaches.

Less-Structured Interviews

Some interviews are done unplanned and are not structured at all. Such interviewing techniques may be appropriate for fact finding, or for counseling interviews. However, they are not best for selection interviewing. These interviews may be conducted by operating managers or supervisors who have had little interview training. An *unstructured interview* occurs when the interviewer improvises by asking questions that are not predetermined. A *semistructured interview* is a guided conversation in which broad questions are asked and new questions arise as a result of the discussion. For example: What would you do differently if you could start over again?

Who Conducts Interviews?

Job interviews can be conducted by an individual, by several individuals sequentially, or by panels or teams. For some jobs, such as entry-level jobs requiring lesser skills, applicants might be interviewed solely by a human resource professional. For other jobs, employers screen applicants by using multiple interviews, beginning with a human resource professional and followed by the appropriate supervisors and managers. Then a selection decision is made collectively. Managers need to ensure that multiple interviews are not redundant.

Other interview formats are also utilized. In a **panel interview**, several interviewers meet with the candidate at the same time so that the same responses are heard. Panel interviews may be combined with individual interviews. However, without proper planning, an unstructured interview can result, and applicants are frequently uncomfortable with the group interview format.

Effective Interviewing

Many people think that the ability to interview is an innate talent, but this contention is difficult to support. Just being personable and liking to talk is no guarantee that someone will be an effective interviewer. Interviewing skills are developed through training. To make interviewing more effective, interviewers should a) Plan the interview; b) Control the interview; and c) use effective questioning techniques.

Some types of questions to avoid in selection interviews include yes/no questions, obvious questions, questions that rarely produce a true answer, leading questions, illegal questions, and questions that are not job-related. Appendix E lists questions that are commonly used in selection interviews.

Problems in the Interview.   Operating managers and supervisors are more likely than HR personnel to use poor interviewing techniques because they do not interview often or lack training. Several problems include:

- *Snap judgments:* Some interviewers decide whether an applicant is suitable within the first two to four minutes of the interview, and spend the rest of the time looking for evidence to support their judgment.
- *Negative emphasis:* When evaluating suitability, unfavorable information about an applicant is often emphasized more than favorable information.
- *Halo effect:* The *halo effect* occurs when an interviewer allows a positive characteristic, such as agreeableness, to overshadow other evidence.

The phrase *devil's horns* describes the reverse of the halo effect; this occurs when a negative characteristic, such as inappropriate dress, overshadows other traits.

- *Biases and stereotyping:* "Similarity" bias occurs when interviewers favor or select people that they believe to be like themselves based on a variety of personal factors. Interviewers also should avoid any personal tendencies to stereotype individuals because of demographic characteristics and differences. For instance, age disparities may be a concern as younger executives are interviewing more senior personnel. Additionally, applicants' ethnic names and accents can negatively impact personal evaluations, and older workers are sometimes less likely to get interviewed and hired than are younger applicants.
- *Cultural noise:* Interviewers must learn to recognize and handle cultural noise, which stems from what applicants believe is socially acceptable rather than what is factual.

BACKGROUND INVESTIGATIONS

Failure to check the backgrounds of people who are hired can lead to embarrassment and legal liability. Hiring workers who commit violent acts on the job is one example. While laws vary from state to state, for jobs in certain industries, such as those that provide services to children, vulnerable adults, security, in-home services, and financial services, background checks are mandated in some states. Nationally background checks are required for people with commercial drivers' licenses who drive tractor-trailer rigs and buses interstate.

Lawyers say that an employer's liability hinges on how well it investigates an applicant's background. Consequently, details provided on the application form should be investigated extensively, and these efforts should be documented.

Negligent hiring occurs when an employer fails to check an employee's background and the employee later injures someone on the job. There is a potential negligent hiring problem when an employer hires an unfit employee, a background check is weak, or an employer does not research potential risk factors that would prevent the positive hire decision. Similarly, **negligent retention** occurs when an employer becomes aware that an employee may be unfit for employment but continues to employ the person, and the person injures someone.

Medical Examinations and Inquiries

Medical information on applicants may be used to determine their physical and mental capabilities for performing jobs. Physical standards for jobs should be realistic, justifiable, and linked to job requirements. Even though workers with disabilities can competently perform many jobs, they sometimes may be rejected because of their physical or mental limitations.

The ADA prohibits the use of preemployment medical exams, except for drug tests, until a job has been conditionally offered. Also, the ADA prohibits a company from rejecting an individual because of a disability and from asking job applicants any question related to current or past medical history until a conditional job offer has been made. Once a conditional offer of employment has been made, then some organizations ask the applicant to complete a preemployment health checklist or the employer pays for a physical examination of the applicant. It should be made clear that the applicant who has been offered the job is not "hired" until successful completion of the physical inquiry.

Drug testing may be conducted as part of a medical exam, or it may be done separately. Use of drug testing as part of the selection process has increased in the past few years. If drug tests are used, employers should remember that their accuracy varies according to the type of test used, the item tested, and the quality of the laboratory where the test samples are sent. Because of the potential impact of prescription drugs on test results, applicants should complete a detailed questionnaire on this matter before the testing. If an individual tests positive for drug use, then an independent medical laboratory should administer a second, more detailed analysis. Whether urine, blood, saliva, or hair samples are used, the process of obtaining, labeling, and transferring the samples to the testing lab should be outlined clearly and definite policies and procedures should be established.

References

References provided by the candidate are of very limited predictive value. Would someone knowingly pick a reference who would speak poorly of them? Of course not. Previous supervisors and employers may provide a better prediction. Good questions to ask previous supervisors or employers include:

- Dates of employment
- Position held
- What were the job duties?
- What strengths/weaknesses did you observe?
- Were there any problems?
- Would you rehire?

Work-related references from previous employers and supervisors provide a valuable snapshot of a candidate's background and characteristics. Telephoning references is common.

Making the Job Offer

The final step of the selection process is offering someone employment. Job offers are often extended over the telephone. Many companies then formalize the offer in a letter that is sent to the applicant. It is important that the offer document be reviewed by legal counsel and that the terms and conditions of employment be clearly identified. Care should be taken to avoid vague, general statements and promises about bonuses, work schedules, or other matters that might change later. These documents should also provide for the individual to sign an acceptance of the offer and return it to the employer, who should place it in the individual's personnel files.

Selecting for "Soft Skills"

Selection in its "scientific" form is about finding valid predictors of what will be needed on a job and picking people who score high on those predictors. These "hard skills" include cognitive skills, education, and technical skills. But these skills may not predict the difference between adequate and outstanding performance. Some argue that "soft skills" provide an important part of the ability to do a job successfully. What are "soft skills"? They are noncognitive abilities that are complementary to outstanding job performance. Examples might include:

Empathy	Leadership
Openness	Integrity
Cooperation	Ethical behavior
Interpersonal style	Effort
Conscientiousness	Emotional intelligence

But selection for soft skills is haphazard. Unlike hard skills, these skills may have to be inferred from past behaviors or from an interview.[11] Tests may be available to help with some soft skills, but the basic process presented in this chapter still must apply. First, identify KSAs, competencies, and job functions through job analysis. Next, decide how those will be identified in an applicant (tests, interviews, experience, etc.). Then use structured behavioral interviewing done by trained interviewers incorporating competency-focused questions. Finally, choose those applicants who are strong in the areas necessary to do the job.

NOTES

1. Rick Be, "Employment Doldrums May Be Easing, Survey Notes," *Workforce Management Online*, August 25, 2009, *www.workforce.com*.

2. U.S. Bureau of Labor Statistics, *www.bls.gov*.

3. Justin Lahart, "Employers Shed Fewer Temp Workers," *The Wall Street Journal*, September 5–6, 2009, A2; Patrick Buckley, et al., "The Use of Automated Employment Recruiting and Screening System for Temporary Professional Employees," *Human Resource Management*, 43 (2004), 233–241.

4. Dan Schaubel, "Skip Job Boards and Use Social Media Instead," *BusinessWeek Online*, July 29, 2009, 14.

5. Tresa Baidas, "Lawyers Warn Employers Against Giving Glowing Reviews on LinkedIn," *National Law Journal*, July 6, 2009, *www.nlj.com*.

6. Stephanie Overman, "Staffing Management: Measure What Matters," *Staffing Management*, October 1, 2008, *www.shrm.org*.

7. Melanie Wanzek, "On Second Thought," *Sunday World Herald*, May 10, 2009, CR1.

8. Arne Kalleberg, "The Mismatched Worker: When People Don't Fit Their Jobs," *Academy of Management Perspectives*, February 2008, 24–40.

9. "Gerber Agrees to Pay $900,000 to Minorities and Females for Hiring Discrimination," *Ceridian Abstracts*, August 26, 2009, *www.hrcompliance. ceridian.com*, 1.

10. Frederick Morgeson, et al., "Reconsidering the Use of Personality Tests in Personnel Selection Contexts," *Personnel Psychology*, 60, 2007, 683–729.

11. Charles Handler, "Dear Workforce . . .," *www.workforce.com*.

INTERNET RESOURCES

JobWeb—For a special report about labor markets and jobs outlook, visit *www.jobweb.com*.

Arbita—This consulting firm provides resources on recruiting-related topics, including a collection of articles and white papers. Visit the website at *www.arbita.net*.

HR-Guide.com—This website offers links to HR websites relating to selection and staffing resources, including information on methods, best practices, tests, and software programs. Visit the site at *www.hr-guide.com*.

UniformGuidelines.com—For a free resource on the use of selection procedures and tests to ensure compliance with federal laws, visit this website at *www.uniformguidelines.com*.

SUGGESTED READINGS

Steven D. Maurer and Yupin Liu, "Developing Effective E-Recruiting Websites: Insights for Managers from Marketers," *Business Horizons*, 50 (2007), 305–314.

Fay Hansen, "Sourcing Disappears as Applications Pile Up for Overwhelmed Recruiters," *Workforce Management Online*, July 23, 2009, *www.workforce.com*.

V. O'Connell, "Test for Dwindling Retail Jobs Spawns a Culture of Cheating," *The Wall Street Journal*, January 7, 2009, A1.

Joann Lublin, "For Job Hunters the Big Interview Is Getting Bigger," *The Wall Street Journal*, June 3, 2008, D1.

CHAPTER 5

Training and Talent Management

HR—MEETING MANAGEMENT CHALLENGES

Improving the performance of employees in an organization frequently means training and managing the talent. Current issues include:

- Designing effective training programs
- Identifying and developing the talent
- Dealing with career issues

Competitive pressures require employees that have current knowledge, ideas, and skills. Employees have to be able to adapt to the changes that inevitably will come for the organization. Talent management is concerned with identifying and developing key human resources. It is a topic currently in vogue.

TRAINING AND HR

Competition forces business organizations to change and adapt to compete successfully. Changes in the way things must be done require training or retraining employees and managers. In this sense, training is an ongoing process for most organizations. Organizations in the United States spend more than $126 billion annually on training and development, or more than $1,000 per employee on average.[1]

Training is the process whereby people acquire capabilities to perform jobs. Training provides employees with specific, identifiable knowledge and skills for use in their present jobs. Organizational training may include teaching of "hard" skills, such as teaching sales representatives how to use intranet resources, a branch manager how to review an income statement, or a machinist apprentice how to set up a drill press. "Soft" skills are critical in many instances and can be taught as well. These skills may include communicating, mentoring, managing a meeting, and working as part of a team.

What kinds of activities usually require training? The most common training topics include, among others, safety, customer service, computer skills, quality initiatives, dealing with sexual harassment, and communication.[2] Further, documented benefits of well-done training include (for both individuals and teams) enhanced skills, greater ability to adapt and innovate,

FIGURE 5-1 Types of Training

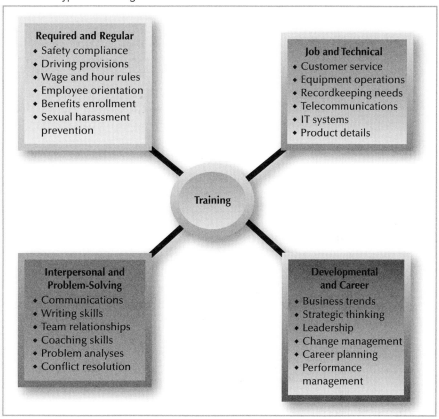

better self-management, and performance improvement. For organizations, research has shown that training brings improvements in effectiveness and productivity, more profitability and reduced costs, improved quality, and increased social capitol.

Training can be designed to meet a number of objectives and can be classified in various ways. Figure 5-1 shows some common groupings.

Strategic Training

Training is used strategically to help the organization accomplish its goals. For example, if sales increases are a critical part of the company's strategy, appropriate training would identify what is causing lower sales and target training to respond as part of a solution.

Strategic training can have numerous organizational benefits. It requires HR and training professionals to get intimately involved with the business and to partner with operating managers to help solve their problems, thus making significant contributions to organizational results. Additionally, a strategic training mind-set reduces the likelihood of thinking that training alone can solve most employee or organizational problems. It is not uncommon for operating managers and trainers to react to most important performance problems by saying, "I need a training program on *X*." With a strategic focus, the organization is more likely to assess whether training actually can address the most important performance issues and what besides training is needed. Training cannot fix all organizational problems.

The nature of technological innovation and change is such that if employees are not trained all the time, they may fall behind and the company could become less competitive. For example, consider the telecommunications industry today compared with ten years ago, with all the new technologies and the accompanying competitive shifts. Without continual training, organizations may not have staff members with the knowledge, skills, and abilities (KSAs) needed to compete effectively.

Training also can affect organizational competitiveness by aiding in the retention of employees. One reason why many individuals stay or leave organizations is career training and development opportunities. Employers that invest in training and developing their employees may enhance retention efforts.

Training as a Revenue Source.   Some organizations have identified that training can be a source of business revenue. For instance, Microsoft, Ceridian, Cisco, Hewlett-Packard, and other technology firms bundle customer training with products and services they sell. Also, manufacturers of industrial equipment offer customers training on machine upgrades and new features. Customers of many of these firms pay for additional training either by course, by participant, or as part of equipment or software purchases.

Integration of Performance with Training.   Job performance, training, and employee learning must be integrated to be effective, and HR plays a role in this integration. Organizations find that training experiences that use real business problems to advance employee learning are better than more traditional approaches. Rather than separating the training experience from the context of actual job performance, trainers incorporate everyday business issues as learning examples, thus increasing the realism of training exercises and scenarios. For example, as part of management training at General Electric, managers are given actual business problems to solve, and they must present their solutions to the business leaders in the firm. Using real situations for practice is yet another way of merging the lines between training, learning, and job performance.

TRAINING FOR GLOBAL STRATEGIES

For a global firm, the most brilliant strategies ever devised will not work unless the company has well-trained employees throughout the world to carry them out. A global look at training is important as firms establish and expand operations worldwide. For U.S. employers, the challenge has increased. According to a report, the number of U.S. job skills certifications declined 18% in one year, while there was a 47% increase in similar certifications in India. The conclusion of the study was that U.S. firms may not remain innovative and strategic leaders much longer, due to the decline in specialized skilled and technical workers.[3] Add this problem to the number of global employees with international assignments, and training clearly must be seen as part of global strategic success.

PLANNING FOR TRAINING

Whether global or national in scope, training benefits from careful planning before it is done. Planning includes looking at the "big picture" in which the training takes place as well as specifics for the design of a particular training effort. For example, the needs for skills have changed over time and things like adaptability, problem solving, and professionalism have increased in value in some firms. Planning to design training to include changes such as these makes for a more effective training program.

Another training planning issue for some companies is knowledge retention for the firm. When retirees leave, they take everything they have learned during a career. Perhaps a retiree is the only one in the company who knows how to operate a piece of machinery or mix a chemical solution. In some areas technology changes so fast that even young people leaving a company may take with them information that cannot easily be replicated. Companies are responding to this knowledge retention need in various ways, including identifying critical employees, having existing critical employees train and mentor others, producing how-to videotapes, and keeping former employees on call for a period of time after their departure.

Training plans allow organizations to identify what is needed for employee performance *before* training begins so that a fit between training and strategic issues is made. Effective training efforts consider the following questions:

- Is there really a need for the training?
- Who needs to be trained?
- Who will do the training?
- What form will the training take?
- How will knowledge be transferred to the job?
- How will the training be evaluated?

Orientation: Planning for New Employees

A good example of one kind of training that requires planning is orientation. Also called "onboarding," orientation is the most important and widely conducted type of regular training done for new employees. **Orientation**, which is the planned introduction of new employees to their jobs, coworkers, and the organization, is offered by most employers. It requires cooperation between individuals in the HR unit and operating managers and supervisors. In a small organization without an HR department, the new employee's supervisor or manager usually assumes most of the responsibility for orientation. In large organizations, managers and supervisors, as well as the HR department, generally work as a team to orient new employees. Unfortunately, without good planning, new employee orientation sessions can come across as boring, irrelevant, and a waste of time to both new employees and their department supervisors and managers.

Among the decisions to be made during planning are what to present and also, equally important, *when* to present it. Too much information on the first day leads to perceptions of ineffective onboarding. Several shorter sessions over a longer period of time, bringing in information as it is needed, are more effective. Effective orientation achieves several key purposes:

- Establishes a favorable employee impression of the organization and the job
- Provides organization and job information
- Enhances interpersonal acceptance by coworkers
- Accelerates socialization and integration of the new employee into the organization
- Ensures that employee performance and productivity begin more quickly

One way of expanding the efficiency of orientation is to use electronic resources. A number of employers place general employee orientation information on company intranets or corporate websites. New employees log on and go through much of the general material on organizational history, structure, products and services, mission, and other background, instead of sitting in a classroom where the information is delivered in person or by videotape. Specific questions and concerns can be addressed by HR staff and others after employees have reviewed the Web-based information. Successfully integrating new hires is important, and measuring the degree of success allows the orientation program to be managed.

A Training System

The way in which a firm plans, organizes, and structures its training affects the way employees experience the training, which in turn influences the effectiveness of the training. Effective training requires the use of a systematic training process. Figure 5-2 shows the four phases of a systematic

FIGURE 5-2 Systematic Training Process

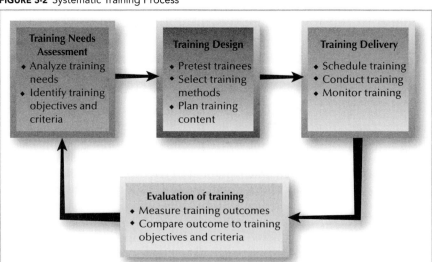

approach: assessment, design, delivery, and evaluation. Using such a process reduces the likelihood that unplanned, uncoordinated, and haphazard training efforts will occur. A discussion of the training process follows.

TRAINING NEEDS ASSESSMENT

Assessing organizational training needs is the diagnostic phase of a training plan. This assessment considers issues of employee and organizational performance to determine if training can help. Needs assessment measures the competencies of a company, a group, or an individual as they relate to what is required. It is necessary to find out what is happening and what should be happening before deciding if training will help, and if it will help, what kind is needed.

The first step in training needs assessment is analyzing what training might be necessary. There are three sources used to analyze training needs.

Organizational analysis comes from various operational measures of organizational performance. Departments or areas with high turnover, customer complaints, high grievance rates, high absenteeism, low performance, and other deficiencies can be pinpointed. Following identification of such problems, training objectives can be developed if training is a solution. During organizational analysis, focus groups of managers can be used to evaluate changes and performance that might require training.

The second way of analyzing training needs is to review *the jobs involved and the tasks performed* in those jobs. By comparing the requirements of jobs with the KSAs of employees, training needs can be identified. For example, at a manufacturing firm, analysis identified the tasks performed by engineers who served as technical instructors for other employees. By listing the tasks required of a technical instructor, management established a program to teach specific instructional skills; thus, the engineers were able to become more successful instructors.

The third means of diagnosing training needs focuses on *individuals and how they perform their jobs.* The following sources are examples that are useful for individual analysis:

- Performance appraisals
- Skill tests
- Individual assessment tests
- Records of critical incidents

- Assessment center exercises
- Questionnaires and surveys
- Job knowledge tools
- Internet input

Once training requirements have been identified using needs analyses, training objectives and priorities can be established by a "gap analysis," which indicates the distance between where an organization is with its employee capabilities and where it needs to be. Training objectives and priorities are then determined to close the gap.

TRAINING DESIGN

Once training objectives have been determined, training design can start. Whether job-specific or broader in nature, training must be designed to address the specific objectives. Effective training design considers the learners, instructional strategies, and how best to get the training from class to the job.

Working in organizations should be a continual learning process. Different approaches are possible because learning is a complex psychological process.

Learner Characteristics

For training to be successful, learners must be ready and able to learn. Learner readiness means that individuals have the ability to learn, which many people certainly have. However, individuals also must have the motivation to learn, have self-efficacy, see value in learning, and have a learning style that fits the training.

Learners must possess basic skills, such as fundamental reading and math proficiency, and sufficient cognitive abilities. Companies may discover that some workers lack the requisite skills to comprehend their training. Some have found that a significant number of job applicants and current employees lack the reading, writing, and math skills needed to learn the jobs.

A person's desire to learn training content, referred to as "motivation to learn," is influenced by multiple factors. For example, differences in gender and ethnicity and the resulting experiences may affect the motivation of adult learners. The student's motivational level also may be influenced by the instructor's motivation and ability, friends' encouragement to do well, classmates' motivational levels, the physical classroom environment, and the training methods used.

Learners must possess **self-efficacy**, which refers to people's belief that they can successfully learn the training program content. For learners to be ready for and receptive to the training content, they must feel that it is possible for them to learn it. As an example, some college students' levels of self-efficacy diminish in math or statistics courses when they do not feel able to grasp the material.

Training that is viewed as useful is more likely to be tried on the job. Perceived utility or value of training is effected by a need to improve, the likelihood that training will lead to improvement, and the practicality of the training for use on the job. Learners must perceive a close relationship between the training and things they want for it to be successful.

People learn in different ways. For example, *auditory* learners learn best by listening to someone else tell them about the training content. *Tactile* learners must "get their hands on" the training resources and use them. *Visual* learners think in pictures and figures and need to see the purpose and process of the training. Trainers who address all these styles by using multiple training methods can design more effective training.

Instructional Strategies

An important part of designing training is to select the right mix of strategies to fit the learners' characteristics. Practice/feedback, overlearning, behavioral modeling, error-based examples, and reinforcement/immediate confirmation are some of the prominent strategies available in designing the training experience.

For some kinds of training, it is important that learners practice what they have learned and get feedback on how they have done so they can improve. **Active practice** occurs when trainees perform job-related tasks and duties during training. It is more effective than simply reading or passively listening.

Overlearning is repeated practice even after a learner has mastered the performance. It may be best used to instill "muscle memory" for a physical activity in order to reduce the amount of thinking necessary and make responses automatic. But overlearning also produces improvement in learner retention.

The most elementary way in which people learn—and one of the best—is through **behavioral modeling**, or copying someone else's behavior. The use of behavioral modeling is particularly appropriate for skill training in which the trainees must use both knowledge and practice. For example, a new supervisor can receive training and mentoring on how to handle disciplinary discussions with employees by observing as the HR director or department manager deals with such problems.

The error-based examples method involves sharing with learners what can go wrong when they do not use the training properly. A good example is sharing with pilots what can happen when they are not aware of a situation they and their aircraft are entering. Situational awareness training that includes error-based examples has been shown to improve air crew situational awareness.[4]

The concept of **reinforcement** is based on the *law of effect*, which states that people tend to repeat responses that give them some type of positive reward and to avoid actions associated with negative consequences. Positively reinforcing correct learned responses while providing negative consequences at some point for wrong responses can change behavior. Closely related is an instructional strategy called **immediate confirmation**, which is based on the idea that people learn best if reinforcement and feedback are given as soon as possible after training.

Transfer of Training

Finally, trainers should design training for the highest possible transfer from the class to the job. Transfer occurs when trainees actually use on the job what knowledge and information they learned in training. The amount of training that effectively gets transferred to the job is estimated to be relatively low, given all the time and money spent on training. It is thought that many employees apply training to their jobs immediately after training, but among those who do not use the training immediately, the likelihood of it being used decreases over time.

TRAINING DELIVERY

Once training has been designed, the actual delivery of training can begin. Regardless of the type of training done, a number of approaches and methods can be used to deliver it. The growth of training technology continues to expand the available choices, as Figure 5-3 shows.

Whatever the approach used, a variety of considerations must be balanced when selecting training delivery methods. The common variables considered are:

- Nature of training
- Subject matter
- Number of trainees
- Individual versus team
- Self-paced versus guided

- Training resources/costs
- E-learning versus traditional learning
- Geographic locations
- Time allotted
- Completion timeline

Internal Training

Internal training generally applies very specifically to the organization and its jobs. It is popular because it saves the cost of sending employees away for training and often avoids the cost of outside trainers. Skills-based technical training is usually conducted inside organizations. Training materials can be created internally as well. Due to rapid changes in technology, the building and updating of technical skills may become crucial internal training needs. Basic technical skills training is also being mandated by federal regulations in areas where the Occupational Safety and Health Administration (OSHA), the Environmental Protection Agency (EPA), and other agencies have jurisdiction. Three types of internal delivery options will be discussed here: informal training, on-the-job training (OJT), and cross training.

FIGURE 5-3 Training Delivery Options

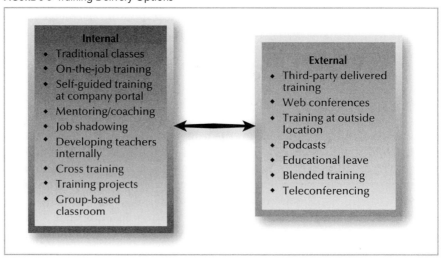

FIGURE 5-4 Stages for On-the-Job Training

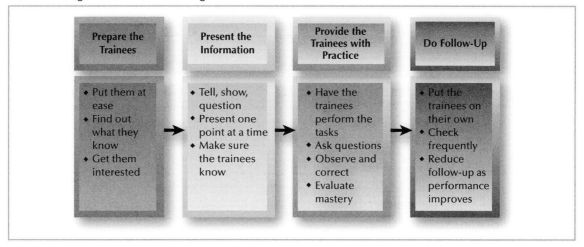

One internal source of training is **informal training**, which occurs through interactions and feedback among employees. Much of what employees know about their jobs they learn informally from asking questions and getting advice from other employees and their supervisors, rather than from formal training programs.

The most common type of training at all levels in an organization is *on-the-job training (OJT)* because it is flexible and relevant to what employees do. Well-planned and well-executed OJT can be very effective. Based on a guided form of training known as job instruction training (JIT), OJT is most effective if a logical progression of stages is used, as shown in Figure 5-4. In contrast with informal training, which often occurs spontaneously, OJT should be planned. The supervisor or manager conducting the training must be able to both teach and show the employees what to do.

However, OJT has some problems. Often, those doing the training may have no experience in training, no time to do it, or no desire to participate in it. Under such conditions, learners essentially are on their own, and training likely will not be effective.

Cross training occurs when people are trained to do more than one job—theirs and someone else's. For the employer, the advantages of cross training are flexibility and development. However, although cross training is attractive to the employer, it is not always appreciated by employees, who often feel that it requires them to do more work for the same pay. To counteract such responses and to make it more appealing to employees, learning "bonuses" can be awarded for successfully completing cross training.

External Training

External training, or training that takes place outside the employing organization, is used extensively by organizations of all sizes. Large organizations use external training if they lack the capability to train people internally or when many people need to be trained quickly. External training may be the best option for training in smaller firms due to limitations in the size of their training staffs and in the number of employees who need various types of specialized training.

Federal, state, and local governments provide a wide range of external training assistance and funding. The Workforce Investment Act (WIA) provides states with block grant programs that target adult education, disadvantaged youth, and family literacy. Employers hiring and training individuals who meet the WIA criteria receive tax credits and other assistance for 6 months or more, depending on the program regulations.

Some employers pay for additional formal education for their employees. Typically, the employee pays for a course that applies to a college degree and is reimbursed upon successful completion of the course. The amounts paid by the employer are considered nontaxable income for the employee up to amounts set by federal laws.

E-Learning: Online Training

E-learning is use of the Internet or an organizational intranet to conduct training online. E-learning is popular with employers. The major advantages are cost savings and access to more employees. Estimates are that corporate training conducted through learning technology will increase in the next few years. Almost 30% of learning hours today are totally technology based, according to one report, and e-learning is preferred by workers under the age of 30.[5]

However, e-learning is advancing gradually, not explosively. It has found favor as part of a "blended" solution that combines it with other forms of learning. By itself, e-learning is not rated among the top effective training practices by training professionals.

Many large employers use interactive two-way television to present classes. The medium allows an instructor in one place to see and respond to a "class" in any number of other locations. With a fully configured system, employees can take courses from anywhere in the world.

Computer-based training involves a wide array of multimedia technologies—including sound, motion (video and animation), graphics, and hypertext—to tap multiple learner senses. Computer-supported simulations within e-learning can replicate the psychological and behavioral requirements of a task, often in addition to providing some amount of physical resemblance to the trainee's work environment.

Virtual reality is also used to create an artificial environment for trainees so that they can participate in the training. Gaming is a possible e-learning tool.

A blended learning approach can use e-learning for building knowledge of certain basics, a Web-based virtual classroom for building skills, and significant in-person traditional instructor-led training sessions and courses. Use of such blended learning provides greater flexibility in the use of multiple training means and enhances the appeal of training activities to different types of employees.

TRAINING EVALUATION

Evaluation of training compares the post-training results to the pre-training objectives of managers, trainers, and trainees. Too often, training is conducted with little thought of measuring and evaluating it later to see how well it worked. Because training is both time consuming and costly, it should be evaluated.

Cost–benefit analysis and return-on-investment (ROI) analysis are commonly used to measure training results, as are various benchmarking approaches.

Cost–Benefit Analysis

Training results can be examined through **cost–benefit analysis**, which is comparison of costs and benefits associated with training. There are four stages in calculating training costs and benefits:

1. *Determine training costs.* Consider direct costs such as design, trainer fees, materials, facilities, and other administration activities.

2. *Identify potential savings results.* Consider employee retention, better customer service, fewer work errors, quicker equipment production, and other productivity factors.

3. *Compute potential savings.* Gather data on the performance results and assign dollar costs to each of them.

4. *Conduct costs and savings benefits comparisons.* Evaluate the costs per participant, the savings per participant, and how the costs and benefits relate to business performance numbers.

Return-on-Investment Analysis and Benchmarking

In organizations, training is often expected to produce an ROI. Still, too often, training is justified because someone liked it, rather than on the basis of resource accountability. ROI simply divides the return produced because of the training by the cost (or investment) of the training.

In addition to evaluating training internally, some organizations use benchmark measures to compare it with training done in other organizations. To do benchmarking, HR professionals gather data on training in their organization and compare them with data on training at other organizations in the same industry and in companies of a similar size. Comparison data are available through the American Society for Training and Development and its Benchmarking Service. This service has training-related data from more than 1,000 participating employers who complete detailed questionnaires annually. Training also can be benchmarked against data from the American Productivity & Quality Center and the Saratoga Institute.

TALENT MANAGEMENT

The need for talent management is brought on by a demographic landscape dominated by the impending retirement of experienced baby boomers, a shortage of young people entering the workforce in western Europe and a decline in the 35–44 age group in the United States. Issues are further complicated by the number of high school graduates who lack writing and verbal communication skills, as well as a work ethic, and the number of college graduates who are weak in writing, leadership, critical thinking, and creativity skills.[6] Where will the successful workforce of the future come from?

The idea that human capital can be a source of competitive advantage for some organizations is gaining ground, but most organizations are not designed or managed to optimize talent performance. Choices for dealing successfully with talent needs are to: (1) emphasize stability in employment and develop talent internally, (2) develop agility as an organization and buy talent as needed, or (3) use some combination of 1 and 2. So the nature of the business and the environment in which it operates to some extent define appropriate strategies for talent management.

Talent management has other characteristics that make it challenging as well. A major one is the nature of "talent" or people. For example, a "deep bench" of talent can be thought of as inventory. But unlike boxes full of empty bottles, talent does not always stay on the shelf until needed—it walks out the door for better opportunities. The shelf life of promising managers and specialists is short if they do not have opportunities where they are currently.

Talent Management "Systems"

Talent management seems to lend itself to the use of various software-based systems that purport to integrate all the pieces of talent management into one manageable whole. For example, one company used a talent management system in:

- Documenting new employee orientations and the onboarding training, regardless of how and where it was done.
- Tracking classroom training and certifications completed by all store employees.
- Automating registration of participants for training and development activities.
- Reporting on completions of training certifications for store employees.
- Compiling and reporting the training and development history of individuals for use with career planning and development.

However, according to one survey, although many companies are planning to use talent management technology, about half still use a manual approach.[7]

Scope of Talent Management

As talent management has evolved, a variety of approaches, ideas, and tools have come along. Some of the most prominent follow.

Target Jobs.   The first issue is to identify the types of jobs that will be the focus of talent management efforts. In some organizations, talent management focuses on the CEO and other executive jobs, rather than more broadly.

Other organizations target senior management jobs, mid-level managers, and other key jobs. However, those groups only represent about one-third of the total workforce, which raises the question of whether talent management efforts would be more useful if they were more widely implemented.

High-Potential Individuals.   Some organizations focus talent management efforts primarily on "high-potential" individuals, often referred to as "high-pos." Attracting, retaining, and developing high-pos have become the emphases for some talent management efforts. Some firms classify individuals as being in the top 10% and then set limits on the number of people who can participate in intensive talent management efforts. Other organizations view talent management more broadly. Targeting primarily high-pos may lead to many other employees seeing their career opportunities as being limited.

Competency Models.   What does a person who is ready to be moved up look like? What competencies should the person have? Competency models show knowledge, skills, and abilities (KSAs) for various jobs. An employer must ask, what talent do we need to achieve this? The answer can be found in a competency model. Competency models help to identify talent gaps. Some companies maintain libraries of competency models. These libraries create a clear path for talent planning. Competency models might be created for executives, managers, supervisors, salespeople, technical professionals, and others.

Talent Pools.   Talent pools are a way to reduce the risk that the company may not need a certain specialty after developing it. The idea is to avoid developing for a narrow specialized job and instead develop a group or pool of talented people with broad general competencies that could fit a wide range of jobs. Once developed, they can be allocated to specific vacancies. Just-in-time training and coaching can make the fit work.

Career Tracks.   Career tracks include a series of steps that one follows to become ready to move up. For example, a potential branch manager in a bank might take rotational assignments in customer sales, teller supervisor, credit cards, and other positions before being considered ready to handle the branch manager's job.

Assessment.   Assessment most often involves tests of one sort or another. Tests for IQ, personality, aptitude, and other factors are used. A portfolio of tests to help predict a person's potential for a job is called an "assessment center."

Development Risk Sharing.   The employer always runs the risk in developing talent that an employee who has been developed will leave with the valuable skills gained through development. An alternative to this risk is to have promising employees volunteer for development on their own time. Executive MBA programs that can be attended on evenings or weekends, extra projects outside a person's current assignment, volunteer projects with nonprofit organizations, and other paths can be used. The employer might contribute through tuition reimbursement or some selected time away from the job, but the risk is at least partly shared by the employee.

SUCCESSION PLANNING

The basis for dealing successfully with staffing "surprises" is succession planning. When a sudden loss of a manager occurs, the void is a serious problem. At that point it is too late to begin to develop a replacement. "Bench strength" and the leadership "pipeline" are metaphors for ways to prevent the void by having replacements ready.

However, succession planning involves more than simply replacement planning. Replacement planning usually develops a list of replacements for given positions. Succession planning must include a well-designed employee development system to reach its potential. It is the process of identifying a plan for the orderly replacement of key employees.

Whether in small or large firms, succession planning is linked to strategic planning through the process shown in Figure 5-5. The process consists of first defining positions that are critical to the strategy, and then making certain top management is involved personally with mentoring, coaching, and talent identification. It may be appropriate to tie some level of reward to executive success in the process. The next step is to assess the talent available in the organization and determine which have the potential, which are ready now for promotion, and which need additional development. The development practices can vary but should be aimed at specific needs in specific individuals. Finally, evaluating the success of the process is important, and appropriate measures are necessary to do so.

All the work involved in the succession planning process should result in two products: (1) identification of potential emergency replacements for critical positions and (2) other successors who will be ready with some additional development. The development necessary should be made clear to the people involved, along with a plan for getting the development.

Benefits of Formal Succession Planning

Employers are doing succession planning formally and informally. As companies become larger, the benefits of formal succession planning become greater. For larger companies, formal planning is recommended. Even government organizations can benefit from formal succession planning. Key benefits include:

- Having a supply of talented employees to fill future key openings
- Providing career paths and plans for employees, which aids in employee retention and performance motivation
- Continually reviewing the need for individuals as organizational changes occur more frequently
- Enhancing the organizational "brand" and reputation of the company as a desirable place to work

FIGURE 5-5 Succession Planning Process

INTEGRATE WITH STRATEGY
- What competencies will be needed?
- Which jobs will be critical?
- How should critical positions be filled?
- Will international assignments be needed?

INVOLVE TOP MANAGEMENT
- Is the CEO personally involved?
- Are top executives mentoring/coaching?
- Are there authority and accountability for succession goals?

ASSESS KEY TALENT
- Does this person have the competencies?
- What competencies are missing?
- Are assessments/performance evaluations/etc. valid?
- Is a results orientation used to identify high positions?
- Are individuals and career goals/interests compatible?

FOLLOW DEVELOPMENT PRACTICES
- How can missing competencies be developed?
- Are there opportunities for those in higher positions to interact with executives/board members?
- Can talent pools be created for job pools?
- What are the rewards to subordinate development?
- Are high position/successors to be told?

MONITOR/EVALUATE
- Are multiple metrics used?
- Are positions filled internally?
- Is the process viewed favorably?

CAREERS AND CAREER PLANNING

A **career** is the series of work-related positions a person occupies throughout his or her life. People pursue careers to satisfy their individual needs. Careers are an important part of talent management, but individuals and organizations view careers in distinctly different ways. Changes in employer approaches to planning for replacement managers based upon a less predictable business environment have put much of the responsibility for a career on the shoulders of individual employees.

However, companies have found that the lack of a career development plan leaves them vulnerable to turnover, and hiring from outside can have drawbacks.[8] When a company attempts to manage careers internally, there may be a typical career path that is identified for employees.

Organization-Centered Career Planning

Careers today are different than they were in the past, and managing them puts a premium on career development by both employers and employees. Effective career planning considers both organization-centered and individual-centered perspectives.

Organization-centered career planning frequently focuses on identifying career paths that provide for the logical progression of people between jobs in an organization. Individuals follow these paths as they advance in organizational units. For example, the right person might enter the sales department as a sales representative, then be promoted to account director, to district sales manager, and finally to vice president of sales.

The systems that an employer uses should be planned and managed to guide managers in developing employees' careers. The career path, or "map," is created and should be shared with the individual employee.

Employees need to know their strengths and weaknesses, and they often discover those through company-sponsored assessments. Then, career paths to develop the weak areas and fine-tune the strengths are developed.

Career paths represent employees' movements through opportunities over time. Although most career paths are thought of as leading upward, good opportunities also exist in cross-functional or horizontal directions.

As noted earlier, not everyone views a career the same way. Further, the way people view their careers depends on the stage of the career. Some research suggests that if employers expect employees to invest more of their personal resources of time and effort in career self-management, they may find it causes conflict with efforts to balance work and life off the job. People may feel they cannot invest great amounts of time beyond their job in career management and have a satisfactory work-life balance as well.[9] This seems especially true for younger employees.

Individual-Centered Career Planning

Organizational changes have altered career plans for many people. Individuals have had to face "career transitions"—in other words they have had to find new jobs. These transitions have identified the importance of **individual-centered career planning**, which focuses on an individual's responsibility for his or her career rather than on organizational needs.

For individuals to successfully manage their own careers, they should perform several activities. Three key activities are:

- *Do self-assessment*
- *Get feedback on reality*
- *Set career goals*

The typical career for individuals today includes more positions, transitions, and organizations—more so than in the past, when employees were less mobile and organizations were more stable as long-term employers. But there are general patterns in people's lives that affect their careers.

Theorists in adult development describe the first half of life as the young adult's quest for competence and for a way to make a mark in the world. According to this view, a person attains happiness during this time primarily through achievement and the acquisition of capabilities.

The second half of life is different. Once the adult starts to measure time from the expected end of life rather than from the beginning, the need for competence and acquisition changes to the need for integrity, values, and well-being. For many people, internal values take precedence over external scorecards or accomplishments such as wealth and job title status.

Early Career Issues.   Early career needs include finding interests, developing capabilities, and exploring jobs. Some organizations do a better job than others of providing those opportunities. Work-at-home programs, mentoring, performance bonuses, time with top executives, extensive training, hiring interns, reimbursement for more education, and rich 401(K) plans are some of the things employers are doing to make jobs more attractive for early career employees.

Career Plateaus.   Those who do not change jobs may face another problem: career plateaus. Many workers define career success in terms of upward mobility. As the opportunities to move up decrease, some employers try to convince employees they can find job satisfaction in lateral movement. Such moves can be reasonable if employees learn new skills that increase individual marketability in case of future layoffs, termination, or organizational restructurings.

An attempt to solve this problem, a **dual-career ladder**, is a system that allows a person to advance up either a management or a technical/professional ladder. Dual-career ladders are now used at many firms, most commonly in technology-driven industries such as pharmaceuticals, chemicals, computers, and electronics. For instance, a telecommunications firm created a dual-career ladder in its IT department to reward talented technical people who do not want to move into management. Different tracks, each with attractive job titles and pay opportunities, are provided. Some health care organizations are using "master" titles for senior experienced specialists such as radiologists and neonatal nurses who do not want to be managers. The masters often are mentors and trainers for younger specialists. Unfortunately, the technical/professional ladder may be viewed as "second-class citizenship" within some organizations.

Retirement Issues.   Whether retirement comes at age 50 or age 70, it can require a major adjustment for many people. Some areas of adjustment faced by many retirees include self-direction, a need to belong, sources of achievement, personal space, and goals. To help address concerns over these issues, as well as anxieties about finances, some employers offer preretirement planning seminars for employees.

Women and Careers

According to the U.S. Bureau of Labor Statistics, the percentage of women in the workforce has more than doubled since 1970, and will reach almost 50% in the decade following 2010. Women are found in all occupations and jobs, but their careers may have a different element than those of men. Women give birth to children, and in most societies they are also primarily responsible for taking care of their children. The effect of this biology and sociology is that women's careers are often interrupted for childbirth and child rearing.[10]

Work, Family, and Careers.   The career approach for women frequently is to work hard before children arrive, plateau or step off the career track when children are younger, and go back to career-focused jobs that allow flexibility when they are older. This approach is referred to as sequencing. But some women who sequence are concerned that the job market will not welcome them when they return, or that the time away will hurt their advancement chances. And indeed, many women's careers are stifled due to their career interruptions.

Glass Ceiling.   Another concern specifically affecting women is the "glass ceiling." This issue describes the situation in which women fail to progress into top and senior management positions. Nationally, women hold about half of managerial/professional positions but only 10% to 15% of corporate officer positions.[11] Some organizations provide leaves of absence, often under FMLA provisions, but take steps to keep women who are away from work involved in their companies. Some have used e-mentoring for women temporarily off their jobs. Other firms use "phased returns" whereby women employees return to work part-time and then gradually return to full-time schedules.

Dual-Career Couples

As the number of women in the workforce continues to increase, particularly in professional careers, so does the number of dual-career couples. The U.S. Bureau of Labor Statistics estimates that more than 80% of all couples are dual-career couples. Marriages in which both mates are managers, professionals, or technicians have doubled over the past two decades.[12] Problem areas for dual-career couples include family issues and job transfers that require relocations.

For dual-career couples with children, family issues may conflict with career progression. Thus, one partner's flexibility may depend on what is "best" for the family. Additionally, it is important that the career development problems of dual-career couples be recognized as early as possible. Whenever possible, having both partners involved in planning, even when one is not employed by the company, may enhance the success of such efforts.

Traditionally, employees accepted transfers as part of upward mobility in organizations. However, for some dual-career couples, the mobility required because of one partner's transfer often interferes with the other's career. In addition to having two careers, dual-career couples often have established support networks of coworkers, friends, and business contacts to cope with both their careers and their personal lives. Relocating one partner in a dual-career couple may mean upsetting this carefully constructed network for the other person or creating a "commuting" relationship.

DEVELOPING HUMAN RESOURCES

Development represents efforts to improve employees' abilities to handle a variety of assignments and to cultivate employees' capabilities beyond those required by the current job. Development can benefit both organizations and individuals. Employees and managers with appropriate experiences and abilities may enhance organizational competitiveness and the ability to adapt to a changing environment. In the development process, individuals' careers also may evolve and gain new or different focuses.

Development differs from training. It is possible to train people to answer customer service questions, drive a truck, enter data in a computer system, set up a drill press, or assemble a television. However, development in areas such as judgment, responsibility, decision making, and communication presents a bigger challenge. These areas may or may not develop through ordinary life experiences of individuals. A planned system of development experiences for all employees, not just managers, can help expand the overall level of capabilities in an organization.

Some important and common management capabilities that may require development include an action orientation, quality decision-making skills, ethical values, and technical skills. Abilities to build teams, develop subordinates, direct others, and deal with uncertainty are equally important but much less commonly developed capabilities for successful managers. For some tech specialties (tech support, database administration, network design, etc.), certain nontechnical abilities must be developed as well: ability to work under pressure, to work independently, to solve problems quickly, and to use past knowledge in a new situation.

Development Needs Analyses

Like employee training, employee development begins with analyses of the needs of both the organization and the individuals. Either the company or the individual can analyze what a given person needs to develop. The goal, of course, is to identify strengths and weaknesses. Methods that organizations use to assess development needs include assessment centers, psychological testing, and performance appraisals.

Assessment Centers. Collections of instruments and exercises designed to diagnose individuals' development needs are referred to as **assessment centers**. Organizational leadership uses assessment centers for both developing and selecting managers. Many types of employers use assessment centers for a wide variety of jobs.

In a typical assessment-center experience, an individual spends two or three days away from the job performing many assessment activities. These activities might include role-playing, tests, cases, leaderless-group discussions, computer-based simulations, and peer evaluations. Frequently, they also include in-basket exercises, in which the individual handles typical work and management problems. For the most part, the exercises represent situations that require the use of individual skills and behaviors. During the exercises, several specially trained judges observe the participants.

Psychological Testing. Psychological tests have been used for several years to determine employees' developmental potential and needs. Intelligence tests, verbal and mathematical reasoning tests, and personality tests are often given. Psychological testing can furnish useful information on individuals about such factors as motivation, reasoning abilities, leadership style, interpersonal response traits, and job preferences.

The biggest problem with psychological testing lies in interpretation, because untrained managers, supervisors, and workers usually cannot accurately interpret test results. After a professional scores the tests and reports the scores to someone in the organization, untrained managers may attach their own meanings to the results.

Performance Appraisals. Well-done performance appraisals can be a source of development information. Performance data on productivity, employee relations, job knowledge, and other relevant dimensions can be gathered in such assessments. In this context, appraisals designed for development purposes, may be different and more useful in aiding individual employee development than appraisals designed strictly for administrative purposes.

HR DEVELOPMENT APPROACHES

Investing in human intellectual capital can occur on or off the job and in "learning organizations." Development becomes imperative as "knowledge work," such as research skills and specialized technology expertise, increases for almost all employers. But identifying the right mix of approaches for development needs requires analyses and planning.

Coaching

The oldest on-the-job development technique is coaching, which is the training and feedback given to employees by immediate supervisors. Coaching involves a continual process of learning by doing. For coaching to be effective, employees and their supervisors or managers must have a healthy and open relationship. Many firms conduct formal courses to improve the coaching skills of their managers and supervisors.

Committee Assignments

Assigning promising employees to important committees may broaden their experiences and help them understand the personalities, issues, and processes governing the organization. For instance, employees on a safety committee can gain a greater understanding of safety management, which would help them to become supervisors. They also may experience the problems involved in maintaining employee safety awareness. However, managers need to guard against committee assignments that turn into time-wasting activities.

Job Rotation

The process of moving a person from job to job is called **job rotation**. It is widely used as a development technique. For example, a promising young manager may spend 3 months in a plant, 3 months in corporate planning, and 3 months in purchasing. When properly handled, such job rotation fosters a greater understanding of the organization and aids with employee retention by making individuals more versatile, strengthening their skills, and reducing boredom.

Assistant Positions

Some firms create assistant positions, which are staff positions immediately under a manager (e.g., Assistant to HR Director). Through such jobs, trainees can work with outstanding managers they might not otherwise have met. Some organizations set up "junior boards of directors" or "management cabinets" to which trainees may be appointed. These assignments provide useful experiences if they present challenging or interesting tasks to trainees.

Classroom Courses and Seminars

Most off-the-job development programs include some classroom instruction. Most people are familiar with classroom training, which gives it the advantage of being widely accepted. But the lecture system sometimes used in classroom instruction encourages passive listening and reduced learner participation, which is a distinct disadvantage. Sometimes trainees have little opportunity to question, clarify, and discuss the lecture material. The effectiveness of classroom instruction depends on multiple factors: group size, trainees' abilities, instructors' capabilities and styles, and subject matter.

Sabbaticals and Leaves of Absence

A **sabbatical** is time off the job to develop and rejuvenate oneself. Some employers provide paid sabbaticals while others allow employees to take unpaid sabbaticals. Popular for many years in the academic world, sabbaticals have been adopted in the business community as well. Some firms give employees 3 to 6 months off with pay to work on "socially desirable" projects. Such projects have included leading training programs in urban ghettos, providing technical assistance in foreign countries, and participating in corporate volunteer programs to aid nonprofit organizations.

Corporate Universities and Career Development Centers

Large organizations may use corporate universities to develop managers and other employees. Corporate universities take various forms. Sometimes regarded as little more than fancy packaging for company training, they may not provide a degree, accreditation, or graduation in the traditional sense. A related alternative, partnerships between companies and traditional universities, can occur where the universities design and teach specific courses for employers.

MANAGEMENT DEVELOPMENT

Although development is important for all employees, it is essential for managers. Without appropriate development, managers may lack the capabilities to best deploy and manage resources (including employees) throughout the organization.

Experience plays a central role in management development. Indeed, experience often contributes more to the development of senior managers than does classroom training, because much of it occurs in varying circumstances on the job over time. Yet, in many organizations it is difficult to find managers for middle-level jobs. Some individuals refuse to take middle-management jobs, feeling that they are caught between upper management and supervisors. Similarly, not all companies take the time to develop their own senior-level managers. Instead, senior managers and executives often are hired from the outside. Figure 5-6 shows experience-based sources of managers' learning and lists some lessons important in effectively developing supervisors, middle managers, and senior-level executives.

A number of approaches are used to mold and enhance the experiences that managers need to be effective. The most widely used methods are supervisor development, leadership development, management modeling, management coaching, management mentoring, and executive education.

Problems with Management Development Efforts

Development efforts are subject to certain common mistakes and problems. Many of the management development problems in firms have resulted from

FIGURE 5-6 Management Lessons Learned from Job Experience

Another common management problem is inadequate planning and a lack of coordination of development efforts. Common problems include the following:

- Failing to conduct adequate needs analysis
- Trying out fad programs or training methods
- Substituting training for selecting qualified individuals

Another common management problem is *encapsulated development*, which occurs when an individual learns new methods and ideas, but returns to a work unit that is still bound by old attitudes and methods. The development was "encapsulated" in the classroom and is essentially not used on the job. Consequently, in this situation, it is common for individuals who participate in development programs paid for by their employers to become discouraged and move to new employers that allow them to use their newly developed capabilities more effectively.

NOTES

1. Herman Aquinis and Kurt Kraiger, "Benefits of Training and Development for Individuals and Teams, Organizations and Society," *Annual Review of Psychology*, 60 (2009), 451–474.
2. Julie Bos, "Maximize Every Training Dollar," *Workforce Management*, November 17, 2008, 39.
3. J. J. Smith, "U.S. Workers Tech Skills Declined While India, Eastern Europe Grew," *SHRM Global HR News*, September 2006, *www.shrm.org/global*.
4. Simon Branbury, et al., "FASA: Development and Validation of a Novel Measure to Assess the Effectiveness of Commercial Airline Pilot Situation Awareness Training," *International Journal of Aviation Psychology*, 17 (2007), 131–152.
5. American Society of Training and Development, *www.astd.org*.
6. Mark Schoeff, Jr., "Skills of Recent High School Graduates Leave Employers Cold," *Workforce Management*, April 13, 2007, 1–2.
7. "Talent Management Continues to Go High Tech," *HR Focus*, October 2009, 8–9.
8. Edward Lawler III, "Choosing the Right Talent," *Workspan*, July 2008, 73–75.
9. Jane Sturges, "All in a Day's Work?" *Human Resource Management Journal*, 18 (2008), 132.
10. Sherry Sullivan and Lisa Mainiero, "Benchmarking Ideas for Fostering Family Friendly Workplaces," *Organizational Dynamics*, 36, 2007, 45–62.
11. Jessica Marquez, "Gender Discrimination Begins Much Earlier than Exec Levels, Report Shows," *Workforce Management*, May 12, 2009, 1–3.
12. Cathy Arnst, "Women Want Careers Just as Much as Men," *Business Week*, March 27, 2009, 1.

INTERNET RESOURCES

American Society for Training & Development— This website on training and development contains information on research, education, seminars, and conferences. Visit the site at *www.astd.org*.

Learnativity.com—For articles and other resources on adult learning, training, and evaluation, visit this website at *www.learnativity.com*.

Taleo Corporation—For a research library on talent management resources, including articles and interactive tools, visit the Taleo website at *www.taleo.com/resources/research*.

Career Planning—This website is a resource for individual career planning. Visit the site at *www.careerplanning.org*.

SUGGESTED READINGS

Julie Bos, "Top Trends in Training and Leadership Development," *Workforce Management*, November 19, 2007, 36.

Malcolm S. Knowles, Elwood F. Holton III, and Richard A. Swanson, *The Adult Learner*, 6th ed. (New York: Elsevier, 2005).

Edward Lawler, *Talent: Making People Your Competitive Advantage* (San Francisco: Jossey-Bass, 2008).

Peter Cappelli, "The Great Circle of Talent Management," *Human Resource Executive Online*, August 20, 2007, *www.hreonline.com*, 1–3; Peter Cappelli, "Talent Management Cycles: Part II," *Human Resource Executive Online*, September 17, 2007, *www.hreonline.com*, 1–3.

Performance

HR—MEETING MANAGEMENT CHALLENGES

An effective performance management system focuses on identifying, measuring, and dealing with employees performance. These issues are discussed in this chapter because effective performance-management systems can contribute to organizational results. Key aspects include:

- Why organizational strategies are linked to a performance management system
- Establishing a legally defensible and effective performance appraisal system
- How to address performance problems and concerns with individuals

Employers want employees who perform their jobs well. Performance management is used to identify, communicate, measure, and reward employees who do just that. Performance management system design is one of the key methods HR management uses to contribute to organizational performance.

THE NATURE OF PERFORMANCE MANAGEMENT

The performance management process starts by identifying the strategic goals an organization needs to accomplish to remain competitive and profitable. Managers then identify how they and their employees can help support organizational objectives by successfully completing work. In a sense, the sum of the work completed in all jobs should advance the strategic plan. By adopting a "big-picture" approach, managers can successfully combine individual efforts in a manner that provides practical measures of organizational effectiveness.

Effective Performance Management

Often performance management is confused with one of its key components—performance appraisal. **Performance management** is a series of activities designed to ensure that the organization gets the performance it needs from its employees. **Performance appraisal** is the process of determining how well employees do their jobs relative to a standard and communicating that information to them.

An effective performance management system should do the following:

- Make clear what the organization expects
- Provide performance information to employees
- Identify areas of success and needed development
- Document performance for personnel records

Performance management starts with the development and understanding of organizational strategy and then becomes a series of steps that involve identifying performance expectations, providing performance direction, encouraging employee participation, assessing job performance, and conducting the performance appraisal. As Figure 6-1 suggests, successful performance management is a circular process that requires a system of administrative tools that effectively structures the dialogue between managers and their employees, and the motivation to utilize the system in a productive way.

A successful performance management system allows managers to better prepare employees to tackle their work responsibilities by focusing on these activities.

Even well-intentioned employees do not always know what is expected or how to improve their performance, which also makes performance management necessary. Additionally, dismissal of a poorly performing employee may

FIGURE 6-1 Components of Performance Management

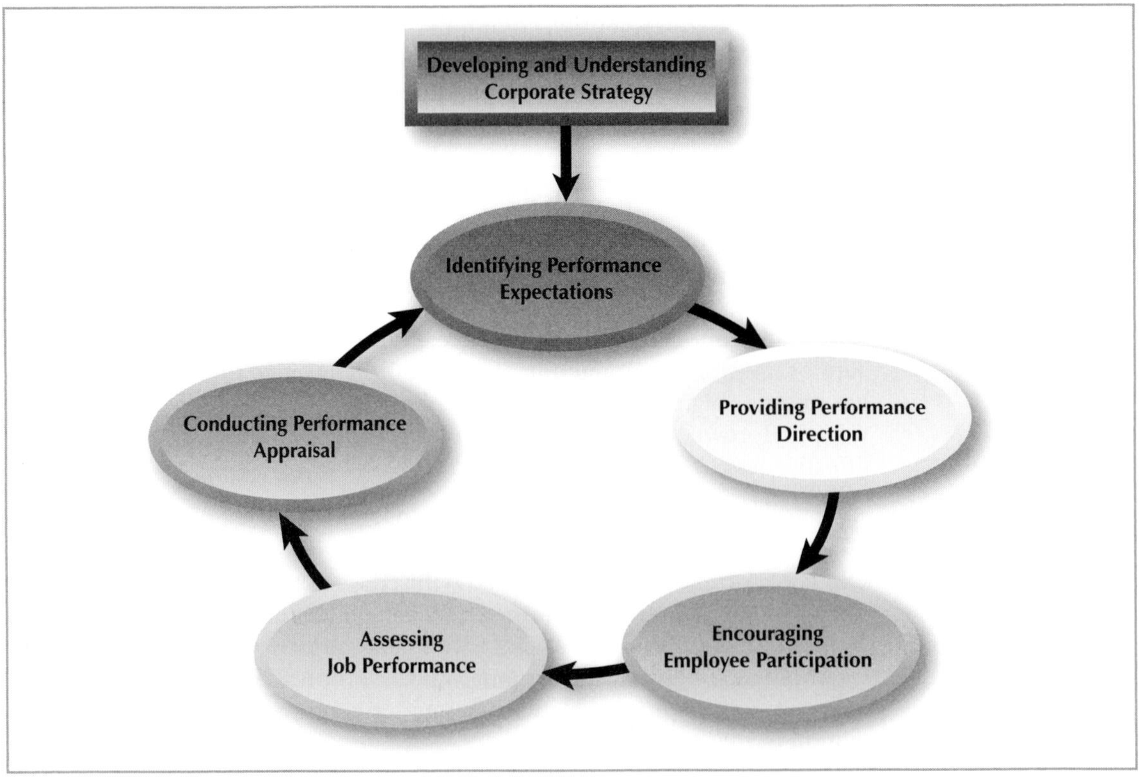

become necessary, and without evidence that the employee has been advised of performance issues, legal problems may result.

Performance management systems and appraisals are very common in the United States and some other countries. However, challenges can be experienced when performance management approaches are used in other countries where multinational organizations have operations, or when they are used with employees who have diverse cultural backgrounds with characteristics very different from those of an American background.

Performance-Focused Organizational Cultures

Organizational cultures vary on many dimensions, and one of these differences involves the degree to which performance is emphasized. Some corporate cultures are based on an *entitlement* approach, meaning that *adequate* performance and stability dominate the organization. Employee rewards vary little from person to person and are not based on individual performance differences. As a result, performance appraisal activities are seen as having few ties to performance and as being primarily a "bureaucratic exercise."

At the other end of the spectrum is a *performance-driven* organizational culture focused on results and contributions. In this context, performance appraisals link results to employee compensation and development. This approach is particularly important when evaluating CEO performance because companies want to hold top leaders accountable for corporate outcomes and motivate them to improve operational and financial results.[1]

It appears that where possible, a performance-based-pay culture is desirable. One study found that 33% of managers and 43% of nonmanagers felt their company was not doing enough about poor performers. The nonmanagers felt that failure to deal with poor performance was unfair to those who worked hard.[2] Additionally, performance-based pay can strengthen the link between employee and organizational goals, increase individual motivation, and augment worker retention, only if an organization develops sound performance plans.

IDENTIFYING AND MEASURING EMPLOYEE PERFORMANCE

Performance criteria vary from job to job, but the most common employee performance measures associated with many jobs include the following:

- Quantity of output
- Quality of output
- Timeliness of output
- Presence/attendance on the job
- Efficiency of work completed
- Effectiveness of work completed

Specific **job duties** are the most important elements in a given job. Duties are identified from job descriptions that contain the most important parts of individual jobs. They help to define what the organization pays employees to do. Therefore, the performance of individuals on important job duties should be measured and compared against appropriate standards, and the results should be communicated to the employee.

To complicate matters, multiple job duties are the rule rather than the exception in most jobs. An individual might demonstrate better performance on some duties than others, and some duties might be more important than others to the organization. Weights can be used to show the relative importance of several duties in one job.

Types of Performance Information

Managers can use three different types of information about employee performance, as Figure 6-2 shows. *Trait-based information* identifies a character trait of the employee—such as attitude, initiative, or creativity—and may or may not be job related.

Behavior-based information focuses on specific behaviors that lead to job success. A human resource director who institutes an "open-door policy" behaves in a manner that likely increases communication with employees. For example, salespeople might use different verbal persuasion strategies with customers because no one approach can be utilized successfully by all individuals.

Results-based information considers employee accomplishments. For jobs in which measurement is easy and obvious, a results-based approach works well. However, in this approach, that which is measured tends to be emphasized, which may leave out equally important but difficult-to-measure parts of work. For example, a car salesperson who gets paid *only* for sales may be unwilling to do paperwork and other work not directly related to selling cars.

Performance measures can be viewed as objective or subjective. The *objective measures* can be observed—for example, the number of cars sold or the

FIGURE 6-2 Types of Performance Information

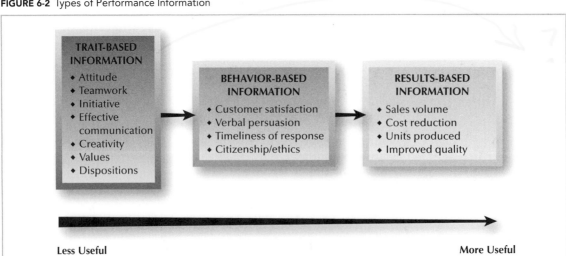

number of invoices processed can be counted. *Subjective measures* require judgment on the part of the evaluator and are more difficult to determine. One example of a subjective measure is a supervisor's ratings of an employee's "attitude," which cannot be seen directly. Consequently, both objective and subjective measures should be used carefully.

Relevance of Performance Criteria

Measuring performance requires focusing on the most important aspects of employees' jobs. For example, measuring the initiative of customer service representatives in an insurance claims center may be less relevant than measuring the number of calls the representatives handle properly. Likewise, evaluating how well a hotel manager is liked by peers is likely to be less relevant than evaluating the policies created by the manager to increase hotel profitability. These examples stress that the most important job criteria or duties should be identified in job descriptions and then conveyed to employees.

Performance Standards

Performance standards define the expected levels of employee performance. Sometimes they are labeled *benchmarks, goals,* or *targets*—depending on the approach taken. Realistic, measurable, clearly understood performance standards benefit both organizations and employees. In a sense, performance standards define what satisfactory job performance is, so performance standards should be established *before* work is performed.

Both numerical and nonnumerical standards can be established. Sales quotas and production output standards are familiar numerical performance standards. A standard of performance can also be based on nonnumerical criteria. Assessing whether someone has met a performance standard, especially a nonnumerical one, can be more difficult, but usually can be done.

Performance Metrics in Service Businesses

Measuring performance in service businesses is difficult, but the process is important. Measuring service performance is difficult because services are very individualized for customers, there is typically great variation in the services that can be offered, and service quality is somewhat subjective. Yet the performance of people in service jobs is commonly evaluated along with the basic productivity measure used in the industry. Some of the most useful sources of performance differences among managers in service businesses are:

- Regional differences in labor costs
- Service agreement differences
- Equipment/infrastructure differences
- Work volume

On an individual employee level, common measures are: cost per employee, incidents per employee per day, number of calls per product, cost per call, sources of demand for services, and service calls per day.

PERFORMANCE APPRAISALS

Performance appraisals are used to assess an employee's performance and provide a platform for feedback about past, current, and future performance expectations. Performance appraisal is variously called *employee rating, employee evaluation, performance review, performance evaluation,* or *results appraisal.*

Performance appraisals are widely used for administering wages and salaries, giving performance feedback, and identifying individual employee strengths and weaknesses. Most U.S. employers use performance appraisals for office, professional, technical, supervisory, middle management, and non-union production workers.

Indeed, performance appraisals be applied to a wide array of work-related questions, and by providing a road map for success, poor performance some-times can be improved. Even after a positive appraisal, employees benefit if appraisals help them to determine how to improve job performance. In addition, even though an employer may not need a reason to terminate an employee, as a practical matter, appraisals can provide justification for such actions should that become necessary.

However, appraisal programs must be carefully developed to fully capital-ize on the talents and efforts of employees. For instance, research has indi-cated that a gap often exists between actual job performance and the ratings of the work.[3] Poorly done performance appraisals lead to disappointing re-sults for all concerned, and there is reason to believe that evaluations can cause bad feelings and damaged relationships if not managed well. Some be-lieve that performance evaluations are an unnecessary part of work because of vague rating terms, self-interest, and/or deception on the part of rating managers. However, having no formal performance appraisal can weaken dis-cipline and harm an employee's ability to improve.

Uses of Performance Appraisals

Organizations generally use performance appraisals in two potentially con-flicting ways. One use is to provide a measure of performance for consider-ation in making pay or other administrative decisions about employees. This *administrative* role often creates stress for managers doing the appraisals and employees as well. The other use focuses on the *development* of individuals. In this role, the manager acts more as a counselor and coach than as a judge, a perspective that can change the overall tone of the appraisal process. The de-velopmental performance appraisal emphasizes identifying current training and development needs, as well as planning employees' future opportunities and career directions. Figure 6-3 shows both uses for performance appraisals.

Administrative Uses of Appraisals.   Three administrative uses of appraisal impact managers and employees the most: (1) determining pay adjustments; (2) making job placement decisions on promotions, transfers, and demotions; and (3) choosing employee disciplinary actions up to and including termina-tion of employment.

FIGURE 6-3 Uses for Performance Appraisals

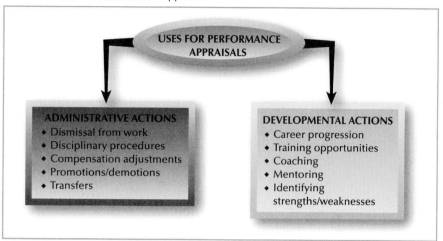

A performance appraisal system is often the link between additional pay and rewards that employees receive and their job performance. Performance-based compensation affirms the idea that pay raises are given for performance accomplishments rather than based on length of service (seniority) or granted automatically to all employees at the same percentage levels. In pay-for-performance compensation systems, historically supervisors and managers have evaluated the performance of individual employees and also made compensation recommendations for the same employees. If any part of the appraisal process fails, better-performing employees may not receive larger pay increases, and the result is perceived inequity in compensation.

U.S. workers say that they see little connection between their performance and the size of their pay increases due to flaws in performance appraisals. However, the use of such appraisals to determine pay is common.

Consequently, many people argue that performance appraisals and pay discussions should be done separately. Two major realities support this view. One is that employees often focus more on the pay received than on the developmental appraisal feedback. The other is that managers sometimes manipulate ratings to justify the pay they wish to give individuals or the amount the market or budget situation suggests should be given.[4] As a result, many employees view the appraisal process as a "game," because compensation increases have been predetermined before the appraisal.

To address these issues, numerous organizations have managers first conduct performance appraisals and discuss the results with employees, and then several weeks later hold a shorter meeting to discuss pay issues. To improve the administrative processes of performance appraisals, many employers have implemented software so that managers can prepare appraisals electronically. Firms are using such HR technology not only to administer appraisals but also to combine employee development and talent management into a package that is integrated.

Developmental Uses of Appraisals.   For employees, a performance appraisal can be a primary source of information and feedback that builds their future development in an organization. By identifying employee strengths, weaknesses, potentials, and training needs through performance appraisal feedback, supervisors can inform employees about their progress, discuss areas in which additional training may be beneficial, and outline future developmental plans.

The manager's role in performance appraisal meetings parallels that of a coach, discussing good performance, explaining what improvements are needed, and showing employees how to improve. It is clear that employees do not always know where and how to improve, and managers should not expect improvement if they are unwilling to provide developmental feedback. Positive reinforcement for desired behaviors contributes to both individual and organizational growth. The purpose of the feedback is both to reinforce satisfactory employee performance and to address performance deficiencies. The developmental function of performance appraisal can also identify areas in which the employee might wish to grow.

Decisions about the Performance Appraisal Process

A number of decisions must be made when designing performance appraisal systems. Some important ones are identifying the type of appraisal system to use, the timing of appraisals, and who will conduct appraisals.

Informal versus Systematic Appraisal Processes.   Performance appraisals can occur in two ways: informally and/or systematically. A supervisor conducts an *informal appraisal* whenever necessary. The day-to-day working relationship between a manager and an employee offers an opportunity for the employee's performance to be evaluated. A manager communicates this evaluation through conversation on the job, over coffee, or by on-the-spot discussion of a specific occurrence. Frequent informal feedback to employees can prevent "surprises" during a formal performance review. However, informal appraisal can become *too* informal. For example, a senior executive at a large firm so dreaded face-to-face evaluations that he delivered one manager's review while both sat in adjoining stalls in the men's room.

A *systematic appraisal* is used when the contact between a manager and employee is formal, and a system is in place to report managerial impressions and observations on employee performance. Systematic appraisals feature a regular time interval, which distinguishes them from informal appraisals. Both employees and managers know that performance will be reviewed on a regular basis, and they can plan for performance discussions.

Timing of Appraisals.   Most companies require managers to conduct appraisals once or twice a year, most often annually. Employees commonly receive an appraisal 60 to 90 days after hiring, again at 6 months, and annually thereafter. *Probationary* or *introductory employees*, who are new and in a trial period, should be informally evaluated often—perhaps weekly for the first month, and monthly thereafter until the end of the introductory period. After that, annual reviews are typical. For employees in high demand, some employers use accelerated appraisals—every 6 months instead of every year. This is done to retain those employees so that more feedback can be given and pay raises may occur more often.

One way to separate the administrative and developmental uses of appraisals is to implement the following appraisal schedule: (1) First hold a performance review and discussion; (2) later hold a separate training, development, and objective-setting session; and (3) within two weeks, have a compensation adjustment discussion. Having three separate discussions provides both the employee and the manager with opportunities to focus on the administrative, developmental, and compensation issues. Using this framework is generally better than addressing all three areas in one discussion of an hour or less, once a year.

Legal Concerns and Performance Appraisals

Because appraisals are supposed to measure how well employees are doing their jobs, it may seem unnecessary to emphasize that performance appraisals must be job related. However, it is important for evaluations to adequately reflect the nature of work, and employees should have fair and nondiscriminatory performance appraisals. Companies need to have appraisal systems that satisfy the courts, as well as performance management needs.

WHO CONDUCTS APPRAISALS?

Performance appraisals can be conducted by anyone familiar with the performance of individual employees. Possible rating situations include the following:

- Supervisors rating their employees
- Employees rating their superiors
- Team members rating each other
- Employees rating themselves
- Outside sources rating employees
- A variety of parties providing multisource, or 360-degree, feedback

Supervisory Rating of Subordinates

The most widely used means of rating employees is based on the assumption that the immediate supervisor is the person most qualified to evaluate an employee's performance realistically and fairly. To help themselves provide accurate evaluations, some supervisors keep performance logs noting their employees' accomplishments so that they can reference these notes when rating performance. For instance, a sales manager might periodically observe a salesperson's interactions with clients so that constructive performance feedback

FIGURE 6-4 Traditional Performance Appraisal Process

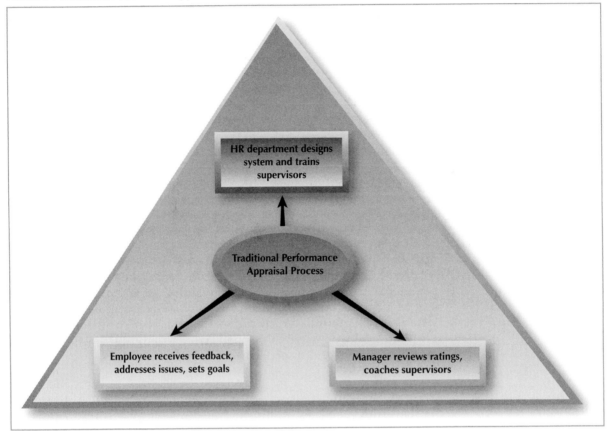

can be provided at a later date. Figure 6-4 shows the traditional review process by which supervisors conduct performance appraisals on employees.

Employee Rating of Managers

A number of organizations ask employees to rate the performance of their immediate managers. Having employees rate managers provides three primary advantages. First, in critical manager-employee relationships, employee ratings can be quite useful for identifying competent managers. The rating of leaders by combat soldiers is one example of such a use. Second, this type of rating program can help make a manager more responsive to employees. This advantage can quickly become a disadvantage if the manager focuses on being "nice" rather than on managing; people who are nice but have no other qualifications may not be good managers in many situations. Finally, employee appraisals can contribute to career development efforts for managers by identifying areas for growth.

A major disadvantage of having employees rate managers is the negative reaction many superiors have to being evaluated by employees. Also, the fear of reprisals may be too great for employees to give realistic ratings. This may prompt workers to rate their managers only on the way the managers treat them, not on critical job requirements. The problems associated with this appraisal approach limit its usefulness to certain situations, including managerial development and improvement efforts.

Team/Peer Rating

Having employees and team members rate each other is another type of appraisal with potential both to help and to hurt. Peer and team ratings are especially useful when supervisors do not have the opportunity to observe each employee's performance but other work group members do. One challenge of this approach is how to obtain ratings with virtual or global teams, in which the individuals work primarily through technology, not in person (i.e., an online college class). Another challenge is obtaining ratings from and for individuals who are on different special project teams throughout the year.

Some contend that any performance appraisal, including team/peer ratings, can negatively affect teamwork and participative management efforts. Although team members have good information on one another's performance, they may not choose to share it in the interest of sparing feelings. Despite the problems, team/peer performance ratings are probably inevitable, especially where work teams are used extensively.

Self-Rating

Self-appraisal works in certain situations. As a self-development tool, it requires employees to think about their strengths and weaknesses and set goals for improvement. Employees working in isolation or possessing unique skills may be particularly suited to self-ratings because they are the only ones qualified to rate themselves. Overall, the use of self-appraisals in organizations has increased.[5] However, employees may use quite different standards and not rate themselves in the same manner as supervisors.

Outsider Rating

People outside the immediate work group may be called in to conduct performance reviews. This field review approach can include someone from the HR department as a reviewer, or completely independent reviewers from outside the organization. Examples include a review team evaluating a college president or a panel of division managers evaluating a supervisor's potential for advancement in the organization. A disadvantage of this approach is that outsiders may not know the important demands within the work group or organization.

The customers or clients of an organization are good sources for outside appraisals. For sales and service jobs, customers may provide useful input on the performance behaviors of employees. For instance, many hospitality organizations such as restaurants and hotels use customer comments cards to gather feedback about the service provided by customer contact personnel, and this information is commonly used for job development purposes.

Multisource/360-Degree Feedback

The use of multisource rating, or 360-degree feedback, has grown in popularity in organizations. Multisource feedback recognizes that for many jobs, employee performance is multidimensional and crosses departmental, organizational, and even global boundaries. Therefore, information needs to be collected from many different sources to adequately and fairly evaluate an incumbent's performance in one of these jobs. The major purpose of 360-degree feedback is *not* to increase uniformity by soliciting like-minded views. Instead, it is designed to capture evaluations of the employee's different roles to provide richer feedback during an evaluation.

Significant administrative time and paperwork are required to request, obtain, and summarize feedback from multiple raters. Using electronic systems to summarize the information can greatly reduce the administrative demands of multisource ratings and increase the effectiveness (i.e., privacy and expediency) of the process.[6]

As originally designed and used, multisource feedback focuses on the use of appraisals for future development of individuals. Conflict resolution skills, decision-making abilities, team effectiveness, communication skills, managerial styles, and technical capabilities are just some of the developmental areas that can be examined. Even in a multisource system, the manager remains a focal point, both to receive the feedback initially and to follow up with the employee appropriately.

The popularity of 360-degree feedback systems has led to the results being used for compensation, promotion, termination, and other administrative decisions. A number of questions have arisen as multisource appraisals have become more common.

Evaluating Multisource Feedback.   Research on multisource/360-degree feedback has revealed both positives and negatives. More variability than expected may be seen in the ratings given by the different sources. Thus, supervisor ratings must carry more weight than peer or subordinate input to resolve the differences. One concern is that those peers who rate poor-performing coworkers tend to inflate the ratings so that the peers themselves can get higher overall evaluation results.

Another concern is whether 360-degree appraisals improve the process or simply multiply the number of problems by the total number of raters. Also, some wonder whether multisource appraisals really create better decisions that offset the additional time and investment required. These issues appear to be less threatening when the 360-degree feedback is used *only for development,* so companies should consider using multisource feedback primarily as a developmental tool to enhance future job performance[7] while effectively reducing the use of multisource appraisals as an administrative tool.

TOOLS FOR APPRAISING PERFORMANCE

Performance can be appraised by a number of methods. Some employers use one method for all jobs and employees, some use different methods for different groups of employees, and others use a combination of methods. The following discussion highlights different tools that can be used and some of the advantages and disadvantages of each approach.

Category Scaling Methods

The simplest methods for appraising performance are category scaling methods, which require a manager to mark an employee's level of performance on a specific form divided into categories of performance. A *checklist* uses a list of statements or words from which raters check statements that are most representative of the characteristics and performance of employees. Often, a scale indicating perceived level of accomplishment on each statement is included, which becomes a type of graphic rating scale.

Graphic Rating Scales

The **graphic rating scale** allows the rater to mark an employee's performance on a continuum indicating low to high levels of a particular characteristic. Because of the straightforwardness of the process, graphic rating scales are commonly used in performance evaluations.[8] Figure 6-5 shows a sample appraisal form that combines graphic rating scales with essays. Three aspects of performance are appraised using graphic rating scales: *descriptive categories* (such as quantity of work, attendance, and dependability), *job duties* (taken from the job description), and *behavioral dimensions* (such as decision making, employee development, and communication effectiveness).

Concerns with Graphic Rating Scales.   Graphic rating scales in many forms are widely used because they are easy to develop and provide a uniform set of criteria to equally evaluate the job performance of different employees. However, the use of scales can cause rater error because the form might not accurately reflect the relative importance of certain job characteristics, and some factors might need to be added to the ratings while others might need to be deleted. If they fit the person and the job, the scales work well. However, if they fit poorly, managers and employees who must use them frequently complain about "the rating form."

A key point must be emphasized. Regardless of the scales used, the focus should be on the job duties and responsibilities identified in job descriptions. The closer the link between the scales and what people actually do, as identified in current and complete job descriptions, the stronger the relationship between the ratings and the job, as viewed by employees and managers. Also, should the performance appraisal results be challenged by legal actions, the closer performance appraisals measure what people actually do, the more likely employers are to prevail in those legal situations.

Behavioral Rating Scales.   In an attempt to overcome some of the concerns with graphic rating scales, employers may use behavioral rating scales designed to assess individual actions instead of personal attributes and characteristics. Different approaches are used, but all describe specific examples of employee job behaviors. In a behaviorally–anchored rating scale (BARS), these examples

FIGURE 6-5 Sample Performance Appraisal Form

Date sent:	4/19/11	

Date sent: 4/19/11   **Return by:**   5/01/11

Name: Joe Hernandez   **Job title:**   Receiving Clerk

Department: Receiving   **Supervisor:**   Marian Williams

Employment status (check one): Full-time ___X___ Part-time _____   **Date of hire:** 5/12/02

Rating period: From: 4/30/10   To: 4/30/11

Reason for appraisal (check one): Regular interval __X__   Introductory ___   Counseling only ___   Discharge ___

Using the following definitions, rate the performance as I, M, or E.

I—Performance is below job requirements and **improvement is needed.**

M—Performance **meets** job requirements and standards.

E—Performance **exceeds** job requirements and standards **most** of the time.

SPECIFIC JOB RESPONSIBILITIES: List the prinicipal activities from the job summary, rate the performance on each job duty by placing an X on the rating scale at the appropriate location, and make appropriate comments to explain the rating.

I ——————————————— M ——————————— E

Job Duty #1: Inventory receiving and checking
Explanation: _____
_____
_____

I ——————————————— M ——————————— E

Job Duty #2: Accurate recordkeeping
Explanation: _____
_____
_____

I ——————————————— M ——————————— E

Attendance (including absences and tardies):   Number of absences ___   Number of tardies ___
Explanation: _____
_____

Overall rating: In the box provided, place the letter—**I, M, or E**—that best describes the employee's overall performance.

Explanation: _____
_____

are "anchored" or measured against a scale of performance levels. When creating a BARS system, identifying important *job dimensions*, which are the most important performance factors in a job description, is done first. Short statements describe both desirable and undesirable behaviors (anchors).

Several problems are associated with the behavioral approaches. First, creating and maintaining behaviorally–anchored rating scales requires extensive time and effort. In addition, various appraisal forms are needed to accommodate different types of jobs in an organization. For instance, because nurses, dietitians, and admissions clerks in a hospital all have distinct job descriptions, a separate BARS form needs to be developed for each.

Comparative Methods

Comparative methods require that managers directly compare the performance levels of their employees against one another, and these comparisons can provide useful information for performance management. An example of this process would be an information systems supervisor comparing the performance of a programmer with that of other programmers. Comparative techniques include ranking and forced distribution.

Ranking.   The **ranking** method lists the individuals being rated from highest to lowest based on their performance levels and relative contributions.[9] One disadvantage of this process is that the sizes of the performance differences between employees are often not fully investigated or clearly indicated. For example, the performances of individuals ranked second and third may differ little, while the performances of those ranked third and fourth differ a great deal. This limitation can be mitigated to some extent by assigning points to indicate performance differences. Ranking also means someone must be last, which ignores the possibility that the last-ranked individual in one group might be equal to the top-ranked employee in a different group. Further, the ranking task becomes unwieldy if the group to be ranked is large.

Forced Distribution.   Forced distribution is a technique for distributing ratings that are generated with any of the other appraisal methods and comparing the ratings of people in a work group. With the **forced distribution** method, the ratings of employees' performance are distributed along a bell-shaped curve. For example, a medical clinic administrator ranking employees on a 5-point scale would have to rate 10% of the employees as a 1 ("unsatisfactory"), 20% as a 2 ("below expectations"), 40% as a 3 ("meets expectations"), 20% as a 4 ("above expectations"), and 10% as a 5 ("outstanding").

Forced distribution has been used in some form by an estimated 30% of all firms with performance appraisal systems. At General Electric, in the "20/70/10" program, managers identify the top 20% and reward them richly so that few will leave. The bottom 10% are given a chance to improve or leave. The forced distribution system is controversial because of both its advantages and its disadvantages, which are discussed next.

One reason why firms have mandated the use of forced distributions for appraisal ratings is to deal with "rater inflation." If employers do not require a forced distribution, performance appraisal ratings often do not match the normal distribution of a bell-shaped curve.

The use of a forced distribution system forces managers to identify high, average, and low performers. Thus, high performers can be rewarded and developed, while low performers can be "encouraged" to improve or leave.

But the forced distribution method suffers from several drawbacks. One problem is that a supervisor may resist placing any individual in the lowest (or the highest) group. Difficulties also arise when the rater must explain to an employee why the employee was placed in one group and others were placed in higher groups.

A number of actions are recommended to address these problems if a forced distribution system is to be used, including many that are similar to those for making other methods of appraisals more legal and effective[10]:

- Use specific, objective criteria and standards to evaluate employees.
- Involve employees in program development.
- Ensure that sufficient numbers of individuals are being rated, so that ranking profiles are relevant.
- Train managers, and review their ratings to ensure job relatedness (no favoritism).

Narrative Methods

Managers and HR specialists may be required to provide written or oral appraisal information. Some appraisal methods are entirely written, rather than relying on predetermined rating scales or ranking structures. Documentation and descriptive text are the basic components of the critical incident method and the essay method.

In the **critical incident** method, the manager keeps a written record of both highly favorable and unfavorable actions performed by an employee during the entire rating period. When a "critical incident" involving an employee occurs, the manager writes it down. For instance, when a sales clerk at a clothing store spends considerable time with a customer helping him purchase a new suit, a manager might document this exceptional service for later review during an annual evaluation. The critical incident method can be used with other methods to document the reasons why an employee was given a certain rating.

The **essay** method requires a manager to write a short essay describing each employee's performance during the rating period. Some "free-form" essays are without guidelines; others are more structured, using prepared questions that must be answered. The rater usually categorizes comments under a few general headings. The essay method allows the rater more flexibility than other methods do. As a result, appraisers often combine the essay with other methods.

The effectiveness of the essay approach often depends on a supervisor's writing skills. Some supervisors do not express themselves well in writing and as a result produce poor descriptions of employee performance, whereas others have excellent writing skills and can create highly positive impressions.

If well composed, essays can provide highly detailed and useful information about an employees' job performance.

Management by Objectives

Management by objectives (MBO) specifies the performance goals that an individual and manager identify together. Each manager sets objectives derived from the overall goals and objectives of the organization; however, MBO should not be a disguised means for a superior to dictate the objectives of individual managers or employees. Other names for MBO include *appraisal by results, target coaching, work planning and review, performance objective setting,* and *mutual goal setting.*

MBO Process.   Implementing a guided self-appraisal system using MBO is a four-stage process. The stages are as follows:

1. *Job review and agreement.*
2. *Development of performance standards.*
3. *Setting of objectives.*
4. *Continuing performance discussions.*

The MBO process seems to be most useful with managerial personnel or employees who have a fairly wide range of flexibility and control over their jobs. When imposed on a rigid and autocratic management system, MBO often has failed. Emphasizing penalties for not meeting objectives defeats the development and participative nature of MBO.

Combinations of Methods

No single appraisal method is best for all situations. Therefore, a performance measurement system that uses a combination of methods may be sensible in certain circumstances. Using combinations may offset some of the advantages and disadvantages of individual methods.

When managers can articulate what they want a performance appraisal system to accomplish, they can choose and mix methods to realize those advantages. For example, one combination might include a graphic rating scale of performance on major job criteria, a narrative for developmental needs, and an overall ranking of employees in a department. Different categories of employees (e.g., salaried exempt, salaried nonexempt, and maintenance) might require different combinations of methods.

TRAINING MANAGERS AND EMPLOYEES IN PERFORMANCE APPRAISAL

Court decisions on the legality of performance appraisals and research on appraisal effectiveness both stress the importance of training managers and employees on performance management and on conducting performance appraisals. Managers with positive views of the performance appraisal system are more likely to use the system effectively. Unfortunately, such training occurs only sporadically or not at all in many organizations.

For employees, performance appraisal training focuses on the purposes of appraisal, the appraisal process and timing, and how performance criteria and standards are linked to job duties and responsibilities. Some training also discusses how employees might rate their own performance and use that information in discussions with their supervisors and managers.

Most systems can be improved by training supervisors in how to do performance appraisals. The following list is not comprehensive, but it does identify some topics covered in appraisal training:

- Appraisal process and timing
- Performance criteria and job standards that should be considered
- How to communicate positive and negative feedback
- When and how to discuss training and development goals
- Conducting and discussing the compensation review
- How to avoid common rating errors

Rater Errors

There are many possible sources of error in the performance appraisal process. One of the major sources is the raters. Although completely eliminating errors is impossible, making raters aware of them through training is helpful.

Varying Standards.   When appraising employees, a manager should avoid applying different standards and expectations to employees performing the same or similar jobs. Such problems often result from the use of ambiguous criteria and subjective weightings by supervisors.

Recency and Primacy Effects.   The **recency effect** occurs when a rater gives greater weight to recent events when appraising an individual's performance. Examples include giving a student a course grade based only on the student's performance in the last week of class and giving a drill press operator a high rating even though the operator made the quota only in the last two weeks of the rating period. The opposite of the recency effect is the **primacy effect,** which occurs when a rater gives greater weight to information received first when appraising an individual's performance.

Central Tendency, Leniency, and Strictness Errors.   A manager may develop a rating pattern. Appraisers who rate all employees within a narrow range in the middle of the scale (i.e., rate everyone as "average") commit a **central tendency error,** giving even outstanding and poor performers an "average" rating.

Rating patterns also may exhibit leniency or strictness. The **leniency error** occurs when ratings of all employees fall at the high end of the scale. The **strictness error** occurs when a manager uses only the lower part of the scale to rate employees. To avoid conflict, managers often rate employees higher than they should. This "ratings boost" is especially likely when no manager or HR representative reviews the completed appraisals.

Rater Bias.   When a rater's values or prejudices distort the rating, this is referred to as **rater bias.** Such bias may be unconscious or quite intentional. For example, a manager's dislike of certain ethnic groups may cause distortion in appraisal information for some people. Use of age, religion, seniority, sex, appearance, or other "classifications" also may skew appraisal ratings if the appraisal process is not properly designed. A review of appraisal ratings by higher-level managers may help correct this problem.

Halo and Horns Effects.   The **halo effect** occurs when a rater scores an employee high on all job criteria because of performance in one area. For example, if a worker has few absences, the supervisor might give the worker a high rating in all other areas of work, including quantity and quality of output, without really thinking about the employee's other characteristics separately. The opposite is the *horns effect*, which occurs when a low rating on one characteristic leads to an overall low rating.

Contrast Error.   Rating should be done using established standards. One problem is the **contrast error,** which is the tendency to rate people relative to one another rather than against performance standards. Although it may be appropriate to compare people at times, the performance rating usually should reflect comparison against performance standards, not against other people.

APPRAISAL FEEDBACK

After completing appraisals, managers need to communicate results in order to give employees a clear understanding of how they stand in the eyes of their immediate superiors and the organization. Organizations commonly require managers to discuss appraisals with employees. The appraisal feedback interview provides an opportunity to clear up any misunderstandings on both sides.

Appraisal Interview

The appraisal interview presents both an opportunity and a danger. It can be an emotional experience for the manager and the employee because the manager must communicate both praise and constructive criticism. A major concern for managers is how to emphasize the positive aspects of the employee's performance while still discussing ways to make needed improvements.[11]

Employees usually approach an appraisal interview with some concern. They may feel that discussions about performance are both personal and important to their continued job success. At the same time, they want to know how their managers feel about their performance. Figure 6-6 summarizes hints for an effective appraisal interview for supervisors and managers.

FIGURE 6-6 Appraisal Interview Hints for Appraisers

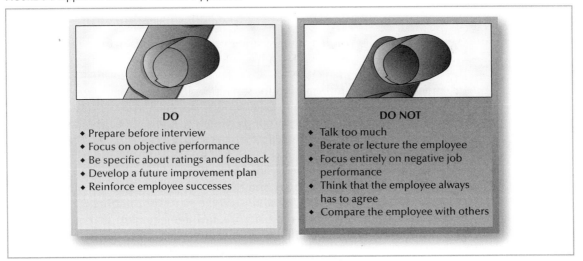

DO	DO NOT
◆ Prepare before interview	◆ Talk too much
◆ Focus on objective performance	◆ Berate or lecture the employee
◆ Be specific about ratings and feedback	◆ Focus entirely on negative job performance
◆ Develop a future improvement plan	◆ Think that the employee always has to agree
◆ Reinforce employee successes	◆ Compare the employee with others

Feedback as a System

The three commonly recognized components of a feedback system are data, evaluation of that data, and some action based on the evaluation. *Data* are factual pieces of information regarding observed actions or consequences. Most often, data are facts that report what happened. Someone must evaluate the meaning or value of the data.

Evaluation is the way the feedback system reacts to the facts, and it requires performance standards. Managers might evaluate the same factual information differently than would customers (e.g., regarding merchandise exchange or credit decisions) or coworkers. Evaluation can be done by the person supplying the data, by a supervisor, or by a group.

For feedback to cause change, some decisions must be made regarding subsequent *action*. Regardless of the process used, the feedback components (data, evaluation, and action) are necessary parts of a successful performance appraisal feedback system.

Reactions of Managers

Managers who must complete appraisals of their employees often resist the appraisal process. Many feel that their role calls on them to assist, encourage, coach, and counsel employees to improve their performance. However, being a judge on the one hand and a coach and a counselor on the other hand may cause internal conflict and confusion for managers.

Knowing that appraisals may affect employees' future careers also may cause altered or biased ratings. This problem is even more likely when managers know that they will have to communicate and defend their ratings to the employees, their bosses, or HR specialists. Managers can easily avoid providing negative feedback to an employee in an appraisal interview and thus avoid unpleasantness in an interpersonal situation by making the employee's ratings positive. But avoidance helps no one. A manager owes an employee a well-done appraisal, no matter how difficult an employee is, or how difficult the conversation about performance might be.

Reactions of Appraised Employees

Employees may well see the appraisal process as a threat and feel that the only way for them to get a higher rating is for someone else to receive a low rating. This win-lose perception is encouraged by comparative methods of rating. Emphasis on the self-improvement and developmental aspects of appraisal appears to be the most effective way to reduce this reaction. However, in most cases, employees will view appraisals done well as what they are meant to be—constructive feedback.

Effective Performance Management

Regardless of the approach used, managers must understand the intended outcome of performance management.[11] When performance management is used to develop employees as resources, it usually works. When one key part of performance management, a performance appraisal, is used to punish employees, performance management is less effective.

Done well, performance management can lead to higher employee motivation and satisfaction. To be effective, a performance management system, including the performance appraisal processes, should be:

- Consistent with the strategic mission of the organization
- Beneficial as a development tool
- Useful as an administrative tool
- Legal and job related
- Viewed as generally fair by employees
- Effective in documenting employee performance

Many of these factors can be enhanced through the effective development of the performance management process. By making sure that raters understand how to consistently evaluate job performance, managers should be able to increase support for the performance management process throughout the organization.

NOTES

1. Patrick Shannon, Colleen O'Neill, Nanci R. Hibschman, and J. Carlos Rivero, "CEO Performance Evaluation: Getting It Right," *Perspective*, Mercer Human Resource Consulting, April 21, 2005.
2. "Survey: Failure to Deal with Poor Performers May Decrease Engagement of Other Employees," *Newsline*, June 22, 2006.
3. Kevin R. Murphy, "Explaining the Weak Relationship Between Job Performance and Ratings of Job Performance," *Industrial and Organizational Psychology*, 1, (2008), 148–160.
4. Samuel A. Culbert, "Get Rid of the Performance Review!" *The Wall Street Journal*, October 20, 2008, R4.

5. Adrienne Fox, "Curing What Ails Performance Reviews," *HR Magazine,* January 2009, 52–56.

6. Leanne Atwater, John F. Brett, and Atira Cherise Charles, "Multisource Feedback: Lessons Learned and Implications for Practice," *Human Resource Management,* 46 (2007), 285–307.

7. Leanne Atwater, John F. Brett, and Atira Cherise Charles, "Multisource Feedback: Lessons Learned and Implications for Practice," *Human Resource Management,* 46 (2007), 285–307; Anne Freedman, "Performance Management: Balancing Values, Results in Reviews," *Human Resource Executive,* August 2006, 62–63.

8. Leslie A. Weatherly, "Performance Management: Getting It Right from the Start," *SHRM Research Quarterly,* 2004.

9. Steve Scullen, Paul Bergey, and Lynda Aiman-Smith, "Forced Distribution Rating Systems and the Improvement of Workforce Potential," *Personnel Psychology,* 58 (2005), 1–31.

10. "A Positive Psychology Handbook for Entrepreneurs," *BusinessWeek, Small Biz,* February/March 2009, 47.

11. Aileen MacMillan, "Raising the Bar on Performance Management Practices to Optimize Performance Reviews and Goal Management," *HR.com,* April 2006, 2–12.

INTERNET RESOURCES

Free Management Library—This website is an integrated online library with resources for profit and nonprofit entities regarding performance management. Visit the site at *www.managementhelp.org.*

LegalWorkplace.Com—For valuable legal management information on performance issues and other HR topics, visit this resource center website at *www.ahipubs.com.*

Personnel Decisions International—This is a website for a firm specializing in the development of people utilizing many different development tools, including managing performance data. Visit the site at *www.personneldecisions.com.*

HR-Software.net—For links to numerous online performance appraisal software systems, visit this website at *www.hr-software.net.*

SUGGESTED READINGS

Herman Aguinis, *Performance Management* (Upper Saddle River, NJ: Pearson/Prentice Hall, 2007), 50–51.

Eric Harmon, Scott Hensel, and T. E. Lukes, "Measuring Performance in Services," *The McKinsey Quarterly,* February, 2006, 2–7.

Lisa Hartley, "Unified Talent Management and the Holy Grail," Best Practices in Performance Management, Special

Advertising Supplement to *Workforce Management* (Taleo), S5; Paul Loucks, "The Need for Web-Based Talent & Performance Management," *Workspan,* October 2007, 68–70.

Laura Roberts, et al., "How to Play to Your Strengths," *Harvard Business Review,* January 2005, 74–80; Peter Drucker, "Managing Oneself," *Harvard Business Review,* January 2005, 100–109.

Total Rewards and Compensation

HR—MEETING MANAGEMENT CHALLENGES

Compensation is always an issue with both management and employees. How can you have a "fair" compensation system? The following points are at the heart of compensation.

- Understand what the organization wants to accomplish with its pay
- Design a rational compensation system
- Comprehend executive compensation

Total rewards are the monetary and non-monetary rewards provided to employees to attract, motivate, and retain them. Critical to an effective rewards approach is the need to balance the interests and costs of the employers with the needs and expectations of employees. In some industries, such as financial services, health care, education, and hospitality, employee payroll and benefits comprise more than 60% of all operating costs. Although actual costs can be easily calculated, the value derived by employers and employees may prove more difficult to identify.

NATURE OF TOTAL REWARDS AND COMPENSATON

Because so many organizational funds are spent on employees, management should match total rewards systems and practices with what the organization is trying to accomplish. To do so, several decision points exist:

- Legal compliance with all appropriate laws and regulations
- Cost-effectiveness for the organization
- Internal, external, and individual equity for employees
- Performance enhancement for the organization
- Performance recognition and talent management for employees
- Enhanced recruitment, involvement, and retention of employees

Employers must balance their costs at a level that rewards employees sufficiently for their knowledge, skills, abilities, and performance accomplishments. During the past several years, total rewards have been a significant focus in HR, and different frameworks have been developed.

Types of Compensation

Rewards can be either intrinsic or extrinsic. *Intrinsic rewards* may include praise for completing a project or meeting performance objectives. Other psychological and social forms of compensation also reflect intrinsic type of rewards. *Extrinsic rewards* are tangible and take both monetary and nonmonetary forms. One tangible component of a compensation program is *direct compensation*, whereby the employer provides monetary rewards for work done and performance results achieved. *Base pay* and *variable pay* are the most common forms of direct compensation. The most common indirect compensation is employee *benefits*.

Base Pay. The basic compensation that an employee receives, usually as a wage or a salary, is called **base pay.** Many organizations use two base pay categories, *hourly* and *salaried*, which are identified according to the way pay is distributed and the nature of the jobs. Hourly pay is the most common means and is based on time.

Employees paid hourly receive **wages,** which are payments calculated based on time worked. In contrast, people paid **salaries** receive the same payment each period regardless of the number of hours worked. Being paid a salary has typically carried higher status for employees than has being paid a wage. However, overtime may have to be paid to certain salaried employees as well as most wage earners as defined by federal and state laws.

Variable Pay. Another type of direct pay is **variable pay,** which is compensation linked directly to individual, team, or organizational performance. The most common types of variable pay for most employees are bonuses and incentive program payments. Executives often receive longer-term rewards such as stock options.

Benefits. Many organizations provide some rewards in an indirect manner. With indirect compensation, employees receive the tangible value of the rewards without receiving actual cash. A **benefit** is a reward—for instance, health insurance, vacation pay, or a retirement pension—given to an employee or a group of employees for organizational membership, regardless of performance. Often employees do not directly pay for all of the benefits they receive. Benefits are discussed in Chapter 8.

Compensation Philosophies

Two basic compensation philosophies lie on opposite ends of a continuum. At one end of the continuum is the *entitlement* philosophy; at the other end is the *performance* philosophy. Most compensation systems fall somewhere in between these two extremes.

The **entitlement philosophy** assumes that individuals who have worked another year are entitled to pay increases, with little regard for performance differences. Many traditional organizations that give automatic increases to their employees every year are practicing the entitlement philosophy. These automatic increases are often referred to as *cost-of-living raises*, even if they are not tied specifically to economic indicators. Further, most of those employees receive the same or nearly the same percentage increase each year.

A **pay-for-performance philosophy** requires that compensation changes reflect performance differences. Organizations operating under this philosophy do not guarantee additional or increased compensation simply for completing another year of organizational service. Instead, they structure pay and incentives to reflect performance differences among employees. Employees who perform satisfactorily maintain or advance their compensation levels more than marginal performers. The bonuses and incentives are based on individual, group, and/or organizational performance.

The total rewards approach reflects a more performance-oriented philosophy because it tends to place more value on individuals' performance, rather than just paying them based on having a job. When determining compensation, managers may also consider elements such as how much an employee knows or how competent an employee is. Some organizations use both compensation and variable pay programs as part of a total rewards approach for all levels of employees. Widespread use of various incentive plans, team bonuses, organizational gainsharing programs, and other designs links growth in compensation and variable pay to results.

Regularly communicating to employees and managers the compensation philosophy helps to reinforce the organizational commitment to it. A recent study found that communication of profit-sharing information increased knowledge, which influenced commitment and satisfaction. Communication also can enhance understanding and perceptions of pay policies, encouraging greater generalized pay satisfaction and career development.[1] Finally, establishing a dialogue with employees about total rewards enables them to be more involved with the development of pay systems that enhance talent and return on investment. A company's compensation philosophy can be used to develop individual talent in an organization.

HR Metrics and Compensation

Employers spend huge amounts of money for employee compensation. Just like any other area of cost, compensation expenditures should be evaluated to determine their effectiveness. Many measures can be used to do this.[2] Employee turnover/retention is one widely used factor. It assumes that compensation systems affect employees' decisions about staying with or leaving the organization. Other more specific measures are used as well, such as the ones shown in Figure 7-1.

The numbers for calculating appropriate measures are readily available to most HR professionals and chief financial officers, but such calculations are not made in many firms. Often the importance of using these numbers is not a priority for managers or CFOs. Ideally, compensation metrics should be computed each year, and then compared with metrics from past years to show how the rate of compensation changes compares with the rate of changes in the organization overall (revenues, expenses, etc.).

FIGURE 7-1 HR Metrics for Compensation

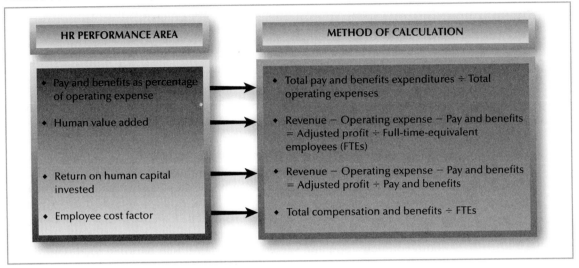

COMPENSATION SYSTEM DESIGN ISSUES

Depending on the compensation philosophies, strategies, and approaches identified for an organization, a number of decisions are made that affect the design of the compensation system. Some important ones are highlighted next.

Compensation Fairness and Equity

Most people in organizations work to gain money for their efforts. Whether employees receive base pay or variable pay, the extent to which they perceive their compensation to be fair often affects their performance, how they view their jobs, and their employers. This factor may lead to lower or higher turnover rates. Pay satisfaction also has been found to be linked to organizational-level performance outcomes.[3]

Equity. The perceived fairness of what a person does (inputs) and what the person receives (outcomes) is called **equity**. Individuals judge equity in compensation by comparing their input (effort and performance) against the effort and performance of others and against the outcomes (the rewards received). These comparisons are personal and are based on individual perceptions, not just facts.

External Equity. If an employer does not provide pay that employees view as equitable compared to other employees performing similar jobs in other organizations, that employer is likely to experience higher turnover. Another drawback is greater difficulty in recruiting qualified and high-demand individuals. By not being competitive, the employer is more likely to attract and retain individuals with less knowledge and fewer skills and abilities, resulting in lower overall organizational performance. Organizations track external equity by using pay surveys, which are discussed later in this chapter, and by looking at the compensation policies of competing employers.

Internal Equity in Compensation.   Internal equity means that employees receive compensation in relation to the knowledge, skills, and abilities (KSAs) they use in their jobs, as well as their responsibilities and accomplishments. Two key issues—procedural justice and distributive justice—relate to internal equity.

Procedural justice is the perceived fairness of the process and procedures used to make decisions about employees, including their pay. As it applies to compensation, the entire process of determining base pay for jobs, allocating pay increases, and measuring performance must be perceived as fair.

A related issue that must be considered is **distributive justice**, which is the perceived fairness in the distribution of outcomes. As one example, if a hardworking employee whose performance is outstanding receives the same across-the-board raise as an employee with attendance problems and mediocre performance, then inequity may be perceived.

To address concerns about both types of justice, some organizations establish compensation appeals procedures. Typically, employees are encouraged to contact the HR department after discussing their concerns with their immediate supervisors and managers.

Pay Secrecy.   Another equity issue concerns the degree of secrecy that organizations have regarding their pay systems. Pay information that may be kept secret in "closed" systems includes how much others make, what raises others have received, and even what pay grades and ranges exist in the organization.

Statistical Analysis.   The management of different fairness and equity issues requires managers to understand the various statistical methodologies that can be used to evaluate current compensation levels. For instance, HR professionals need to check how corporate pay programs compare to the compensation being offered by competing firms so that compensation can be adjusted to reflect the company's pay philosophy. HR professionals also must determine the degree to which compensation is distributed fairly within the organization based on such factors as job level, experience, training, and other human capital factors.

Market Competitiveness and Compensation

The market competitiveness of compensation has a significant impact on how equitably employees view compensation. Providing competitive compensation to employees, whether globally, domestically, or locally, is a concern for all employers. Some organizations establish specific policies about where they wish to be positioned in the labor market. These policies use a *quartile strategy*, as illustrated in Figure 7-2.

"Meet the Market" Strategy.   Most employers choose to position themselves in the *second quartile* (median), in the middle of the market, as identified by pay data from surveys of other employers' compensation plans. Choosing this level attempts to balance employer cost pressures and the need to attract

FIGURE 7-2 Compensation Quartile Strategies

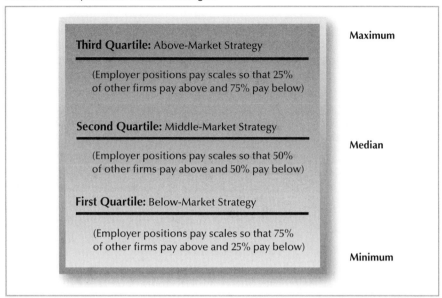

and retain employees, by providing mid-level compensation scales that "meet the market" for the employer's jobs.

"Lag the Market" Strategy. An employer using a *first-quartile* strategy may choose to "lag the market" by paying below market levels, for several reasons. If the employer is experiencing a shortage of funds, it may be unable to pay more. Also, when an abundance of workers is available, particularly those with lower skills, a below-market approach can be used to attract sufficient workers at a lesser cost. Some employers hire illegal immigrants at below-market rates because of the large numbers of those individuals who want to work in the United States. The downside of this strategy is that it increases the likelihood of higher worker turnover. If the labor market supply tightens, then attracting and retaining workers becomes more difficult.

"Lead the Market" Strategy. A *third-quartile* strategy uses an aggressive approach to "lead the market." This strategy generally enables a company to attract and retain sufficient workers with the required capabilities and to be more selective when hiring. Because it is a higher-cost approach, organizations often look for ways to increase the productivity of employees receiving above-market wages.

Selecting a Quartile. The pay levels and pay structures used can affect organizational performance. Individual employee pay levels will vary around the quartile level, depending on experience, performance, and other individual factors. Deciding in which quartile to position pay structures is a function of a number of considerations. The financial resources available, competitive pressures, and the market availability of employees with different capabilities are external factors. For instance, some employers with extensive benefits programs or broad-based incentive programs may choose a first-quartile strategy so that their overall compensation costs and levels are not excessive.

Competency-Based Pay

The design of most compensation programs rewards employees for carrying out their tasks, duties, and responsibilities. The job requirements determine which employees have higher base rates. Employees receive more for doing jobs that require a greater variety of tasks, more knowledge and skills, greater physical effort, or more demanding working conditions. However, the design of some compensation programs emphasizes competencies rather than the tasks performed.

Competency-based pay rewards individuals for the capabilities they demonstrate and acquire. In knowledge-based pay (KBP) or skill-based pay (SBP) systems, employees start at a base level of pay and receive increases as they learn to do other jobs or gain additional skills and knowledge and thus become more valuable to the employer. For example, a printing firm operates two-color, four-color, and six-color presses. The more colors, the more skills required of the press operators. Under a KBP or SBP system, press operators increase their pay as they learn how to operate the more complex presses, even though sometimes they may be running only two-color jobs. A recent study determined that receiving SBP is related to learning and skill enhancement, which demonstrates that such compensation systems can be effective.[4]

When an organization moves to a competency-based system, considerable time must be spent identifying the required competencies for various jobs. Reliance on items such as college diplomas and degrees may need to change such that more emphasis is placed on demonstrated knowledge and competencies rather than degrees. *Progression* of employees must be possible, and employees must be paid appropriately for all their competencies. Any *limitations* on the numbers of people who can acquire more competencies should be clearly identified. *Training* in the appropriate competencies is particularly important. Also, a competency-based system needs to acknowledge or certify employees as they acquire certain competencies, and then to verify the maintenance of those competencies. In summary, use of a competency-based system requires significant investment of management time and commitment.

LEGAL CONSTRAINTS ON PAY SYSTEMS

Pay systems must comply with many government constraints. The important areas addressed by the laws include minimum-wage standards and hours of work. The following discussion examines the laws and regulations affecting base compensation.

Fair Labor Standards Act (FLSA)

The major federal law affecting compensation is the Fair Labor Standards Act (FLSA), which was originally passed in 1938. Compliance with FLSA provisions is enforced by the Wage and Hour Division of the U.S. Department of Labor. To meet FLSA requirements, employers must keep accurate time records and maintain those records for 3 years. Penalties for wage and hour violations often include awards of up to 2 years of back pay for affected current and former employees.

The provisions of both the original act and subsequent revisions focus on the following major areas:

- Establish a minimum wage.
- Discourage oppressive use of child labor.
- Encourage limits on the number of hours employees work per week, through overtime provisions (exempt and nonexempt statuses).

Minimum Wage.   The FLSA sets a minimum wage to be paid to the broad spectrum of covered employees. The actual minimum wage can be changed only by congressional action. A lower minimum wage is set for "tipped" employees, such as restaurant servers, but their compensation must equal or exceed the minimum wage when average tips are included. Minimum-wage levels have sparked significant political discussions and legislative maneuvering at both the federal and state levels for the past decade. Consequently, a three-stage increase in the federal minimum wage occurred beginning in 2007 as part of the Fair Minimum Wage Act of 2007, which recently was set with the current minimum wage of $7.25 an hour. Note that if a state's minimum wage is higher, employers must meet the state level rather than the federal level.

Discussion also surrounds the payment of a "living wage" versus the minimum wage. A **living wage** involves earnings that are supposed to meet the basic needs of an individual working for an organization, including food, clothing, and shelter. In the United States, many cities have passed local living-wage legislation.

Child Labor Provisions.   The child labor provisions of the FLSA set the minimum age for employment with unlimited hours at 16 years. For hazardous occupations, the minimum is 18 years of age. Individuals 14 to 15 years old may work outside school hours with certain limitations. Many employers require age certificates for employees because the FLSA makes the employer responsible for determining an individual's age. A representative of a state labor department, a state education department, or a local school district generally issues such certificates.

Exempt and Nonexempt Statuses.   Under the FLSA, employees are classified as exempt or nonexempt. **Exempt employees** hold positions for which employers are not required to pay overtime. **Nonexempt employees** must be paid overtime. The current FLSA regulations used to identify whether or not a job qualifies for exempt status classifies exempt jobs into five categories:

- Executive
- Administrative
- Professional (learned or creative)
- Computer employees
- Outside sales

FIGURE 7-3 Determining Exempt Status under the FLSA

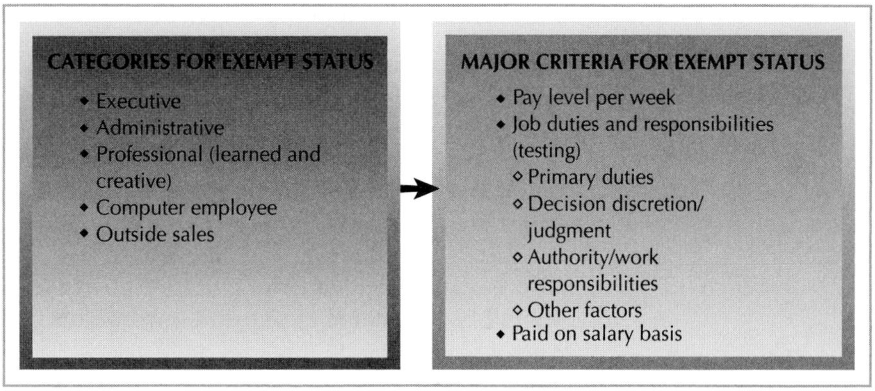

CATEGORIES FOR EXEMPT STATUS	MAJOR CRITERIA FOR EXEMPT STATUS

• Executive
• Administrative
• Professional (learned and creative)
• Computer employee
• Outside sales
	• Pay level per week
	• Job duties and responsibilities (testing)
	  ◦ Primary duties
	  ◦ Decision discretion/judgment
	  ◦ Authority/work responsibilities
	  ◦ Other factors
	• Paid on salary basis

As Figure 7-3 indicates, the regulations identify several factors to be considered in exempt status: salaried pay levels per week, duties and responsibilities, and other criteria that must exist for jobs to be categorized as exempt. To review the details for each exemption, go to the U.S. Department of Labor's website at www.dol.gov.

The FLSA does not require employers to pay overtime for *salaried exempt* jobs, although some organizations have implemented policies to pay a straight rate for extensive hours of overtime. For instance, some electric utilities pay first-line supervisors extra using a special rate for hours worked over 50 a week during storm emergencies. A number of salaried exempt professionals in various IT jobs also receive additional compensation for working extensively more than 40 hours per week.

Overtime. The FLSA establishes overtime pay requirements. Its provisions set overtime pay at one and one-half times the regular pay rate for all hours over 40 a week, except for employees who are not covered by the FLSA. Overtime provisions do not apply to farm workers, who also have a lower minimum-wage schedule.

The workweek is defined as a consecutive period of 168 hours (24 hours × 7 days) and does not have to be a calendar week. If they wish to do so, hospitals and nursing homes are allowed to use a 14-day period instead of a 7-day week, as long as overtime is paid for hours worked beyond 8 in a day or 80 in a 14-day period. No daily number of hours requiring overtime is set, except for special provisions relating to hospitals and other specially designated organizations. Thus, if a manufacturing firm operates on a 4-day/10-hour schedule, no overtime pay is required by the act.

The most difficult part is distinguishing who is and is not exempt. Some recent costly settlements have prompted more white-collar workers to sue for overtime pay. Retail managers, reporters, sales reps, personal bankers, engineers, computer programmers, and claims adjusters have won in some cases, as being nonexempt workers.

Common Overtime Issues. For individuals who are nonexempt, employers must consider a number of issues. These include the following:

- *Compensatory time off:* "Comp" hours are given to public-sector nonexempt employees in lieu of payment for extra time worked at the rate of one and one-half times the number of hours over 40 that are worked in a week. Comp time is currently not available in the private sector and cannot be legally offered to employees working for private for-profit organizations.
- *Incentives for nonexempt employees:* Employers must add the amount of direct work-related incentives to a person's base pay. Then overtime pay should be calculated as one and one-half times the higher (adjusted) rate of pay.
- *Training time:* Time spent in training must be counted as time worked by nonexempt employees unless it is outside regular work hours, not directly job-related, or falls under various other aspects. College degree programs may not be affected by these provisions.
- *Travel time:* Travel time must be counted as work time if it occurs during normal work hours, even on nonworking days, unless the nonexempt person is a passenger in a car, bus, train, airplane, or other similar mode of transportation. The complex clarifications regarding travel regulations affecting overtime should be reviewed by HR specialists to ensure compliance.

Independent Contractor Regulations

The growing use of contingent workers by many organizations has focused attention on another group of legal regulations—those identifying the criteria that independent contractors must meet. For an employer, classifying someone as an independent contractor rather than an employee offers a major advantage. The employer does not have to pay Social Security, unemployment, or workers' compensation costs. These additional payroll levies may add 10% or more to the costs of hiring the individual as an employee. Most federal and state entities rely on the criteria for independent contractor status identified by the Internal Revenue Service (IRS). However, the misclassification of employees as independent contractors is becoming an increasingly significant legal concern for organizations.[5]

Behavioral Control. Some key differences between an employee and an independent contractor have been identified by the IRS. The first set of factors consists of behavioral control factors, which indicate the extent to which an employer can control what a worker does and how a worker performs. One key area includes *business instructions given to the worker*, such as where and when to work, in what sequences, and with what tools and equipment, as well as how to purchase supplies and services. The other area is *business training given to the worker*, such as when someone must be trained to perform in a specific manner, rather than accomplishing results.

Financial Control. This set of factors focuses on the extent to which an employer can control the business facets of a worker's job. Considerations include how many *unreimbursed business expenses* a worker has and what investments a worker makes independently to do the job. Other financial factors include whether a worker *provides services to other firms*, how the *business pays the worker*, and if the worker can make a *profit or loss*.

Relationship-Type Factors. A number of other items can help clarify whether a relationship is truly independent or not, such as having *written contracts* and the *extent of services provided*. Also, if the employer *provides benefits*, such as insurance or pensions, it is more likely that the person is an employee, and not an independent contractor. For additional details, go to www.irs.gov.

Acts Affecting Government Contractors

Several compensation-related acts apply to firms having contracts with the U.S. government. The Davis-Bacon Act of 1931 affects compensation paid by firms engaged in federal construction projects valued at over $2,000. It deals only with federal construction projects and requires that the "prevailing" wage be paid on all such projects. The *prevailing wage* is determined by a formula that considers the rate paid for a job by a majority of the employers in the appropriate geographic area.

Two other acts require firms with federal supply or service contracts exceeding $10,000 to pay a prevailing wage. Both the Walsh-Healy Public Contracts Act and the McNamara-O'Hara Service Contract Act apply only to those who are working directly on a federal government contract or who substantially affect its performance.

Lilly Ledbetter Fair Pay Act

As a result of limited time allowed under law for claiming pay discrimination based on sex, religion, color, disability, and other protected characteristics, the Lilly Ledbetter Fair Pay Act was signed by President Obama in January 2009. Before the law was passed, individuals had to submit complaints of pay discrimination to the EEOC within a 180- or 300-day window, which was based on the state where the person was employed. This new legislation effectively negates any statute of limitations for filing a complaint, so claims of pay discrimination can now be made at any time after the alleged misconduct.[6]

DEVELOPMENT OF A BASE PAY SYSTEM

A base compensation system is developed using current job descriptions and job specifications. These information sources are used when *valuing jobs* and analyzing *pay surveys*—activities that are designed to ensure that the pay system is both internally equitable and externally competitive. The data compiled in these two activities are used to design *pay structures*, including *pay grades* and minimum-to-maximum *pay ranges*. After pay structures are established, individual jobs must be placed in the appropriate pay grades and employees' pay must be adjusted according to length of service and performance. Finally, the pay system must be monitored and updated.

Employers want their employees to perceive their pay levels as appropriate in relation to pay for jobs performed by others inside the organization. Frequently, employees and managers make comments such as "This job is more important than that job in another department, so why are the two jobs paid about the same?" Two general approaches for valuing jobs are available: job evaluation and market pricing. Both approaches are used to determine the values of jobs in relation to other jobs in an organization, and they are discussed next.

Valuing Jobs with Job Evaluation Methods

Job evaluation is a formal, systematic means to identify the relative worth of jobs within an organization. Several job evaluation methods are available for use by employers of different sizes.

Point Method.   The most widely used job evaluation method, the point method, looks at compensable factors in a group of similar jobs and places weights, or *points*, on them. A **compensable factor** identifies a job value commonly present throughout a group of jobs. Compensable factors are derived from job analysis and reflect the nature of different types of work performed in the organization.

The point method is the most popular because it is relatively simple to use and it considers the components of a job rather than the total job. However, point systems have been criticized for reinforcing traditional organizational structures and job rigidity. Although not perfect, the point method of job evaluation is generally better than the ranking and classification methods because it quantifies job elements.

Legal Issues and Job Evaluation.   Because job evaluation affects the employment relationship, specifically the pay of individuals, some legal issues are of concern. Critics have charged that traditional job evaluation programs place less weight on knowledge, skills, and working conditions for many female-dominated jobs in office and clerical areas than on the same factors for male-dominated jobs in craft and manufacturing areas. Employers counter that because they base their pay rates heavily on external equity comparisons in the labor market, they are simply reflecting rates the "market economy" sets for jobs and workers, rather than discriminating on the basis of gender.

Valuing Jobs Using Market Pricing

Some employers have scaled back their use of "internal valuation" through traditional job evaluation methods. They have instead switched to **market pricing**, which uses market pay data to identify the relative value of jobs based on what other employers pay for similar jobs. Jobs are arranged in groups tied directly to similar survey data amounts.

Key to market pricing is identifying relevant market pay data for jobs that are good "matches" with the employer's jobs, geographic considerations, and company strategies and philosophies about desired market competitiveness levels. That is why some firms have used market pricing as part of strategic decisions in order to ensure market competitiveness of their compensation levels and practices.

Advantages of Market Pricing.   The primary advantage cited for the use of market pricing is that it closely ties organizational pay levels to what is actually occurring in the market, without being distorted by "internal" job evaluation. An additional advantage of market pricing is that it allows an employer to communicate to employees that the compensation system is truly "market linked," rather than sometimes being distorted by internal issues. Employees often see a compensation system that was developed using market pricing as having "face validity" and as being more objective than a compensation system that was developed using the traditional job evaluation methods.

Disadvantages of Market Pricing.   The foremost disadvantage of market pricing is that for numerous jobs, pay survey data are limited or may not be gathered in methodologically sound ways. A closely related problem is that the responsibilities of a specific job in a company may be somewhat different from those of the "matching" job identified in the survey.[7]

Finally, tying pay levels to market data can lead to wide fluctuations based on market conditions. For evidence of this, one has only to look back at the extremes of the IT job market during the past decade, when pay levels varied significantly. For these and other types of jobs, the debate over the use of job evaluation versus market pricing is likely to continue because both approaches have pluses and minuses associated with them.

Pay Surveys

A **pay survey** is a collection of data on compensation rates for workers performing similar jobs in other organizations. Both job evaluation and market pricing are tied to surveys of the pay that other organizations provide for similar jobs.

Because jobs may vary widely in an organization, it is particularly important to identify **benchmark jobs**—ones that are found in many other organizations. Often these jobs are performed by individuals who have similar duties that require similar KSAs. For example, benchmark jobs commonly used in clerical/office situations are accounts payable processor, customer service representative, and receptionist. Benchmark jobs are used because they provide "anchors" against which individual jobs can be compared. An employer may obtain surveys conducted by other organizations, access Internet data, or conduct its own survey. Many different surveys are available from a variety of sources.

Internet-Based Pay Surveys.   HR professionals can access a wide range of pay survey data online. In many cases, pay survey questionnaires are distributed electronically rather than as printed copies, and HR staff members complete the questionnaires electronically. It is anticipated that during the next 5 years, most pay surveys will be conducted using electronic, Web-based technology.

The Internet provides a large number of pay survey sources and data. However, use of these sources requires caution because their accuracy and completeness may not be verifiable or may not be applicable to individual firms and employees.

Using Pay Surveys. The proper use of pay surveys requires evaluating a number of factors to determine if the data are relevant and valid. The following questions should be answered for each survey:

- *Participants:* Does the survey cover a realistic sample of the employers with whom the organization competes for employees?
- *Broad-based:* Does the survey include data from employers of different sizes, industries, and locales?
- *Timeliness:* How current are the data (determined by the date the survey was conducted)?
- *Methodology:* How established is the survey, and how qualified are those who conducted it?
- *Job matches:* Does the survey contain job summaries so that appropriate matches to job descriptions can be made?

PAY STRUCTURES

Once job valuations and pay survey data are gathered, pay structures can be developed. Data from the valuation of jobs and the pay surveys may lead to the establishment of several different pay structures for different job families, rather than just one structure for all jobs. A **job family** is a group of jobs having common organizational characteristics. Organizations can have a number of different job families. Examples of some common pay structures based on different job families include: (1) hourly and salaried; (2) office, plant, technical, professional, and managerial; and (3) clerical, IT, professional, supervisory, management, and executive. The nature, culture, and structure of the organization are considerations for determining how many and which pay structures to have.

Pay Grades

In the process of establishing a pay structure, organizations use **pay grades** to group individual jobs having approximately the same job worth. Although no set rules govern the establishment of pay grades, some overall suggestions can be useful. Generally, 11 to 17 grades are used in small and medium-sized companies, such as companies with fewer than 500 to 1,000 employees. Two methods are commonly used to establish pay grades: job evaluation data and use of job market banding.

Setting Pay Grades Using Job Evaluation Points. One approach to determining pay grades uses job evaluation points or other data generated from the traditional job evaluation methods discussed earlier in the chapter. This process ties pay survey information to job evaluation data by plotting a **market line** that shows the relationship between job value as determined by job evaluation points and job value as determined by pay survey rates.

Setting Pay Grades Using Market Banding. Closely linked to the use of market pricing to value jobs, **market banding** groups jobs into pay grades based on similar market survey amounts. The midpoint of the survey average is used to develop pay range minimums and maximums, the methods of which are discussed later in this chapter.

Pay Ranges

Once pay grades are determined, the pay range for each pay grade must be established. Using the market line as a starting point, the employer can determine minimum and maximum pay levels for each pay grade by making the market line the midpoint line of the new pay structure (see Figure 7-4). For example, in a particular pay grade, the maximum value may be 20% above the midpoint located on the market line, and the minimum value may be 20% below it. Once pay grades and ranges have been computed, then the current pay of employees must be compared with the draft ranges. A number of employers are reducing the number of pay grades and expanding pay ranges by broadbanding.

Broadbanding. The practice of using fewer pay grades with much broader ranges than in traditional compensation systems is called **broadbanding.** Combining many grades into these broadbands is designed to encourage horizontal movement and therefore more skill acquisition. About one-quarter of all employers in one survey are using broadbanding.[8] The main advantage of broadbanding is that it is more consistent with the flattening of organizational levels and the growing use of jobs that are multidimensional. The primary reasons for using broadbanding are: (1) to create more flexible organizations, (2) to encourage competency development, and (3) to emphasize career development.

Individual Pay

Once managers have determined pay ranges, they can set the pay for specific individuals. Setting a range for each pay grade gives flexibility by allowing individuals to progress within a grade instead of having to move to a new grade each time they receive a raise. A pay range also allows managers to reward the better-performing employees while maintaining the integrity of the pay system. Regardless of how well a pay structure is constructed, there usually are a few individuals whose pay is lower than the minimum or higher than the maximum due to past pay practices and different levels of experience and performance. Two types of such employees are discussed next.

FIGURE 7-4 Example of Pay Grades and Pay Ranges

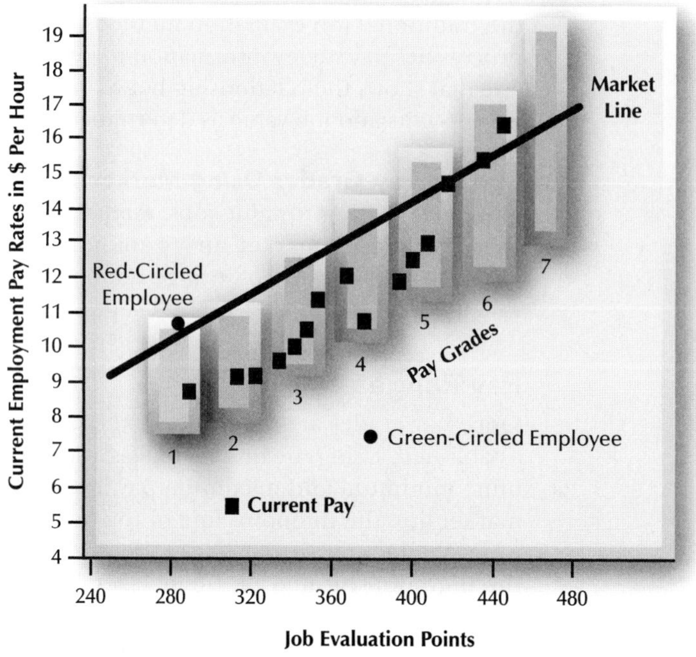

Grade	Point Range	Minimum Pay	Midpoint Pay	Maximum Pay
1	Below 300	7.50	9.17	10.87
2	300–329	7.96	9.75	11.54
3	330–359	8.98	11.00	13.02
4	360–389	10.00	12.25	14.50
5	390–419	11.01	13.49	15.97
6	420–449	11.79	14.74	17.69
7	Over 450	12.79	15.99	19.18

Red-Circled Employees.   A **red-circled employee** is an incumbent who is paid above the range set for the job. For example, assume that an employee's current pay is $11.92 an hour, but the pay range for that person's pay grade is $7.96 to $11.54 an hour. The person would be red-circled. Management would try over a year or so to bring the employee's rate into grade.

Several approaches can be used to bring a red-circled person's pay into line. Although the fastest way would be to cut the employee's pay, that approach is not recommended and is seldom used. Instead, the employee's pay may be frozen until the pay range can be adjusted upward to get the employee's pay rate back into the grade. Another approach is to give the employee a small lump-sum payment but not adjust the pay rate when others are given raises.

Green-Circled Employees.   An individual whose pay is below the range set for a job is a **green-circled employee**. Promotion is a major contributor to this situation. Generally, it is recommended that the green-circled individual receive fairly rapid pay increases to reach the pay grade minimum. More frequent increases can be used if the minimum is a large amount above the incumbent's current pay.

Pay Compression.   One major problem many employers face is **pay compression,** which occurs when the pay differences among individuals with different levels of experience and performance become small. Pay compression occurs for a number of reasons, but the major one involves situations in which labor market pay levels increase more rapidly than current employees' pay adjustments.

In response to shortages of particular job skills in a highly competitive labor market, managers may occasionally have to pay higher amounts to hire people with those scarce skills. For example, suppose the job of specialized information systems analyst is identified as a $48,000 to $68,000 salary range in one company, but qualified individuals are in short supply and other employers are paying $70,000. To fill the job, the firm likely will have to pay the higher rate. Suppose also that several good analysts who have been with the firm for several years started at $55,000 and have received 4% increases each year. These current employees may still be making less than the $70,000 paid to attract and retain new analysts with less experience from outside. Making certain that pay rates for company jobs are market-based and pay raises are based on performance-based reviews are ways to mitigate salary compression.[9]

DETERMINING PAY INCREASES

Decisions about pay increases are often critical ones in the relationships between employees, their managers, and the organization. Individuals express expectations about their pay and about how much of an increase is "fair," especially in comparison with the increases received by other employees. This is why HR professionals must be actively involved in the communication of pay increases to help manage perceptions of any changes made to employees' compensation.

Pay increases can be determined in several ways: performance, seniority, cost-of-living adjustments, across-the-board increases, and lump-sum increases. These methods can be used separately or in combination.

Performance-Based Increases

As mentioned earlier, some employers have shifted to more pay-for-performance philosophies and strategies. Consequently, they have adopted the following means to provide employees with performance-based increases.

Targeting High Performers. This approach focuses on providing the top-performing employees with significantly higher pay raises. Some organizations target the top 10% of employees for significantly greater increases while providing more standard increases to the remaining satisfactory performers.

The primary reason for having such significant differentials focuses on rewarding and retaining the critical high-performing individuals.[10] Key to rewarding exceptional performers is identifying how much their accomplishments have been above the normal work expectations. The more "standard" increases for the average performers are usually aligned with labor market pay adjustments, so that those individuals are kept competitive. The lower performers are given less because of their performance issues, which "encourages" them to leave their organizations.

Pay Adjustment Matrix. A system for integrating appraisal ratings and pay changes must be developed and applied equally. Often, this integration is done through the development of a *pay adjustment matrix*, or *salary guide chart*. Use of pay adjustment matrices bases adjustments in part on a person's **compa-ratio**, which is the pay level divided by the midpoint of the pay range. To illustrate, the following is an example of the compa-ratio for an employee called *J*:

$$\text{Employee } J = \frac{\$13.35 \text{ (current pay)}}{\$15.00 \text{ (midpoint)}} \times 100 = 89 \text{ (Compa-ratio)}$$

Salary guide charts reflect a person's upward movement in an organization. That movement often depends on the person's performance, as rated in an appraisal, and on the person's position in the pay range, which has some relation to experience as well. A person's placement on the chart determines what pay raise the person should receive. According to the chart shown in Figure 7-5, if employee *J* is rated as exceeding expectations (3) with a compa-ratio of 89, that person is eligible for a raise of 7% to 9%.

Two interesting elements of the sample matrix illustrate the emphasis on paying for performance. First, individuals whose performance is below expectations receive small to no raises. This approach sends a strong signal that poor performers will not continue to receive increases just by completing another year of service. Second, as employees move up the pay range, they must exhibit higher performance to obtain the same percentage raise as those lower in the range performing at the "meets performance expectations" level (see Figure 7-5). This approach is taken because the firm is paying above the market midpoint but receiving only satisfactory performance rather than above-market performance. Charts can be constructed to reflect the specific pay-for-performance policies and philosophy in an organization.

Standardized Pay Adjustments

Several different methods are used to provide standardized pay increases to employees. The most common ones are discussed next.

FIGURE 7-5 Pay Adjustment Matrix

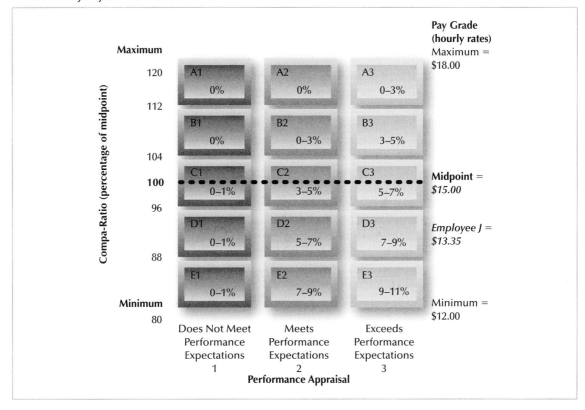

Seniority. The time spent in an organization or on a particular job, called **seniority,** can be used as the basis for pay increases. Many employers have policies that require a person to be employed for a certain length of time before being eligible for pay increases. Pay adjustments based on seniority often are set as automatic steps once a person has been employed the required length of time, although performance must be at least satisfactory in many nonunion systems.

Cost-of-Living Adjustments. A common pay-raise practice is the use of a *cost-of-living adjustment (COLA)*. Often, these adjustments are tied to changes in the Consumer Price Index (CPI) or some other general economic measure. However, numerous studies have revealed that the CPI overstates the actual cost of living, and, as stated previously, COLA increases do little to recognize employees for their relative contributions to the organization.

Across-the-Board Increases. Unfortunately, some employers give across-the-board raises and call them *merit raises,* which they are not. Usually the percentage raise is based on standard market percentage changes or financial budgeting determinations not specifically linked to the COLA. If all employees get the same percentage pay increase, it is legitimately viewed as having little to do with merit or good performance. For this reason, employers should reserve the term *merit* for any amount above the standard raise, and they should state clearly which amount is for performance and which amount is the "automatic" portion.

Lump-Sum Increases.   Most employees who receive pay increases, either for merit or for seniority, receive an increase in the amount of their regular monthly or weekly paycheck. For example, an employee who makes $12.00 an hour and then receives a 3% increase will move to $12.36 an hour.

In contrast, a **lump-sum increase (LSI)** is a one-time payment of all or part of a yearly pay increase. The pure LSI approach does not increase the base pay. Therefore, in the example of a person making $12.00 an hour, if an LSI of 3% is granted, the person receives a lump sum of $748.80 ($0.36 an hour $\times$ 2,080 working hours in the year). However, the base rate remains at $12.00 an hour, which slows down the progression of the base wages.

An LSI plan offers advantages and disadvantages. The major advantage of an LSI plan is that it heightens employees' awareness of what their performance levels "merited." Another advantage is that the firm can use LSIs to slow down the increase of base pay and thus reduce or avoid the compounding effect on succeeding raises. One disadvantage of LSI plans is that workers who take a lump-sum payment may become discouraged because their base pay has not changed. Unions generally resist LSI programs because of their impact on pensions and benefits, unless the total amount used in those computations includes the LSI.

EXECUTIVE COMPENSATION

Most organizations administer compensation for executives somewhat differently than compensation for other employees. An executive typically is someone in the top two levels of an organization, such as chief executive officer (CEO), president, senior vice president, chief operating officer, executive vice president, chief financial officer, or senior HR Executive. At the heart of most executive compensation plans is the idea that executives should be rewarded if the organization grows in profitability and value over a period of years.

Elements of Executive Compensation

Because many executives are in high tax brackets, their compensation often is provided in ways that offer significant tax savings, which means that their total compensation packages may be more significant than just their base pay. Thus, executives often are interested in current compensation and the mix of items in the total package.

Executive Salaries and Benefits.   Salaries of executives vary by the type of job, size of organization, the industry, and other factors. In some organizations, particularly nonprofits, salaries often make up 90% or more of total compensation. In contrast, in large corporations, salaries may constitute less than half of the total package. Survey data on executive salaries are often reviewed by boards of directors to ensure that their organizations are competitive.

Many executives are covered by *regular benefits plans* that are also available to nonexecutive employees, including traditional retirement, health insurance, and vacation plans. In addition, executives may receive *supplemental benefits* that other employees do not receive such as corporate-owned life insurance, company-paid financial planning, and estate-planning. *Deferred compensation* is another way of helping executives with tax liabilities caused by incentive compensation plans.

Executive Perquisites (Perks). In addition to the regular benefits received by all employees, perquisites often are received by executives. **Perquisites (Perks)** are special benefits—usually noncash items. Perks also can offer substantial tax savings because some of them are not taxed as income. Some commonly used executive perks are company cars, health club and country club memberships, first-class air travel, use of private jets, stress counseling, and chauffeur services.

Annual and Long-Term Executive Incentives and Bonuses. Annual incentives and bonuses for senior managers and executives can be determined in several ways. One way is to use a discretionary system whereby the CEO and the board of directors decide bonuses; the absence of formal, measurable targets detracts significantly from this approach. Another way is to tie bonuses to specific measures, such as return on investment, earnings per share, and net profits before taxes.

Executive performance-based incentives tie executive compensation to the long-term growth and success of the organization. However, whether these incentives really emphasize the long term or merely represent a series of short-term rewards is controversial. Short-term rewards based on quarterly or annual performance may not result in the kind of long-run-oriented decisions necessary for the company to perform well over many years. As would be expected, the total amount of pay-for-performance incentives varies by management level, with CEOs receiving significantly more than subsidiary or other senior managers.

A *stock option* gives individuals the right to buy stock in a company, usually at an advantageous price. Various types of stock option plans are the most widely used executive incentive. Despite the prevalence of such plans, research has found little relationship between providing CEOs with stock options and subsequent firm performance. The two items may not be closely linked in some firms.

"Reasonableness" of Executive Compensation

The notion of providing monetary incentives that are tied to improved performance results makes sense to most people. However, in the United States, there is an ongoing debate about whether executive compensation, especially that of CEOs, is truly linked to performance. Given the astronomical amounts of some executive compensation packages, this concern is justified.

The reasonableness of executive compensation is often justified by comparison to compensation market surveys, but these surveys usually provide a range of compensation data that requires interpretation. Some useful questions that have been suggested for determining whether executive pay is "reasonable" include the following:

- Would another company hire this person as an executive?
- How does the executive's compensation compare with that for executives in similar companies in the industry?
- Is the executive's pay consistent with pay for other employees within the company?
- What would an investor pay for the level of performance of the executive?

Link between Executive Compensation and Corporate Performance.
Of all the executive compensation issues that have been raised, the one that is discussed most frequently is whether executive compensation levels, especially for CEOs, are sufficiently linked to organizational performance. Board members of some organizations have viewed CEO compensation as not being as closely linked to performance as needed, resulting in CEO total compensation being seen as too high.[11]

The most important reason for giving pay as incentives is that it is thought to be effective in motivating employees and increasing corporate performance and stock values. Another common reason for using variable compensation is related to the ability to attract and keep employees. These reasons apply to executives as well as to other employees. But in order for compensation based on these reasons to be effective, executive compensation packages must be linked to performance.

One key aspect in evaluating this topic is the performance measures used. In many settings, financial measures such as return on equity, return to shareholders, earnings per share, and net income before taxes are used to measure performance. However, a number of firms also incorporate nonfinancial organizational measures of performance when determining executive bonuses and incentives. Customer satisfaction, employee satisfaction, market share, productivity, and quality are other areas measured for executive performance rewards.

Measurement of executive performance varies from one employer to another. Some executive compensation packages use a short-term focus of one year, which may lead to large rewards for executive performance in a given year even though corporate performance over a multiyear period is mediocre, especially if the yearly measures are not carefully chosen.

A number of other executive compensation issues and concerns exist. Figure 7-6 highlights some of the criticisms and counterarguments in regard to executive compensation.

FIGURE 7-6 Common Executive Compensation Criticisms

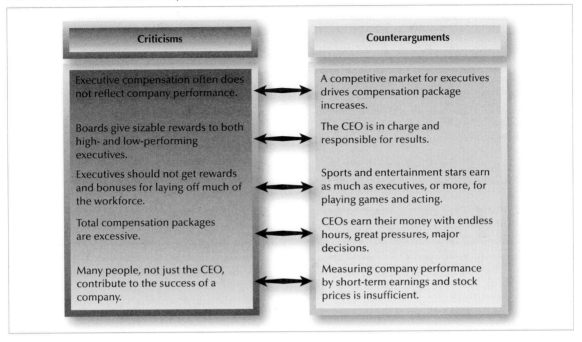

Executive Compensation and Boards of Directors. In most organizations, the board of directors is the major policy-setting entity and must approve executive compensation packages. Corporate directors receive compensation for board and committee meetings and other activities.[12] The **compensation committee** usually is a subgroup of the board of directors that is composed of directors who are not officers of the firm. A compensation committee generally makes recommendations to the board of directors on overall pay policies, salaries for top officers, supplemental compensation such as stock options and bonuses, and additional perquisites for executives.

One major concern voiced by many critics is that the base pay and bonuses of CEOs are often set by the members of board compensation committees, many of whom are CEOs or executives of other companies with similar compensation packages. Also, the compensation advisors and consultants to the CEOs often collect large fees, and critics charge that those fees distort the objectivity of the advice given.

To counter criticism, some corporations have changed the composition of the compensation committees by taking actions such as prohibiting "insider" company officers from serving on them. Also, some firms have empowered the compensation committees to hire and pay compensation consultants without involving executive management. Finally, better disclosure can provide the board with a fuller picture of a chief's entire compensation package.

NOTES

1. "Pay Communication: A Reality Check," *Workspan*, October 2008, 52–59; Terry Satterfield, "Pay Satisfaction: A Practical Approach to a Challenging Issue," *Workspan*, August 2008, 47–50.

2. For examples, see Dow Scott, Dennis Morajda, and Thomas D. McMillien, "Evaluating Pay Program Effectiveness," *WorldatWork Journal*, Second Quarter 2006, 50–59.

3. S. C. Currell, et al., "Pay Satisfaction and Organizational Outcomes," *Personnel Psychology*, 58 (2005), 613–640.

4. Erich C. Dierdorff and Eric A. Surface, "If You Pay for Skills, Will They Learn? Skill Change and Maintenance Under a Skill-Based Pay System," *Journal of Management*, 34 (2008), 721–743.

5. Thomas R. Bundy, "Worker Misclassification: The Next Big Legal Concern?" *Employee Relations Law Journal*, 33 (2007), 18–26.

6. Bill Leonard, "President Signs Wage Bias Law," *HR Magazine*, March 2009, 13; Towers Perrin, "New Law Makes Companies More Vulnerable to Complaints of Pay Discrimination," *www.towersperrin.com*.

7. Charles H. Fay and Madhura Tare, "Market Pricing Concerns," *WorldatWork Journal*, Second Quarter 2007, 61–69.

8. Mercer Human Resource Consulting, *2006 Compensation Planning Survey* (New York: Mercer Corporation, 2006).

9. Linda Ulrich, "Money Talks: Identifying, Preventing, and Alleviating Systematic Salary Compression Issues," *Workspan*, November 2008, 42–46.

10. Jessica Marquez, "Raising the Performance Bar," *Workforce Management*, April 24, 2006, 31–32.

11. Steven N. Kaplan, "Are U.S. CEOs Overpaid?" *Academy of Management Perspectives*, May 2008, 5–20; Edward Lawler III and David Finegold, "CEO Compensation: What Board Members Think," *WorldatWork Journal*, Third Quarter, 2007, 38–47.

12. "Compensation for Corporate Directors Rose Modestly in 2008," *Towers-Perrin Monitor*, October, 2009, *www.towersperrin.com*.

INTERNET RESOURCES

WorldatWork—This website provides information on products and services as well as research on compensation and benefits. Visit the site at *www.worldatwork.org*.

Compensation Resources, Inc.—Specialty services such as developing, designing, and implementing compensation plans are provided by this consulting firm. Visit its website at *www.compensationresources.com*.

Institute of Management and Administration (IOMA)—For information on salary sources that are reviewed by the IOMA, visit the website at *www.ioma.com*.

National Compensation Survey (NCS)—This website provides comprehensive measures of occupational wages, employment cost trends, and benefit incidence and detailed plan provisions. Visit the site at *www.bls.gov/ncs/home.htm*.

SUGGESTED READINGS

Laura Sejen, "Merging Reward and Talent Management to Strengthen Company Performance," *Workspan*, January 2009, 66–69.

For additional details on different methods, see *Job Evaluation: Methods to the Process* (Scottsdale, AZ: WorldatWork), 2005, 159 pp.

Peter Acker and John Cummings, "What in the World Is Happening with Long-Term Incentives?" *Workspan*, September 2008, 64–68.

Xiamoneg Zhang, et al., "CEOs on the Edge: Earnings Manipulation and Stock-Based Incentives," *Academy of Management Journal*, 51 (2008), 241–258.

Variable Pay and Benefits

HR—MEETING MANAGEMENT CHALLENGES

Variable pay and benefits offer employers opportunities to increase productivity and retention respectively. The opportunities presented by incentives and benefits will be present only if employers understand how they can work and their drawbacks. It is important to consider the following:

- Individual, group, and organization incentives can increase motivation
- Sales compensation provides opportunities to increase sales
- Benefits can be designed to fit the company's strategy

Tying pay to performance holds a promise that employers and employees both find attractive. For employees it can mean more pay and for employers it can mean more output per employee and therefore more productivity. Incentive pay must be tied to performance to be successful. Employers often fill the role of major provider of benefits for citizens. Although federal regulations require U.S. employers to provide certain benefits, U.S. employers voluntarily provide many others.

VARIABLE PAY: INCENTIVES FOR PERFORMANCE

Variable pay is compensation linked to individual, group/team, and/or organizational performance. Variable pay plans attempt to provide tangible rewards, traditionally known as *incentives,* to employees for performance beyond normal expectations. The philosophical foundation of incentives rests on several basic assumptions:

- Some jobs contribute more to organizational success than others.
- Some people perform better and are more productive than others.
- Employees who perform better should receive more compensation.
- Many employees' total compensation should be tied directly to performance and results.

Incentives can take many forms. For example, they can include simple praise, "recognition and reward" programs that award trips and merchandise, bonuses for performance accomplishments, and rewards for successful results for the company. A variety of possibilities exist, but a successful plan will include a combination of different types of incentives.

Developing Successful Pay-for-Performance Plans

Employers adopt variable pay or incentive plans for a number of reasons. Key reasons that many employers adopt these plans are as follows:

- Link strategic business goals and employee performance
- Enhance organizational results and reward employees financially for their contributions
- Recognize different levels of employee performance through different rewards
- Achieve HR objectives, such as increasing retention, reducing turn-over, recognizing training, and rewarding safety

As economic conditions have changed in industries and among employ-ers, the use of variable pay incentives has changed as well. Under variable pay programs, employees can have a greater sharing of the gains or declines in organizational performance results.

Variable pay plans can be considered successful if they meet the objectives the organization had for them when they were initiated and if they work with the organizational culture and the financial resources of the organization. Both financial and nonfinancial rewards for performance are important in pay-for-performance plans. The manner in which targets are set and mea-sured is important.[1] Three elements that affect the success of variable pay systems are discussed next. These are highlighted in Figure 8-1.

Does the Plan Fit the Organization?   The success of any incentive pay program relies on its consistency with the culture of the organization. When it comes to variable pay-for-performance plans, one size does not fit all. A plan that has worked well for one company will not necessarily work well for

FIGURE 8-1 Effective Variable Pay Plans

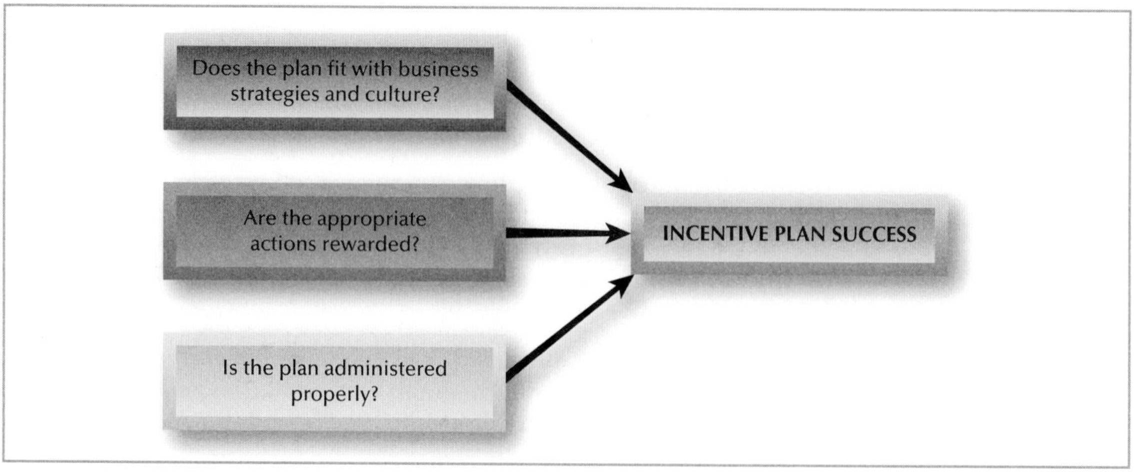

another. For an incentive plan to work, it must be linked to the objectives of the organization, its financial resources, and its desired performance results.

Does the Plan Reward Appropriate Actions?   Variable pay systems should be tied as much as possible to desired performance. Employees must see a direct relationship between their efforts and their financial and nonfinancial rewards. Because people tend to produce what is measured and rewarded, organizations must make sure that what is being rewarded is clearly linked to what is needed. Linking pay to performance may not always be appropriate. For instance, if the output cannot be measured objectively, management may not be able to correctly reward the higher performers with more pay. Managers may not even be able to accurately identify the higher performers. For example, in an office where tasks are to provide permits for building renovations, individual contributions may not be identifiable or appropriate.

Is the Plan Administered Properly?   A variable pay plan may be complex or simple, but it will be successful only if employees understand what they have to do to be rewarded. The more complicated a plan is the more difficult it will be to communicate it meaningfully to employees. Experts generally recommend that a variable pay plan include several performance criteria. But having multiple areas of focus should not overly complicate the calculations necessary for employees to determine their own incentive amounts. Managers also need to be able to explain clearly what future performance targets need to be met and what the rewards will be.

Metrics for Variable Pay Plans

Firms in the United States are spending significant amounts on variable pay plans as incentives. For instance, according to one survey, incentive expenditures in one year totaled $46 billion. Interestingly, more than $30 billion was paid on incentive merchandise and about $13 billion was spent on travel incentives. With such incentive expenditures increasing each year, it is crucial that the results of variable pay plans be measured to determine the success of the programs.[2]

Various metrics can be used, depending on the nature of the plan and the goals set for it. Figure 8-2 shows some examples of different metrics that

FIGURE 8-2 Metric Options for Variable Pay Plans

ORGANIZATIONAL PERFORMANCE
- Actual change vs. planned change
- Revenue growth
- Return on investment
- Average employee productivity change

SALES PROGRAMS
- Increase in market share
- Customer acquisition rate
- Growth of existing customer sales
- Customer satisfaction

HR RELATED
- Employee satisfaction
- Turnover costs
- Absenteeism cost
- Workers' comp claims
- Accident rates

can be used to evaluate variable play plans. Regardless of the variable pay plan, employers should gather and evaluate data to determine if the expenditures are justified by increased organizational operating performance. If the measures and analyses show positive results, the nature of the plan is truly a pay-for-performance one. If not, the plan should be changed to one that is more likely to be successful.

Successes and Failures of Variable Pay Plans

Even though variable pay has grown in popularity, some attempts at incentives have succeeded while others have not. Incentives *do* work, but they are not a panacea because their success depends on multiple factors.[3] The positive view that many employers have of variable pay is not shared by all workers. If individuals see incentives as desirable, they are likely to put forth the extra effort to attain the performance objectives that trigger the incentive payouts. But not all employees believe that they are rewarded when doing a good job, and not all employees are motivated by their employers' incentive plans.

Given the complexity of these plans, the following factors can contribute to the success of incentive plans:

- Develop clear, understandable plans that are continually communicated.
- Use realistic performance measures.
- Keep the plans current and linked to organizational objectives.
- Clearly link performance results to payouts that truly recognize performance differences.
- Identify variable pay incentives separately from base pay.

Three Categories of Variable Pay

The incentives offered in variable pay plans can be classified into three categories: individual, group/team, and organizational. There are advantages and disadvantages to each.

Individual incentives are given to reward the effort and performance of individuals. Some common means of providing individual variable pay are piece-rate systems, sales commissions, and individual bonuses. Others include special recognition rewards such as trips or merchandise.

When an organization rewards an entire group/team for its performance, cooperation among the members may increase. The most common *group/team incentives* are gainsharing or goalsharing plans, in which the employees on a team that meets certain goals, as measured against performance targets, share in the gains.

Organizational incentives reward people according to the performance results of the entire organization. These programs often share some of the financial gains made by the firm with employees through payments calculated as a percentage of the employees' base pay. The most prevalent forms of organization-wide incentives are profit-sharing plans and employee stock plans.

Figure 8-3 shows some of the programs that fall under each type of incentive pay plan. These programs are discussed next.

FIGURE 8-3 Categories of Variable Pay Plans

INDIVIDUAL INCENTIVES

Individual incentive systems tie personal effort to additional rewards. Conditions necessary for the use of individual incentive plans are as follows:

- Individual performance must be identified.
- Individual competitiveness must be desirable.
- Individualism must be stressed in the organizational culture.

Piece-Rate Systems

The most basic individual incentive systems are piece-rate systems. Under **straight piece-rate system,** wages are determined by multiplying the number of units produced (such as garments sewn or service calls handled) by the piece rate for one unit. Because the cost is the same for each unit, the wage for each employee is easy to figure, and labor costs can be accurately predicted.

A *differential piece-rate system* pays employees one piece-rate wage for units produced up to a standard output and a higher piece-rate wage for units produced over the standard. Managers often determine the quotas or standards by using time and motion studies.

Bonuses

Individual employees may receive additional compensation in the form of a **bonus,** which is a one-time payment that does not become part of the employee's base pay. Individual bonuses are used at all levels in some firms and are the most popular short-term incentive plan.

A bonus can recognize performance by an employee, a team, or the organization as a whole. When performance results are good, bonuses go up. When performance results are not met, bonuses go down. Most employers base part of an employee's bonus on individual performance and part on company results, as appropriate. Numerous CEOs receive bonuses based on specific results. A unique type of bonus used is a "spot" bonus, so called because it can be awarded at any time. Spot bonuses are given for a number of reasons, perhaps for extra time worked, extra efforts, or an especially demanding project. Often, spot bonuses are given in cash, although some firms provide managers with gift cards, travel vouchers, or other noncash rewards. The keys to successful use of spot bonuses are to keep the amounts reasonable and to provide them only for exceptional performance accomplishments.

GROUP/TEAM INCENTIVES

The use of groups/teams in organizations has implications for incentive compensation. Although the use of groups/teams has increased substantially in the past few years, the question of how to compensate their members equitably remains a significant challenge.

Team incentives can take the form of either cash bonuses for the team or items other than money, such as merchandise or trips. But group incentive situations may place social pressure on members of the group. Everyone in the group succeeds or fails. Therefore, some argue that team incentives should be given to team members equally, although not everyone agrees.

Design of Group/Team Incentive Plans

In designing group/team incentive plans, organizations must consider a number of issues. The main concerns are how and when to distribute the incentives, and who will make decisions about the incentive amounts.

Several decisions about how to distribute and allocate group/team rewards must be made. The two primary ways for distributing those rewards are as follows:

1. *Same-size reward for each member:* All members receive the same payout, regardless of job level, current pay, seniority, or individual performance differences.

2. *Different-size reward for each member:* Employers vary individual rewards depending on such factors as contribution to group/team results, current pay, years of experience, and skill levels of jobs performed.

Generally, more organizations use the first approach. The combination of equal team member award payouts and individual pay differences rewards performance by making the group/team incentive equal while also recognizing that individual differences exist and are important to many employees. The size of the group/team incentive can be determined either by using a percentage of base pay for the individuals or the group/team as a whole, or by offering a specific dollar amount.

To reinforce the effectiveness of working together, some group/team incentive programs allow members to make decisions about how to allocate the rewards to individuals. In some situations, members vote; in some, a group/team leader decides. In other situations, the incentive "pot" is divided equally, thus avoiding conflict and recognizing that all members contributed to the team results. However, many companies have found group/team members unwilling to make decisions about coworkers' incentives.

Types of Group/Team Incentives

Group/team reward systems use various ways of compensating individuals. The components include individual wages and salaries in addition to the other rewards. Most organizations that use group/team incentives continue to pay individuals based either on the jobs performed or the individuals' competencies and capabilities. The two most common types of group/team incentives are team results and gainsharing.

Group/Team Results.   Pay plans for groups/teams may reward all members equally on the basis of group output, cost savings, or quality improvement. The design of most group/team incentives is based on a "self-funding" principle. That means the money to be used as incentive rewards is obtained through improvement of organizational or group results, and can be structured as either a group or company-wide incentive.

Gainsharing.   The system of sharing with employees greater-than-expected gains in profits and/or productivity is **gainsharing.** Also called *teamsharing* or *goalsharing,* the focus is to increase "discretionary efforts," which are the difference between the maximum amount of effort a person can exert and the minimum amount of effort that person needs to exert to keep from being fired.

To develop and implement a gainsharing or goalsharing plan, management must identify the ways in which increased productivity, quality, and financial performance can occur and decide how some of the resulting gains should be shared with employees. Measures such as labor costs, overtime hours, and quality benchmarks often are used. Both organizational measures and departmental measures may be targeted, with the weights for gainsharing split between the two categories.

ORGANIZATIONAL INCENTIVES

An organizational incentive system compensates all employees according to how well the organization as a whole performs during the year. The basic concept behind organizational incentive plans is that overall results depend on organization-wide efforts and cooperation. The purpose of these plans is to produce better results by rewarding cooperation throughout the organization. For example, conflict between marketing and production can be overcome if management uses an incentive system that emphasizes organization-wide profit and productivity. To be effective, an organizational incentive program should include everyone from nonexempt employees to managers and executives. Two common organizational incentive systems are profit sharing and employee stock plans.

Profit Sharing

As the name implies, **profit sharing** distributes some portion of organizational profits to employees. One research study found that profit-sharing plans in small firms can help to enhance employee commitment and increase job-related performances of individuals.[4] The primary objectives of profit-sharing plans can include the following:

- Increase productivity and organizational performance
- Attract or retain employees
- Improve product/service quality
- Enhance employee morale

Typically, the percentage of the profits distributed to employees is set by the end of the year before distribution, although both timing and payment levels are considerations. In some profit-sharing plans, employees receive portions of the profits at the end of the year; in others, the profits are deferred, placed in a fund, and made available to employees on retirement or on their departure from the organization.

Drawbacks of Profit-Sharing Plans.   When used throughout an organization, including with lower-level workers, profit-sharing plans can have some drawbacks. First, employees must trust that management will disclose accurate financial and profit information. Second, profits may vary a great deal from year to year, resulting in windfalls or losses beyond the employees' control. Third, payoffs are generally far removed by time from employees' efforts; therefore, higher rewards may not be obviously linked to better performance.

Employee Stock Plans

Two types of organizational incentive plans use stock ownership in the organization to reward employees. The goal of these plans is to get employees to think and act like "owners."

A **stock option plan** gives employees the right to purchase a fixed number of shares of company stock at a specified exercise price for a limited period of time. If the market price of the stock exceeds the exercise price, employees can then exercise the option and buy the stock. The number of firms giving stock options to nonexecutives has declined in recent years, primarily due to changing laws and accounting regulations.

Employee Stock Ownership Plans.   Firms in many industries have an **employee stock ownership plan (ESOP),** which is designed to give employees significant stock ownership in their employers.

Establishing an ESOP creates several advantages. The major one is that the firm can receive favorable tax treatment on the earnings earmarked for use in the ESOP. Another is that an ESOP gives employees a "piece of the action" so that they can share in the growth and profitability of their firm. Employee ownership may motivate employees to be more productive and focused on organizational performance.

SALES COMPENSATION

The compensation paid to employees involved with sales and marketing is partly or entirely tied to individual sales performance. Salespeople who sell more products and services receive more total compensation than those who sell less. Sales incentives are perhaps the most widely used individual incentives. The intent is to stimulate more effort from salespeople so they earn more money.

Types of Sales Compensation Plans

Sales compensation plans can be of several general types, depending on the degree to which total compensation includes some variable pay tied to sales performance. A look at three general types of sales compensation and some challenges to sales compensation follows.

Salary Only.   Some companies pay salespeople only a salary. The *salary-only approach* is useful when an organization emphasizes serving and retaining existing accounts over generating new sales and accounts. This approach is frequently used to protect the income of new sales representatives for a period of time while they are building up their clientele. Generally, the employer extends the salary-only approach for new sales representatives to no more than six months, at which point it implements one of the other systems discussed below.

Straight Commission.   A widely used individual incentive system in sales jobs is the **commission**, which is compensation computed as a percentage of sales in units or dollars. Commissions are integrated into the pay given to sales workers in three common ways: straight commission, salary-plus-commission, and bonuses.

In the *straight commission system,* a sales representative receives a percentage of the value of the sales the person has made. Consider a sales representative working for a consumer products company who receives no compensation if that person makes no sales, but who receives a percentage of the total amount of all sales revenues that person has generated. The advantage of this system is that it requires the sales representative to sell in order to earn. The disadvantage is that it offers no security for the sales staff.

To offset this insecurity, some employers use a **draw** system, in which sales representatives can draw advance payments against future commissions. The amounts drawn are then deducted from future commission checks.

Salary-Plus-Commission or Bonuses.   The form of sales compensation used most frequently is the *salary-plus-commission,* which combines the stability of a salary with the performance aspect of a commission. A common split is 80–20% or 70–30% salary to commission, although the split varies by industry and can be based on numerous other factors. Some organizations pay salespeople salaries and then offer bonuses that are a percentage of the base pay, tied to how well each employee meets various sales targets or other criteria. A related method is using *lump-sum bonuses,* which may lead to salespeople working more intensively to get more sales results than the package approach.

Sales Compensation Challenges

Sales incentives work well, especially when they are tied to the broad strategic initiatives of the organization and its specific marketing and sales strategies. However, as economic and competitive changes have occurred, employers in many industries have faced challenges in their sales. Firms can analyze more thoroughly their sales compensation costs, assess how the sales pay is increasing or decreasing performance efforts by employees, and then evaluate the extent to which the sales and profit goals are being met.

Effectiveness of Sales Incentive Plans.   So many organizations have sales incentive plans that it would be logical to think those plans are effective. However, many sales compensation plans are not seen as effective by either salespeople or managers and executives. One problem that can occur is constantly making too many changes in sales incentives, resulting in confusion by many people. Frequent changes reduce the effectiveness of plans and create problems with the sales representatives and managers. HR professionals may be involved in designing, revising, and communicating sales incentive plans, as well as responding to the complaints and concerns of sales representatives.

EMPLOYEE BENEFITS

An employer may provide benefits to workers for being part of the organization. A **benefit** is an indirect reward given to an employee or group of employees for organizational membership. Benefits often include retirement plans, vacations with pay, health insurance, educational assistance, and many more programs.

Benefits are costly for the typical U.S. employer, averaging from 30% to 40% of payroll expenses. In highly unionized manufacturing and utility industries, they may be over 70% of payroll. The costs of benefits are increasing, sometimes faster than inflationary rates, causing some organizations to require employees to help pay for these benefits.

Benefits and HR Strategy

In the United States, a challenge for employers is how to best manage the balancing act between the growing costs of benefits and the use of those benefits in accomplishing organizational goals. For instance, organizations can choose to compete for or retain employees by providing different levels of base compensation, variable pay, and benefits. Indeed, when a lagging economy causes organizations to downsize or cut various programs, some companies have remained focused on benefits, exploring new benefits options and adopting a more comprehensive approach to compensation management. This is why benefits should be looked at as a vital part of the total rewards "package" when determining organizational strategies regarding compensation.

It is important that benefits be used to help create and maintain competitive advantages. Benefits should not be viewed entirely as cost factors because they can positively affect HR efforts. Given the intense competition for competent workers, companies should consider investing in benefits packages that are attractive for those employees.

Employers may offer benefits to aid recruiting and retention, impact organizational performance, and meet legal requirements. Also, some employers see benefits as reinforcing the company philosophy of social and corporate citizenship. Employers that provide good benefits are viewed more positively within a community and the industry by customers, civic leaders, current employees, and workers in other firms. Conversely, employers who are seen as skimping on benefits, cutting benefits, or taking advantage of workers may be viewed more negatively.

The primary reasons executives see for offering benefits is to attract and retain talent and meet responsibilities to employees. According to a survey by an international consulting firm, 48% of executives see benefits as extremely important to a company's competitive effectiveness and another 41% saw benefits as somewhat important.[5]

A major advantage of benefits is that they generally are not taxed as income to employees. For this reason, benefits represent a somewhat more valuable reward to employees than an equivalent cash payment. This feature makes benefits a desirable form of compensation to employees if they understand the value provided by the benefits.

Benefits Plan Design

Benefits plans can provide flexibility and choices for employees, or they can be standardized for all employees. Increasingly, employers are finding that providing employees with some choices and flexibility allow individuals to tailor their benefits to their own situations. However, the more choices available, the higher the administrative demands placed on organizations. A number of key decisions are part of benefits design:

- How much total compensation, including benefits, can be provided?
- What part of the total compensation of individuals should benefits constitute?
- Which employees should be provided which benefits?
- What expense levels are acceptable for each benefit offered?
- What is being received by the organization in return for each benefit?
- How flexible should the package of benefits be?

Part-Time Employee Benefits.   Another key design issue is whether or not to provide benefits coverage to part-time employees. Many employers do not provide part-time employee benefits, except some time-off leave benefits.

Part-time employees who do receive benefits usually do so in proportion to the percentage of full-time work they provide.

Flexible Benefits.   As mentioned, as part of both benefits design and administration, many employers offer employees choices for benefits. A **flexible benefits plan** allows employees to select the benefits they prefer from groups of benefits established by the employer. Sometimes called a *flex plan* or *cafeteria plan*, these plans have a variety of "dishes," or benefits, available so that each employee can select an individual combination of benefits within some overall limits.

Because many flexible plans have become so complex, they require more administrative time and information systems to track the different choices made by employees. Despite the disadvantages, flex plans will likely continue to grow in popularity.

HR and Benefits Administration.   With the myriad of benefits, it is easy to see why many organizations must make coordinated efforts to administer benefits programs. Benefits administration responsibilities can be split between HR specialists and operating managers. HR specialists play the more significant role, but managers must assume responsibility for some of the communication aspects of benefits administration. One significant trend affecting HR is that outsourcing of benefits administration may be necessary.

HR Technology and Benefits

The spread of HR technology, particularly Internet-based systems, has significantly changed the benefits administration time and activities for HR staff members. Internet and computer-based systems are being used to communicate benefits information, conduct employee benefits surveys, and facilitate benefits administration. Recent research shows that these systems can decrease expenses, increase positive communication, and effectively connect people across many different HR functions, including benefits management.[6]

Information technology allows employees to change their benefits choices, track their benefits balances, and submit questions to HR staff members and external benefits providers. Some systems provide prepackaged connections with benefits providers so that information technology requirements are minimized. Use of online benefits enrollment has increased significantly. The greatest use has been to allow employees to sign up for, change, or update their benefits choices through Web-based systems.

Benefits Measurement

The significant costs associated with benefits require that analyses be conducted to determine the payoffs for the benefits. With the wide range of benefits that are offered, numerous HR metrics can be used such as the following:

- Benefits as a percentage of payroll (pattern over a multiyear period)
- Benefits expenditures per full-time-equivalent (FTE) employee

- Benefits costs by employee group (full-time vs. part-time, union vs. nonunion, management, professional, technical, office, etc.)
- Benefits administration costs (including staff time multiplied by the staff pay and benefits costs per hour)
- Health care benefits costs per participating employee

Metrics are used to measure the return on the expenditures for various benefits programs provided by employers. Some common benefits that employers track using HR metrics are workers' compensation, wellness programs, prescription drug costs, leave time, tuition aid, and disability insurance. The point is that both benefits expenditures generally, and costs for individual benefits specifically, need to be measured and evaluated as part of strategic benefits management.

Benefits Cost Control

Because benefits expenditures have risen significantly in the past few years, particularly for health care, employers are focusing more attention on measuring and controlling benefits costs, even reducing or dropping benefits offered to employees.

Another common means of benefits cost control is cost sharing, which refers to having employees pay for more of their benefits costs. This is commonly used for health insurance costs. Three other means of health insurance cost control are using wellness programs, adding employee health education efforts, and changing prescription drug programs.

Benefits Communication

Benefits communication and satisfaction of employees with their benefits are linked. For instance, employees often do not fully understand their health benefits, a situation that can cause individual dissatisfaction. Consequently, many employers should consider developing special benefits communication systems to inform employees about the monetary value of the benefits they provide. Employers can use various means, including videos, CDs, emails, electronic alerts, newsletters, and employee meetings. All these efforts are done to ensure that employees are knowledgeable about their benefits. Some of the important information to be communicated includes the value of the plans offered, why changes have to be made, and the fundamental financial costs of the plans. The Employee Retirement Income Security Act (ERISA) also requires sponsors of health programs to write a *summary plan description* that details the rights and benefits associated with particular plans, and these documents must be easy to understand.[7]

Benefits Statements.   Some employers give individual employees a "personal statement of benefits" that translates benefits into dollar amounts. Increasingly, firms are using the Internet to provide statements, with estimates that 60% of employers are doing so.[8] These statements often are used as part of a total rewards education and communication effort. The Employee

Retirement Income Security Act (ERISA) also requires that employees receive an annual pension-reporting statement, which also can be included in the personal benefits statement.

TYPES OF BENEFITS

A wide range of benefits are offered by employers. Some are mandated by laws and government regulations, while others are offered voluntarily by employers as part of their HR strategies.

Government-Mandated Benefits

There are many mandated benefits that employers in the United States must provide to employees by law. Social Security (federal) and unemployment insurance (state) are funded through a tax paid by the employer based on the employee's compensation. Workers' compensation laws exist in all states. In addition, under the Family and Medical Leave Act (FMLA), employers must offer unpaid leave to employees with certain medical or family difficulties. Other mandated benefits are funded in part by taxes, through Social Security. The Consolidated Omnibus Budget Reconciliation Act (COBRA) mandates that an employer continue to provide health care coverage—albeit paid for by the employees—for a time after employees leave the organization. The Health Insurance Portability and Accountability Act (HIPAA) requires that most employees be able to obtain coverage if they were previously covered in a health plan and provides privacy rights for medical records.

A major reason for additional mandated benefits proposals is that federal and state governments would like to shift many of the social costs for health care and other expenditures to employers. This shift would relieve some of the budgetary pressures facing government entities that otherwise might have to raise taxes and/or cut spending.

The federal plan for universal health care benefits for individuals has been passed, but given the complexity of the bill and uncertainty over how it will work, it is unclear exactly how such coverage will impact organizations, sponsors of health benefits, and health care providers. Additional mandated benefits have been proposed for many other areas but not adopted are as follows:

- Child-care assistance
- Pension plan coverage that can be transferred by workers who change jobs
- Core benefits for part-time employees working at least 500 hours a year
- Paid time off for family leave
- Paid time off for pregnancy and child bearing

Voluntary Benefits

Employers voluntarily offer other types of benefits to help them compete for and retain employees. By offering additional benefits, organizations are assuming a need to provide greater security and benefits support to workers

FIGURE 8-4 Types of Benefits

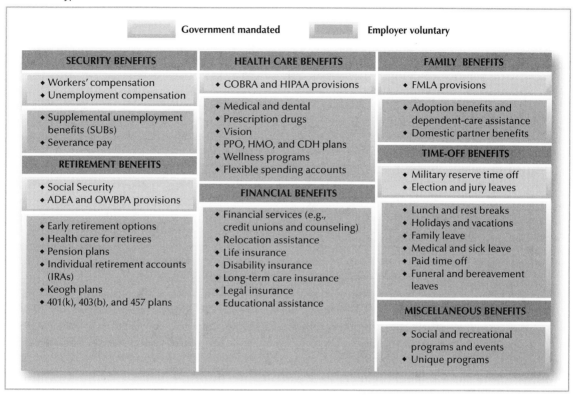

with widely varied personal circumstances. In addition, as jobs become more flexible and varied, both workers and employers recognize that choices among benefits are necessary, as evidenced by the growth in flexible benefits and cafeteria benefit plans. Figure 8-4 lists seven types of mandated and voluntary benefits. The following sections describe them by type.

SECURITY BENEFITS

A number of benefits provide employee security. These benefits include some mandated by laws and others offered by employers voluntarily. The primary benefits found in most organizations include workers' compensation, unemployment compensation, and severance pay.

Workers' Compensation

Workers' compensation provides benefits to persons who are injured on the job. State laws require most employers to supply workers' compensation coverage by purchasing insurance from a private carrier or state insurance fund or by providing self-insurance. Government employees in the United States are covered under the Federal Employees Compensation Act, administered by the U.S. Department of Labor. The workers' compensation system requires employers to give cash benefits, medical care, and rehabilitation services to employees for injuries or illnesses occurring within the scope of their employment. In exchange, employees give up the right to pursue legal actions and awards.

Unemployment Compensation

Another benefit required by law is unemployment compensation, established as part of the Social Security Act of 1935. Because each U.S. state operates its own unemployment compensation system, provisions differ significantly from state to state. The tax is paid to state and federal unemployment compensation funds. The percentage paid by individual employers is based on "experience rates," which reflect the number of claims filed by workers who leave.

An employee who is out of work and is actively looking for employment normally receives up to 26 weeks of pay, at the rate of 50% to 80% of normal pay. Most employees are eligible. However, workers fired for misconduct or those not actively seeking employment generally are ineligible.

Severance Pay

As a security benefit, **severance pay** is voluntarily offered by employers to individuals whose jobs are eliminated or who leave by mutual agreement with their employers. Employer severance pay provisions often provide severance payments corresponding to an employee's level within the organization and the person's years of employment. The Worker Adjustment and Retraining Notification Act (WARN) of 1988 requires that many employers give 60 days' notice if a mass layoff or facility closing is to occur. The act does not require employers to give severance pay.

HEALTH CARE BENEFITS

Employers provide a variety of health care and medical benefits, usually through insurance coverage. The most common plans cover medical, dental, prescription drug, and vision care expenses for employees and their dependents.

Increases in Health Benefits Costs

For several decades, the costs of health care have escalated at rates well above those of inflation and changes in workers' earnings. For instance, the reduction in the number of obstetricians caused by litigation fears and the price of malpractice insurance has increased costs due to higher premiums and diagnostic testing. In addition, the costs of health care have increased by two percentage points over increases in the GDP across many developed nations for close to 50 years. As a result of large increases such as these, many employers find that dealing with health care benefits is time consuming and expensive.

Uninsured Workers. Some of the health benefits cost pressures are due to health care providers having to cover the costs for the rising number of individuals in the United States without health insurance coverage. A number of uninsured workers are illegal immigrants; others work for employers that do not provide benefits. The costs are shifted to those with health insurance paid for by employers, making this a high-profile political issue that has driven attention to health care reform.

Retirees' Health Benefits Costs. Another group whose benefits costs are rising is retirees whose former employers still provide health benefits coverage. To control retiree health benefits costs, some firms are cutting their benefits or requiring retirees to pay higher rates for health benefits. Approximately 75% of employers in one survey have increased health insurance premiums in recent years. Many of the retirees worked for their employers for 20, 30, or more years, yet the reward for their long service increasingly is a reduction in health care benefits. As a result, many individuals are delaying retirement until age 65 so that Medicare coverage can be secured.

Controlling Health Care Benefits Costs

Employers offering health care benefits are taking a number of approaches to controlling their costs. The most prominent ones are changing copayments and employee contributions, using managed care, switching to mini-medical plans or consumer-driven health plans, and increasing health preventive and wellness efforts.

Changing Copayments and Employee Contributions. The **copayment** strategy requires employees to pay a portion of the cost of insurance premiums, medical care, and prescription drugs. Requiring new or higher copayments and employee contributions is the most prevalent cost-control strategy identified by many employers surveyed.

These changes are facing significant resistance by employees, especially those who have had *first-dollar coverage.* With this type of coverage, all expenses, from the first dollar of health care costs, are paid by the employee's insurance. Experts claim that when first-dollar coverage is included in a basic health plan, many employees see a doctor for even minor illnesses, which results in an escalation of the benefits costs.

Using Managed Care. Several other types of programs attempt to reduce health care costs paid by employers. **Managed care** consists of approaches that monitor and reduce medical costs through restrictions and market system alternatives. Managed care plans emphasize primary and preventive care, the use of specific providers who will charge lower prices, restrictions on certain kinds of treatment, and prices negotiated with hospitals and physicians.

The most prominent managed care approach is the **preferred provider organization (PPO),** a health care provider that contracts with an employer or an employer group to supply health care services to employees at a competitive rate. Employees have the freedom to go to other providers if they want to pay the differences in costs. *Point-of-service plans* are somewhat similar, offering financial incentives to encourage employees to use designated medical providers.

Another managed care approach is a **health maintenance organization (HMO),** which provides services for a fixed period on a prepaid basis. The HMO emphasizes both prevention and correction. An employer contracts with an HMO and its staff of physicians and medical personnel to furnish complete medical care, except for hospitalization. The employer pays a flat rate per enrolled employee or per enrolled family. The covered individuals may then go to the HMO for health care as often as needed.

Mini-Medical Plans.   Another type of plan that has grown in usage in the past few years is the *mini-medical plan*. This type of plan provides limited health benefits coverage for employees. In the past, these plans have been used more with part-time and lower wage level employees. But more employers are using these plans for full-time employees of all types. A typical mini-medical plan limits the number of doctor visits paid per year to fewer than 10, covers only certain prescription drugs, provides very limited hospital coverage, and caps total annual health benefits costs at $10,000 or less.

Consumer-Driven Health Plans

Some employers are turning to employee-focused health benefits plans. The most prominent is a **consumer-driven health (CDH) plan,** which provides employer financial contributions to employees to help cover their health-related expenses. A growing number of employers have switched to CDH plans, and others are actively considering switching to these plans. CDH plans are being offered by both large and small businesses and that more workers are signing up for them.

In these plans, which are also called *defined-contribution health plans,* an employer places a set amount into each employee's "account" and identifies a number of health care alternatives that are available. Then individual employees select from those health care alternatives and pay for part of the costs from their accounts.

There are two advantages to such plans for employers. One is that more of the increases in health care benefits costs are shifted to employees, because the employer contributions need not increase as fast as health care costs. Second, the focus of controlling health care usage falls on employees, who may have to choose when to use and not use health care benefits.

Health Savings Accounts.   Often **Health savings accounts (HSAs)** are combined with high-deductible insurance to cut employer costs. Such insurance is defined as plans that have between $1,150 and $5,800 in deductibles for individuals, and between $2,300 and $11,600 in deductibles for families.[9] Other components of an HSA include the following:

- Both employees and employers can make contributions to an account.
- Individual employees can set aside pretax amounts for medical care into an HSA.

- Unused amounts in an individual's account can be rolled over annually for future health expenses.
- Incentives are included to encourage employees to spend less on health expenses.
- Contributions must be uniform for all employees enrolled in HSA accounts unless they are based on a cafeteria program.

Health Care Preventive and Wellness Efforts

Preventive and wellness efforts can occur in a variety of ways. Many employers offer programs to educate employees about health care costs and how to reduce them. Newsletters, formal classes, and many other approaches are all designed to help employees understand why health care costs are increasing and what they can do to control them. Many employers have programs that offer financial incentives to improve health habits. These wellness programs reward employees who stop smoking, lose weight, and participate in exercise programs, among other activities.

HIPAA Provisions.   The Health Insurance Portability and Accountability Act (HIPAA) of 1996 allows employees to switch their health insurance plans when they change employers, and to get new health coverage with the new company regardless of preexisting health conditions. The legislation also prohibits group insurance plans from dropping coverage for a sick employee and requires them to make individual coverage available to people who leave group plans.

One of the greatest impacts of HIPAA comes from its provisions regarding the privacy of employee medical records. These provisions require employers to provide privacy notices to employees.

RETIREMENT BENEFITS

The aging of the workforce in many countries is affecting retirement planning for individuals and retirement plan costs for employers and governments. In the United States, the number of citizens at least 55 years or older has increased significantly in recent years, and older citizens currently constitute a large portion of the population. Simultaneously, the age of retirement has declined, as it has been doing for decades. With more people retiring earlier and living longer, retirement benefits are becoming a greater concern for employers, employees, and retired employees.

Unfortunately, most U.S. citizens have inadequate savings and retirement benefits for funding their retirements. According to a study by the Employee Benefit Research Institute, almost 70% of individuals over age 55 have inadequately saved for retirement.[10] These individuals are heavily dependent on employer-provided retirement benefits. But many employers with fewer than 100 workers do not offer retirement benefits. Also, the economic downturn caused a reduction in the value of worker retirement accounts and contributions, leading many older employees to continue with their employment. Some individuals are relying solely on Social Security payments, which were not designed to provide full retirement income.

Social Security

The Social Security Act of 1935, with its later amendments, established a system providing *old-age, survivor's, disability,* and *retirement* benefits. Administered by the federal government through the Social Security Administration, this program provides benefits to previously employed individuals. Employees and employers share in the cost of Social Security through a tax on employees' wages or salaries.

Pension Plans

A **pension plan** is a retirement program established and funded by the employer and employees. Organizations are not required to offer pension plans to employees, and fewer than half of U.S. workers are covered by them. Small firms offer pension plans less often than do large ones.

Defined-Benefit Pension Plans. A "traditional" pension plan, in which the employer makes the contributions and the employee will get a defined amount each month upon retirement, is no longer the norm in the private sector. Through a **defined-benefit plan,** employees are promised a pension amount based on age and service. The employees' contributions are based on actuarial calculations on the *benefits* to be received by the employees after retirement and the *methods* used to determine such benefits. A defined-benefit plan gives employees greater assurance of benefits and greater predictability in the amount of benefits that will be available for retirement. Defined-benefit plans are often preferred by workers with longer service, as well as by small business owners.

Defined-Contribution Pension Plans. In a **defined-contribution plan,** the employer makes an annual payment to an employee's pension account. The key to this plan is the *contribution rate;* employee retirement benefits depend on fixed contributions and employee earnings levels. Profit-sharing plans, employee stock ownership plans (ESOPs), and 401(k) plans are common defined-contribution plans. Because these plans hinge on the investment returns on the previous contributions, the returns can vary according to profitability or other factors. Therefore, employees' retirement benefits are somewhat less secure and predictable. But because of their structure, these plans are sometimes preferred by younger, shorter-service employees.

Cash Balance Pension Plans. Some employers have changed traditional pension plans to hybrids based on ideas from both defined-benefit and defined-contribution plans. One such plan is a **cash balance plan,** in which retirement benefits are based on an accumulation of annual company contributions, expressed as a percentage of pay, plus interest credited each year. With these plans, retirement benefits accumulate at the same annual rate until an employee retires. Because cash balance plans spread funding across a worker's entire career, these plans work better for mobile younger workers.

Pension Plan Concepts

Pension plans can be either contributory or noncontributory. In a **contributory plan,** money for pension benefits is paid in by both employees and the employer. In a **noncontributory plan,** the employer provides all the funds for pension benefits. As expected, the noncontributory plans are generally preferred by employees and labor unions.

Certain rights are attached to employee pension plans. Various laws and provisions have been passed to address the right of employees to receive benefits from their pension plans. Called **vesting,** this right assures employees of a certain pension, provided they work a minimum number of years.

Individual Retirement Options

The availability of several retirement benefit options makes the pension area more complex. The most prominent options are individual retirement accounts (IRAs) and 401(k), 403(b), 457, and Keogh plans. These plans may be available in addition to company-provided pension plans and usually are contributory plans.

The **401(k) plan** gets its name from section 401(k) of the federal tax code. This plan is an agreement in which a percentage of an employee's pay is withheld and invested in a tax-deferred account. Many employers match employee 401(k) contributions, up to a percentage of the employee's pay. As a result, a significant number of employees contribute to 401(k) plans. The use of 401(k) plans and of the assets in them has grown significantly in the past few years. Employers frequently have programs to encourage employees to contribute to 401(k) plans.

Employee Retirement Income Security Act

The widespread criticism of many pension plans led to passage of the Employee Retirement Income Security Act (ERISA) in 1974. The purpose of this law is to regulate private pension plans so that employees who put money into them or depend on a pension for retirement funds actually receive the money when they retire.

ERISA essentially requires many companies to offer retirement plans to all employees if they offer retirement plans to any employees. Accrued benefits must be given to employees when they retire or leave. The act also sets minimum funding requirements, and plans not meeting those requirements are subject to financial penalties imposed by the IRS. Additional regulations require that employers pay plan termination insurance to ensure payment of employee pensions should the employers go out of business. To spread out the costs of administration and overhead, some employers use plans funded by multiple employers.

Retiree Benefits and Legal Requirements

Some employers choose to offer retiree health benefits that may be paid for by the retirees, the company, or both. The costs of such coverage have risen dramatically. To ensure that firms adequately reflect the liabilities for retiree health benefits, the Financial Accounting Standards Board issued Rule 106, which requires employers to establish accounting reserves for funding retiree health care benefits. For instance, one problem with retiree pension benefits is that a number of firms are facing unfunded pension liabilities.

Pension Protection Act of 2006.   The Pension Protection Act of 2006 has numerous reporting requirements that must be met by employers. These requirements make employers disclose the assets and liabilities of pension plans. The act also requires that employers increase funding to cover unfunded liabilities they face. Many of the provisions focus specifically on the liabilities created by defined-benefit plans that employers must cover.

FINANCIAL BENEFITS

Employers may offer workers a wide range of special benefits that provide financial support to employees. Figure 8-5 illustrates some common financial benefits. Employers find that such benefits can be useful in attracting and retaining employees. Workers like receiving these benefits, which often are not taxed as income.

Insurance Benefits

In addition to health-related insurance, some employers provide other types of insurance. These benefits offer major advantages for employees because many employers pay some or all of the costs. Even when employers do not pay any of the costs, employees still benefit because of the lower rates available through

FIGURE 8-5 Common Types of Financial Benefits

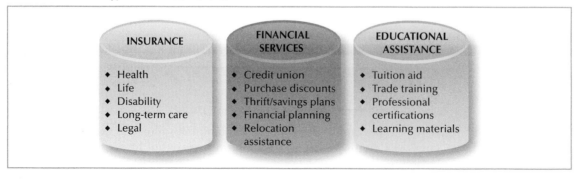

group programs. The most common types of insurance benefits are life insurance, disability insurance, long-term care insurance, and legal insurance.

Financial Services

Financial benefits include a wide variety of items. A *credit union* sponsored by the employer provides saving and lending services for employees. *Purchase discounts* allow employees to buy goods or services from their employers at reduced rates. For example, a furniture manufacturer may allow employees to buy furniture at wholesale cost plus 10%, or a bank may offer employees use of a safe deposit box and free checking. Employee *thrift plans, savings plans,* or *stock investment plans* of different types may be available.

Financial planning and counseling are especially valuable services for executives, many of whom may need information on investments and tax shelters, as well as comprehensive financial counseling, because of their higher levels of compensation.

Educational Assistance

Another benefit that saves financial resources of employees comes in the form of educational assistance and tuition aid, which pays some or all of the costs associated with formal education courses and degree programs. Often the costs of books and laboratory materials are covered. Unless the education paid for by the employer meets certain conditions, the cost of educational aid must be counted as taxable income by employees.

FAMILY-ORIENTED BENEFITS

Balancing family and work demands presents a major challenge to many workers at all levels of organizations. Therefore, employers have established a variety of family-oriented benefits. Since 1993, employers also have been required to provide certain benefits to comply with the Family and Medical Leave Act (FMLA).

Family and Medical Leave Act

The FMLA covers all federal, state, and private employers with 50 or more employees who live within 75 miles of the workplace. Only employees who have worked at least 12 months and 1,250 hours in the previous year are eligible for leave under the FMLA. The law requires that employers allow eligible employees to take a total of 12 weeks' leave during any 12-month period for one or more of three situations:

- Birth, adoption, or foster care placement of a child
- Caring for a spouse, a child, or a parent with a serious health condition
- Serious health condition of the employee

A **serious health condition** is one requiring in-patient, hospital, hospice, or residential medical care or continuing physician care, or problems that exist beyond three days including treatment provided. An employer may require an employee to provide a certificate from a doctor verifying such an illness. The FMLA provides a number of guidelines regarding employee leaves:

- Employees taking family and medical leave must be able to return to the same job or a job of equivalent status or pay.
- Health benefits must be continued during the leave at the same level and conditions. If, for a reason other than serious health problems, the employee does not return to work, the employer may collect the employer-paid portion of the premiums from the nonreturning employee.
- The leave may be taken intermittently rather than in one block, subject to employee and employer agreements, when birth, adoption, or foster child care is the cause. For serious health conditions, employer approval is not necessary.
- Employees can be required to use all paid-up vacation and personal leave before taking unpaid leave.
- Employees are required to give 30-day notice, where practical.

Some provisions associated with the FMLA started January 16, 2009, expanding coverage for some employees and revising specific criteria of the regulations. One of the most noteworthy revisions to the FMLA involves providing 26 weeks of leave to individuals providing care to injured family members who served in the military.

Family-Care Benefits

Family issues are growing in importance for many organizations and for many workers. Many employers provide maternity and paternity benefits to employees who give birth. Some firms also provide adoption benefits.

Balancing work and family responsibilities is a major challenge for many workers. Some employers are addressing the child-care issue in the following ways:

- Providing referral services to help parents locate child-care providers
- Establishing discounts at day-care centers, which may be subsidized by the employer
- Arranging with hospitals to offer sick-child programs partially paid for by the employer
- Developing after-school programs for older school-age children, often in conjunction with local public and private school systems
- Offering on-site child-care centers

Another family issue of importance is caring for elderly relatives. An increasing number of organizations are offering benefits that help employees more effectively balance their work and elder-care responsibilities. Besides time off provided by the FMLA, some of these benefits include subsidies for elder-care expenses, referrals to elder-care providers, and elder-care assistance for emergencies.[11]

Measuring the Effectiveness of Family Benefits

Employers that have provided child-care and other family-friendly assistance have found the programs beneficial for several reasons. The greatest advantage is in aiding employee retention.[12] Employees are more likely to stay with employers who aid them with work-life balancing. Child-care benefits can produce significant savings, primarily due to decreased employee absenteeism and turnover. Analyses of elder-care costs-benefits show similar results. To determine such metrics, costs for recruiting, training, turnover, and lost productivity often are included.

Benefits for Domestic Partners

As lifestyles change in the United States, employers are being confronted with requests for benefits from employees who are not married but have close personal relationships with others. The terms often used to refer to individuals with such arrangements are *domestic partners* and *spousal equivalents*. The employees who are submitting these requests are: (1) unmarried employees who are living with individuals of the opposite sex and (2) gay and lesbian employees who have partners.

TIME-OFF AND OTHER BENEFITS

Time-off benefits represent a significant portion of total benefits costs. Employers give employees paid time off for a variety of circumstances. Paid lunch breaks and rest periods, holidays, and vacations are common.

Holiday and Vacation Pay

Most employers provide pay for a variety of holidays. In the United States, employers commonly offer 10 to 12 holidays annually. Employers in many other countries are required to provide a significantly higher number of holidays, approaching 20 to 30 days in some cases. In both the United States and other countries, the number of holidays offered can vary depending on state/provincial laws and union contracts.

Paid vacations are a common benefit. Employers often use graduated vacation-time scales based on employees' lengths of service. Some organizations have a "use it or lose it" policy whereby accrued vacation time cannot be carried over from year to year. Some employers have policies to "buy back" unused vacation time. Other employers, such as banks, may have policies requiring employees to take a minimum number of vacation days off in a row. Regardless of the vacation policies used, employees are often required to work the day before and the day after vacation time off.

Leaves of Absence

Employers grant *leaves of absence*, taken as time off with or without pay, for a variety of reasons. All the leaves discussed here add to employer costs even if unpaid. That is because the missing employee's work must be covered, either by other employees working additionally or by temporary employees working under contract.

Leaves are given for a variety of purposes. Some, such as *military leave, election leave*, and *jury leave*, are required by various state and federal laws. *Funeral leave* or *bereavement leave* is another common type of leave offered.

Medical and *sick leave* are closely related. Many employers allow employees to miss a limited number of days because of illness without losing pay. More than 50% of all U.S. workers receive paid sick leave. But U.S. employers do not provide paid sick leave to as many workers percentagewise as do the employers in other developed countries. Some employers allow employees to accumulate unused sick leave, which may be used in case of catastrophic illnesses. Others pay their employees for unused sick leave.

Paid-Time-Off Plans

A growing number of employers have made use of a **paid-time-off (PTO) plan,** which combines all sick leave, vacation time, and holidays into a total number of hours or days that employees can take off with pay. Many of those employers have found PTO plans to be more effective than other means of reducing absenteeism and in having time off scheduled more efficiently. Other advantages cited by employers with PTO plans are ease of administration and as an aid for recruiting and retention and for increasing employee understanding and use of leave policies.

NOTES

1. Bruce Ellig, "What Pay for Performance Should Measure," *WorldatWork Journal,* Second Quarter, 2008, 64–75.
2. Leo Jakobson, "$46 Billion Spent on Incentives," *Incentive,* November 2007, 27–28.
3. Patricia K. Zinghelm and Jay R. Schuster, "Revisiting Effective Incentive Design," *WorldatWork Journal,* First Quarter, 2005, 50–58.
4. A. Bayo-Moriones and M. Larraa-Kintana, "Profit-Sharing Plans and Affective Commitment," *Human Resource Management,* March–April 2009, 207–226.
5. "An Executive Perspective on Employee Benefits," *McKinsey Quarterly Survey,* April 2006, 1, *www .mckinseyquarterly.com;* "Incorporate 'Employer of Choice' Goals into Strategic, Benefits Planning," *Best Practices in HR,* September 22, 2006, 3.
6. Thomas W. Gainey and Brian S. Klaas, "The Use and Impact of e-HR: A Survey of HR Professionals," *People and Strategy,* 31 (2008) , 50–55.
7. Robert Whiddon, "Ranking Health Plans on Satisfaction," *Employee Benefits News,* June 15, 2008;

Dennis Ackley, "Communication: The Key to Putting the Benefit Back in Benefits," *Workspan,* February 2006, 31–34; Betty Sosnin, "What's in Your Summary Plan Description?" *HR Magazine,* August 2007, 63–70.
8. Jill Elswick, "Loaded Statements: Web-Based Total Compensation Statements Keep Employees in the Know," *BenefitNews.com,* May 2005, *www .benefitnews.com.*
9. Christine Keller and Christopher E. Condeluci, "Tax Relief and Health Care Act Should Prompt Re-examination of HSAs," *SHRM HR Legal Report,* July–August 2007, 1–8.
10. *EBRI 2010 Retirement Confidence Study, www .ebri.org.*
11. Stephanie Armour, "Juggling Work, Care for Aging Parent: Some Companies Help Their Workers," *USA Today,* June 26, 2007, 3B.
12. Reagan Baughman, Daniela DiNardi, and Douglas Holtz-Eakin, "Productivity and Wage Effects of 'Family Friendly' Fringe Benefits," *International Journal of Manpower,* 24 (2003), 247.

INTERNET RESOURCES

HR-Guide.com—This website discusses incentives and gainsharing in detail. Visit the site at *www.hr-guide.com*.

MyStockOptions.com—For tools to communicate with, educate, and train employees about stock options, visit this website at *www.mystockoptions.com*.

BenefitNews.Com—This website is a resource for surveys, archived articles, and the latest trends and information regarding employee benefits. Visit the site at *www.benefitnews.com*.

Work-Life and Human Capital Solutions—This website provides organizations with information and resources for employees on work and family issues such as child care and elder care. Visit the site at *www.workfamily.com*.

SUGGESTED READINGS

M. J. Gibbs, et al., "Performance Measure Properties and Incentive System Design," *Industrial Relations*, 48 (2009), 237–264.

Bonnie Schindler, "Understanding Private Company Incentive Pay Practices," *Workspan*, March 2008, 43–48; Dan Kleinman, "Getting Our Bonus Expectations Right," *Workspan*, July 2009, 75–76.

For an overview and details, see Jerry S. Rosenbloom, *The Handbook of Employee Benefits: Design, Funding, and Administration*, 6th ed. (New York: McGraw-Hill, 2005).

"An Employee's Guide to Health Benefits under COBRA: The Consolidation Omnibus Budget Reconciliation Act of 1986," U.S. Department of Labor Manual, Employee Benefits Security Administration, *www.dol.gov*.

Risk Management and Employee Relations

HR—MEETING MANAGEMENT CHALLENGES

Employer protection activities help manage risks and maintain a safe and healthy work environment. This chapter highlights the factors affecting risk management in organizations as well as those affecting of employee relations. Key issues are:

- Ensuring that worker health, safety, and security are consistently addressed
- Having employee relations, rights and responsibilities addressed by HR policies and practices
- Controlling and measuring employee absenteeism as well as using discipline appropriately

Components of risk management are workplace safety, employee health and wellness, and workplace and worker security. The employment relationship is a reciprocal one in which both employer and employee have contractual rights as well as responsibilities. Employers must address such issues as privacy, use of electronic communications, absenteeism, and discipline.

RISK MANAGEMENT, HEALTH, SAFETY, AND SECURITY

In the United States and most developed nations, the concept of using prevention and control to minimize or eliminate a wide range of risks in workplaces has been expanding. **Risk management** involves responsibilities to consider physical, human, and financial factors to protect organizational and individual interests.[1] Its scope can range from workplace safety and health to disaster preparation. A well-done HR risk management program can affect the bottom line through direct savings in workers' compensation costs, civil liability damages, and litigation expenses, as well as by increasing the likelihood of winning bids and government contracts.

The first emphasis in HR risk management in most organizations is health, safety, and security. The terms *health, safety,* and *security* are closely related. The broader and somewhat more nebulous term is **health,** which refers to a general state of physical, mental, and emotional well-being. A healthy person is free from illness, injury, or mental and emotional problems that impair normal human activity. Health management practices in organizations strive to maintain employees' overall well-being.

Typically, **safety** refers to a condition in which the physical well-being of people is protected. The main purpose of effective safety programs in organizations is to prevent work-related injuries and accidents. The purpose of **security** is protecting employees and organizational facilities. With the growth of workplace violence and other risk management issues, security has become a concern for employers and employees alike.

Current State of Health, Safety, and Security

In a recent year in the United States, about 4 million nonfatal injuries and illnesses occurred at work. That was down from previous years. Specific rates vary depending on the industry, type of job, and other factors. The number of workplace injuries also varies by employer size, with smaller employers having more injuries per employee.

While injury accidents in general are down, injuries resulting in disabilities among American workers are growing. The problem seems to be related partly to unhealthy lifestyles. The aging workforce also is a factor. Older workers have lower frequencies of disability, but when they are out of work due to injuries, it is usually for a longer period of time.

To reduce risk of lawsuits, a number of companies have turned to employment practices liability insurance (EPLI), mandatory arbitration, and internal conflict resolution programs. EPLI can provide some protection from employment-related lawsuits, but generally it is available only if employment practices, policies, recordkeeping, past claims, training, complaints, and problems pass muster. Mandatory arbitration requires all employees to agree, as a condition of employment, that they will participate in arbitration rather than instituting a lawsuit to settle any employment differences.

LEGAL REQUIREMENTS FOR SAFETY AND HEALTH

Employers must comply with a variety of federal and state laws when developing and maintaining healthy, safe, and secure workforces and working environments. Three major legal areas are workers' compensation legislation, the Americans with Disabilities Act, and child labor laws.

Workers' Compensation

Workers' compensation laws in some form are on the books in all states today. Under these laws, employers contribute to an insurance fund to compensate employees for injuries received while on the job. Premiums paid reflect the accident rates of the employers, with employers that have higher incident rates being assessed higher premiums. These laws usually provide payments to replace wages for injured workers, depending on the amount of lost time and the wage level. They also provide payments to cover medical bills and for retraining if a worker cannot go back to the current job. Most state laws also set a maximum weekly amount for determining workers' comp benefits.

One aspect of workers' compensation coverage relates to the use of tele-commuting by employees. In most situations, while working at home for employers, individuals are covered under workers' compensation laws. There-fore, if an employee is injured while doing employer-related work at home, the employer likely is liable for the injury.

Workers' compensation costs have become a major issue for many em-ployers. These costs usually represent from 2% to 10% of payroll for most em-ployers. The major contributors to increases have been higher medical costs and litigation expenses.[2] However, the frequency of workers' compensation claims for lost time has decreased some in all industry groups.

The Family and Medical Leave Act (FMLA) affects workers' compensation as well. Because the FMLA allows eligible employees to take up to 12 weeks of leave for their serious health conditions, injured employees may ask to use that leave time in addition to the leave time allowed under workers' comp, even if it is unpaid. Some employers have policies that state that FMLA leave runs concurrently with any workers' comp leave.

Americans with Disabilities Act and Safety Issues

Employers sometimes try to return injured workers to light-duty work to re-duce workers' compensation costs. However, under the Americans with Dis-abilities Act (ADA), when making accommodations for injured employees through light-duty work, employers may undercut what are really essential job functions. Also, making such accommodations for injured employees for a pe-riod of time may require employers to make similar accommodations for job applicants with disabilities. Health and safety recordkeeping practices have been affected by an ADA provision that requires all medical-related informa-tion to be maintained separately from all other confidential files.

Child Labor Laws

Safety concerns are reflected in restrictions affecting younger workers, espe-cially those under the age of 18. Child labor laws, found in section XII of the Fair Labor Standards Act (FLSA), set the minimum age for most employment at 16 years. For "hazardous" occupations, 18 years is the minimum. Figure 9-1 lists 17 occupations that the federal government considers hazardous for chil-dren who work while attending school.

In addition to complying with workers' compensation, ADA, and child labor laws, most employers must comply with the Occupational Safety and Health Act of 1970. This act has had a tremendous impact on the workplace. The act is administered by the Occupational Safety and Health Administration.

OCCUPATIONAL SAFETY AND HEALTH ACT

The Occupational Safety and Health Act of 1970 was passed "to assure so far as possible every working man or woman in the Nation safe and healthful working conditions and to preserve our human resources." Every employer

FIGURE 9-1 Selected Child Labor Hazardous Occupations (minimum age: 18 years)

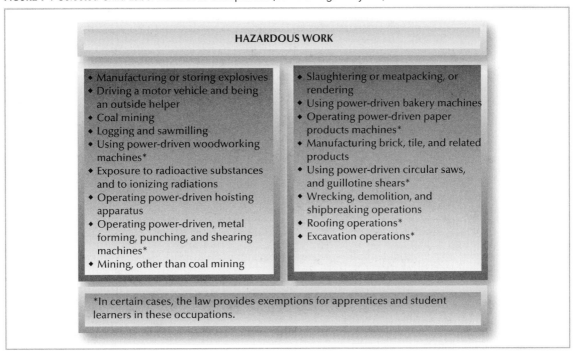

HAZARDOUS WORK

- Manufacturing or storing explosives
- Driving a motor vehicle and being an outside helper
- Coal mining
- Logging and sawmilling
- Using power-driven woodworking machines*
- Exposure to radioactive substances and to ionizing radiations
- Operating power-driven hoisting apparatus
- Operating power-driven, metal forming, punching, and shearing machines*
- Mining, other than coal mining

- Slaughtering or meatpacking, or rendering
- Using power-driven bakery machines
- Operating power-driven paper products machines*
- Manufacturing brick, tile, and related products
- Using power-driven circular saws, and guillotine shears*
- Wrecking, demolition, and shipbreaking operations
- Roofing operations*
- Excavation operations*

*In certain cases, the law provides exemptions for apprentices and student learners in these occupations.

that is engaged in commerce and has one or more employees is covered by the act. Farmers having fewer than 10 employees are exempt. Employers in specific industries, such as coal mining, are covered under other health and safety acts. Federal, state, and local governments are covered by separate statutes and provisions.

The Occupational Safety and Health Act of 1970 established the Occupational Safety and Health Administration, known as OSHA, to administer its provisions. By making employers and employees more aware of safety and health considerations, OSHA has significantly affected organizations. OSHA regulations appear to have contributed to reductions in the number of accidents and injuries in some cases. But in other industries, OSHA has had little or no effect.

OSHA Enforcement Standards

To implement OSHA regulations, specific standards were established to regulate equipment and working environments. Two provisions have been recognized as key to employers' responsibility to comply with OSHA. These are as follows:

- *General duty*: The act requires that the employer has a "general duty" to provide safe and healthy working conditions, even in areas where OSHA standards have not been set.[3] Employers who know or reasonably should know of unsafe or unhealthy conditions can be cited for violating the general duty clause.

- *Notification and posters*: Employers are required to inform their employees of safety and health standards established by OSHA. Also, OSHA posters must be displayed in prominent locations in workplaces.

OSHA Recordkeeping Requirements

Employers are generally required to maintain a detailed annual record of the various types of injuries, accidents, and fatalities for inspection by OSHA representatives and for submission to the agency. OSHA guidelines state that facilities whose accident records are below the national average rarely need inspecting. But those with high "days away from work scores" may get letters from OSHA and perhaps an inspection.

Four types of injuries or illnesses are defined by the Occupational Safety and Health Act. They are as follows:

- *Injury- or illness-related deaths*: fatalities at workplaces or caused by work-related actions
- *Lost-time or disability injuries*: job-related injuries or disabling occurrences that cause an employee to miss regularly scheduled work on the day following the accident
- *Medical care injuries*: injuries that require treatment by a physician but do not cause an employee to miss a regularly scheduled work turn
- *Minor injuries*: injuries that require first aid treatment and do not cause an employee to miss the next regularly scheduled work turn

OSHA Inspections

The Occupational Safety and Health Act provides for on-the-spot inspections by OSHA representatives, called compliance officers or inspectors. In *Marshall v. Barlow's, Inc.*, the U.S. Supreme Court held that safety inspectors must produce a search warrant if an employer refuses to allow an inspector into the plant voluntarily. The Court also ruled that an inspector does not have to show probable cause to obtain a search warrant. A warrant can be obtained easily if a search is part of a general enforcement plan.[4]

When an OSHA compliance officer arrives, managers should ask to see the inspector's credentials. Next, the HR representative for the employer should insist on an opening conference with the compliance officer. The compliance officer may request that a union representative, an employee, and a company representative be present while the inspection is conducted.

OSHA has been criticized on several fronts. Because the agency has so many worksites to inspect, employers have only a relatively small chance of being inspected. Some suggest that employers pay little attention to OSHA enforcement efforts for this reason. Employers, especially smaller ones, continue to complain about the complexity of complying with OSHA standards and the costs associated with penalties and with making changes required to remedy problem areas.

SAFETY MANAGEMENT

Well-designed and well-managed safety programs can pay dividends in reduced accidents and associated costs, such as workers' compensation and possible fines. Further, accidents and other safety concerns usually decline as a result of management efforts that emphasize safety. Often, the difference between high-performing firms with good occupational safety records and other firms is that the former have effective safety management programs. Both HR and operating managers must be involved in coordinating health, safety, and security efforts. Successful safety management includes several components highlighted next.

Organizational Commitment and a Safety Culture

At the heart of safety management is an organizational commitment to a comprehensive safety effort that should be coordinated at the top level of management and include all members of the organization. Three approaches are used by employers in managing safety. Figure 9-2 shows the organizational, engineering, and individual approaches and their components. Successful programs may use all three in dealing with safety issues.

Safety Policies, Discipline, and Recordkeeping

Designing safety policies and rules and disciplining violators are important components of safety efforts. Frequently reinforcing the need for safe behavior

FIGURE 9-2 Approaches to Effective Safety Management

APPROACHES TO EFFECTIVE SAFETY MANAGEMENT

ORGANIZATIONAL APPROACH
- Designing jobs
- Developing and implementing safety policies
- Using safety committees
- Coordinating accident investigations

ENGINEERING APPROACH
- Designing work settings and equipment
- Reviewing equipment
- Applying ergonomic principles

INDIVIDUAL APPROACH
- Reinforcing safety motivation and attitudes
- Providing employee safety training
- Rewarding safety through incentive programs

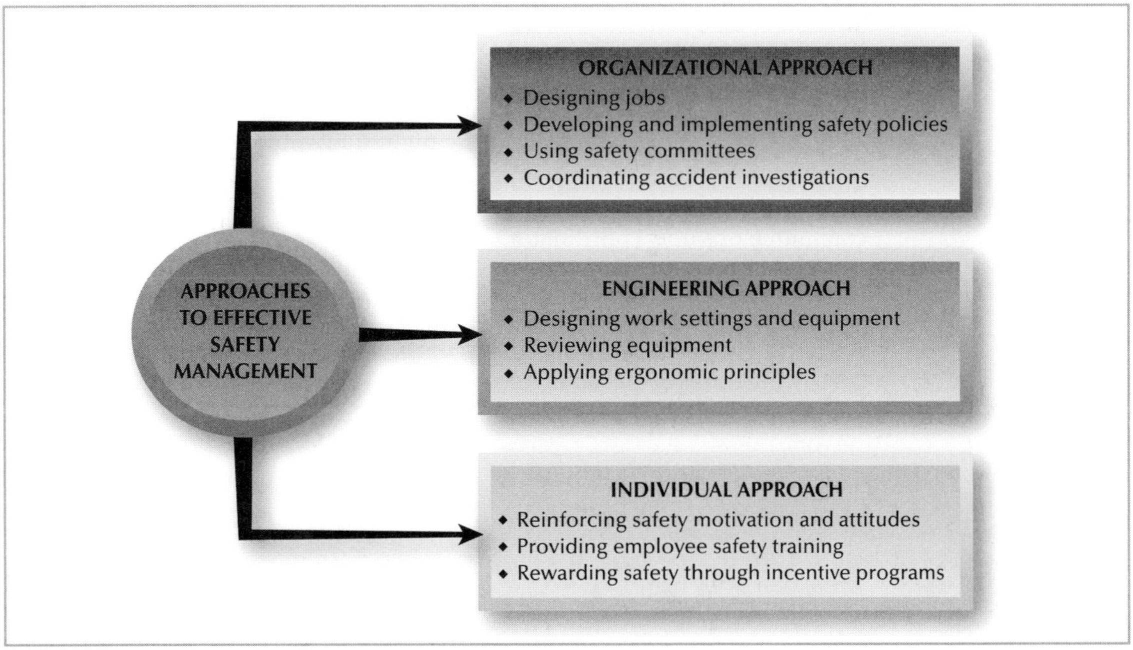

and frequently supplying feedback on positive safety practices are also effective ways of improving worker safety. Such safety-conscious efforts must involve employees, supervisors, managers, safety specialists, and HR staff members.

For policies about safety to be effective, good recordkeeping about accidents, causes, and other details is necessary. Without records, an employer cannot track its safety performance, compare benchmarks against other employers, and may not realize the extent of its safety problems.

Safety Training and Communication

Good safety training reduces accidents, and can be done in various ways. Regular training sessions with supervisors, managers, and employees are often coordinated by HR staff members. Communication of safety procedures, reasons why accidents occurred, and what to do in an emergency is part of that training. Without effective communication, training is insufficient. To reinforce safety training, continuous communication to develop safety consciousness is necessary.

Safety Committees

Employees frequently participate in safety planning through safety committees, often composed of workers from a variety of levels and departments. A safety committee generally meets at regularly scheduled times, has specific responsibilities for conducting safety reviews, and makes recommendations for changes necessary to avoid future accidents. Usually, at least one member of the committee comes from the HR department.

Inspection, Investigation, and Evaluation

It is not necessary to wait for an OSHA inspector to check the work area for safety hazards. Inspections may be done regularly by a safety committee or by a company safety coordinator. Problem areas should be addressed immediately to keep work productivity at the highest possible levels. OSHA inspects organizations with above-average rates of lost workdays more frequently. When accidents occur, they should be investigated by the employer's safety committee or safety coordinator.

The phases of accident investigation are in Figure 9-3. While identifying why an accident occurred is useful, taking steps to prevent similar accidents from occurring is even more important.

FIGURE 9-3 Phases of Accident Investigation

Measuring Safety Efforts

Organizations should monitor and evaluate their safety efforts. Just as organizational accounting records are audited, a firm's safety efforts should be audited periodically as well. Accident and injury statistics should be compared with previous accident patterns to identify any significant changes. This analysis should be designed to measure progress in safety management.

Safety efforts can be measured. Some common ones are workers' compensation costs per injury/illness; percentage of injuries/illnesses by department, work shifts, and job categories; and incident rate comparisons with industry and benchmark targets. Regardless of the specific measures used, it is critical to be able to track and evaluate safety management efforts using relevant HR metrics.

EMPLOYEE HEALTH

Employee health problems are varied—and somewhat inevitable. They can range from minor illnesses such as colds to serious illnesses related to the jobs performed. Employers face a variety of workplace health issues, some of which are discussed next.

Substance Abuse

Use of illicit substances or misuse of controlled substances, alcohol, or other drugs is called **substance abuse.** The millions of substance abusers in the workforce cost global employers billions of dollars annually, although recently there has been a decline in illegal drug use by employees. Most companies have a drug-screening policy that focuses on preemployment testing.

A company should have a written policy covering alcohol and drugs and the possession of illegal drugs at work. Such a policy should prohibit employees from coming to work under the influence of alcohol or drugs. The policy should be communicated in writing, and each employee should sign off and understand that failure to take a test can lead to adverse inference.[5]

Employers' concerns about substance abuse stem from the ways it alters work behaviors, causing increased tardiness, increased absenteeism, a slower work pace, a higher rate of mistakes, and less time spent at the work station. It can also cause an increase in withdrawal (physical and psychological) and antagonistic behaviors, which may lead to workplace violence. Alcohol testing and drug testing are used by many employers, especially following an accident or some other reasonable cause. Some employers also use random testing programs.

Types of Drug Tests. There are several different types of tests for drug use: urinalysis, radioimmunoassay of hair, surface swiping, and fitness-for-duty testing. The innovative fitness-for-duty tests can be used alone or in conjunction with drug testing. These tests can distinguish individuals under the influence of alcohol or prescription drugs to the extent that their abilities to perform their jobs are impaired. Some firms use fitness-for-duty tests to detect work performance safety problems before putting a person behind dangerous equipment.

Handling Substance Abuse Cases.   The Americans with Disabilities Act (ADA) affects how management can handle substance abuse cases. Current users of *illegal* drugs are specifically excluded from the definition of *disabled* under the act. However, those addicted to *legal* substances (e.g., alcohol and prescription drugs) are considered disabled under the ADA. Also, recovering substance abusers are considered disabled under the ADA.

To encourage employees to seek help for their substance abuse problems, a *firm-choice option* is usually recommended and has been endorsed legally. In this procedure, a supervisor or a manager confronts the employee privately about unsatisfactory work-related behaviors.

Emotional/Mental Health

Many individuals are facing work, family, and personal life pressures. A variety of emotional/mental health issues arise at work that must be addressed by employers. It is important to note that emotional/mental illnesses such as schizophrenia and depression are considered disabilities under the ADA.

Depression is another common emotional/mental health concern. The effects of depression are seen at all organizational levels, from warehouses and accounting offices to executive suites. Employees who appear to be depressed are guided to employee assistance programs and helped with obtaining medical treatment.

Health and Older Employees

The graying of the workforce has been mentioned previously, but there are implications for health and safety. All signs point to an abundance of older workers, as many are showing signs of working beyond age 65. As noted earlier, there is a diminishing pool of successful younger workers to replace them. Data show that older workers have fewer injuries, but are out of work longer when they do, and these injuries cost more to fix.

Health Promotion

Employers concerned about maintaining a healthy workforce must move beyond simply providing healthy working conditions and begin promoting employee health and wellness in other ways. **Health promotion** is a supportive approach of facilitating and encouraging healthy actions and lifestyles among employees. Health promotion efforts can range from providing information and increasing employee awareness of health issues to creating an organizational culture supportive of employee health enhancements.

Wellness programs are designed to maintain or improve employee health before problems arise by encouraging self-directed lifestyle changes. Programs emphasize healthy lifestyles and environment, including reduced cholesterol and heart disease risks and individualized exercise programs and follow-up. These programs use information and subtle psychology to motivate people to live healthier lifestyles. They typically focus on exercise, nutrition, sleep, stress, and life balance.

Employee Assistance Programs. One method organizations use as a broad-based response to health issues is an **employee assistance program (EAP),** which provides counseling and other help to employees having emotional, physical, or other personal problems. In such a program, an employer typically contracts with a counseling agency for the service. Employees who have problems may then contact the agency, either voluntarily or by employer referral, for assistance with a broad range of problems. Counseling costs are paid for by the employer, either in total or up to a preestablished limit. Done well, EAPs can help reduce health care and other costs.

SECURITY CONCERNS AT WORK

Traditionally, when employers have addressed worker health and safety, they have been concerned about reducing workplace accidents, improving safety practices, and reducing health hazards at work. However, in the past decade, providing security for employees has become important. Notice that virtually all of the areas discussed in the following text have significant HR implications. Heading the list of security concerns is workplace violence.

Workplace Violence

Workplace violence is an attack directed at someone at work or on duty. For example, physical assault, threats, harassment, intimidation, and bullying all qualify. There are a number of warning signs and characteristics of a potentially violent person at work. Individuals who have committed the most violent acts have had a relatively common profile. A profound humiliation or rejection, the end of a marriage, the loss of a lawsuit, termination from a job, or other sources of stress may make a difficult employee turn violent. Too often violence that begins at home with family or "friends" can spill over to the workplace. Also, many abused women report being harassed frequently at work, by telephone or in person, by abusing partners.

Dealing with Workplace Violence. The increase in workplace violence has led many employers to develop policies and practices for trying to prevent and respond to workplace violence. Policies can identify how workplace violence is to be dealt with in conjunction with disciplinary actions and referrals to EAPs. Training of managers is important, as well as creating a *violence response team*, composed of security personnel, key managers, HR staff members, and selected employees.

Security Management

A comprehensive approach to security management is needed to address a wide range of issues, including workplace violence. HR managers may have responsibility for security programs or may work closely with security managers or consultants.

Security Audit. In a **security audit,** HR staff conduct a comprehensive review of organizational security. Sometimes called a *vulnerability analysis,* such an audit uses managers inside the organization (e.g., the HR manager and the facilities manager) and outsiders (e.g., security consultants, police officers, fire officials, and computer security experts) to assess security issues.

Typically, a security audit begins with a survey of the area around the facility. Such factors as lighting in parking lots, traffic flow, location of emergency response services, crime in the surrounding neighborhood, and the layout of the buildings and grounds are evaluated.

Controlled Access. A key part of security involves controlling access to the physical facilities of the organization. Many workplace homicides occur during robberies. Therefore, employees who are most vulnerable, such as taxi drivers and convenience store clerks, can be provided bulletproof partitions and restricted access areas.

Controlling computer access may be an important part of securing IT resources. Coordination with information technology resources to change passwords, access codes, and otherwise protect company information may be important.

Employee Screening and Selection. A key facet of providing security is screening job applicants. HR management is somewhat limited by legal constraints on what can be done with the use of psychological tests and checking of references. However, firms that do not screen employees adequately may be subject to liability if an employee commits crimes later.

DISASTER PREPARATION AND RECOVERY PLANNING

During the past several years, a number of significant disasters have occurred. Some have been natural disasters, such as hurricanes, major snowstorms, flooding in various states, tornadoes, and forest fires. There also has been concern about terrorism, and some firms have been damaged by fires and explosions. All of these situations have led to HR management having an expanded role in disaster planning.

Disaster Planning

For disaster planning to occur properly, three components must be addressed by HR, as shown in Figure 9-4. Imagine that a hurricane destroys the work

FIGURE 9-4 Disaster Planning Components

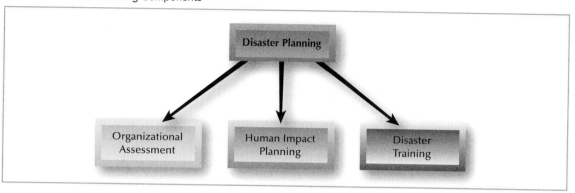

facility where employees work, as well as many of the employees' homes. Or picture an explosion or terrorist attack that prohibits workers from getting to their workplaces. Such situations illustrate why each of the components has human dimensions to be addressed.

Organizational Assessment.   Organizational assessment includes establishing a disaster planning team, often composed of representatives from HR, security, information technology, operations, and other areas. The purpose of this team is to conduct an organizational assessment of how various disasters might affect the organization and its employees. Then a disaster recovery plan is developed to identify how the organization will respond to different situations.

Human Impact Planning.   A number of areas are part of human impact planning, including items such as having backup databases for numerous company details, along with employee contact information. Who will take responsibilities for various duties and how these efforts will be coordinated must be identified.

Disaster Training.   All of the planning efforts may be wasted if managers and employees are not trained on what to do when disasters occur. This training covers a wide range of topics, including the following: first aid/CPR, hazardous materials containment, disaster escape means, employer contact methods, and organizational restoration efforts.

But training is not sufficient without conducting exercises or simulations for managers and employees to use the training. Regular tests to ensure that information technology and databases are security accessible outside of the main location should occur. Testing responses if a workplace violence attack occurs may identify additional activities needed in an organization. Training must be a continuing consideration and must reflect updated disaster planning efforts.[6]

Disaster Planning for Disease

One issue during the past few years has been the spread of various kinds of viruses and flu throughout the world. The global nature of business travel has increased the likelihood of the spread of a deadly virus. Two key issues are whether to evacuate expatriate employees from locations where flu occurs and how to protect local employees if the flu symptoms occur in their area.

EMPLOYER AND EMPLOYEE RIGHTS AND RESPONSIBILITIES

Four interrelated HR issues are considered part of this topic: *employee rights, HR policies, absenteeism,* and *discipline.* Employees come to work with some rights, but many more are granted or constrained by the HR policies and rules an employer sets. For example, such rules include policies on absenteeism. Further, discipline used against those who fail to follow policies and rules has both employee and employer rights dimensions.

Rights generally do not exist in the abstract. Instead, **rights** are powers, privileges, or interests granted by law, nature, or tradition. **Statutory rights** are the result of specific laws or statutes passed by federal, state, or local governments. Various federal, state, and local laws have granted employees certain rights at work, such as equal employment opportunity, collective bargaining, and workplace safety. These laws and their interpretations also have been the subjects of a considerable number of court cases because employers also have rights.

Rights are offset by **responsibilities,** which are obligations to perform certain tasks and duties. Employment is a reciprocal relationship in that both the employer and the employee have rights and obligations. The reciprocal nature of rights and responsibilities suggests that both parties to an employment relationship should regard the other as having rights and should treat the other with respect.

Employment Contracts

When individuals become employees, they will encounter both employment rights and responsibilities. Employment rights and responsibilities can be spelled out formally in written employment contracts or in employer handbooks and policies disseminated to employees. Contracts can formalize the employment relationship.

Traditionally, employment contracts have been used mostly for executives and senior managers, but the use of employment contracts is filtering down in the organization to include highly specialized professional and technical employees who have scarce skills. An **employment contract** is a formal agreement that outlines the details of employment. Depending on the organization and individuals involved, employment agreements may contain a number of provisions.

Employment contracts may include **noncompete agreements,** which prohibit individuals who leave an organization from working with an employer in the same line of business for a specified period of time. A noncompete agreement may be presented as a separate contract or as a clause in an employment contract. Though primarily used with newly hired employees, some firms have required existing employees to sign noncompete agreements.

Implied Contracts

The idea that a contract (even an implied or unwritten one) exists between individuals and their employers affects the employment relationship. The rights and responsibilities of the employee may be spelled out in a job description, in an employment contract, in HR policies, or in a handbook, but often they are not. The rights and responsibilities of the employee may exist *only* as unwritten employer expectations about what is acceptable behavior or performance on the part of the employee. When the employer fails to follow up on the implied promises, the employee may pursue remedies in court.

RIGHTS AFFECTING THE EMPLOYMENT RELATIONSHIP

As employees have increasingly regarded themselves as free agents in the workplace and as the power of unions has changed in the United States, the struggle between individual employee and employer "rights" has become heightened. Employers frequently do not fare well in court in employee "rights" cases. Several concepts from law and psychology influence the employment relationship: employment-at-will, wrongful or constructive discharge, just cause, due process, and distributive and procedural justice.

Employment-at-Will

Employment-at-will (EAW) is a common-law doctrine stating that employers have the right to hire, fire, demote, or promote whomever they choose, unless there is a law or a contract to the contrary. Conversely, employees can quit whenever they want and go to another job under the same terms. An employment-at-will statement in an employee handbook usually contains wording such as the following:

> *This handbook is not a contract, express or implied, guaranteeing employment for any specific duration. Although we hope that your employment relationship with us will be long term, either you or the Employer may terminate this relationship at any time, for any reason, with or without cause or notice.*

Wrongful Discharge.   Employers who run afoul of EAW restrictions may be guilty of **wrongful discharge,** which is the termination of an individual's employment for reasons that are illegal or improper. Employers should take several precautions to reduce wrongful-discharge liabilities. Having a well-written employee handbook, training managers, and maintaining adequate documentation are key.

Some state courts have recognized certain nonstatutory grounds for wrongful-discharge suits. Additionally, courts generally have held that unionized workers cannot pursue EAW actions as at-will employees because they are covered by the grievance arbitration process. As EAW has changed in interpretations and more wrongful-discharge lawsuits have been brought, employers have become more concerned about legal liability issues.[7]

Closely related to wrongful discharge is **constructive discharge,** which is deliberately making conditions intolerable to get an employee to quit. Under normal circumstances, an employee who resigns rather than being dismissed cannot later collect damages for violation of legal rights. An exception to this rule occurs when the courts find that the working conditions were made so intolerable as to *force* a reasonable employee to resign. Then, the resignation is considered a discharge.

Just Cause and Due Process

Just cause is reasonable justification for taking employment-related action. The need for a "good reason" for disciplinary actions such as dismissal usually can be found in union contracts, but not in at-will situations. The United States has different just-cause rules than do some other countries. Even though definitions of *just cause* vary, the overall concern is fairness. To be viewed by others as *just*, the disciplinary action must be justified by the facts in the individual case.

Due process, like just cause, is about fairness. Due process is the requirement that the employer use a fair process to determine if there has been employee wrongdoing and that the employee have an opportunity to explain and defend his or her actions. Figure 9-5 shows some factors to be considered when combining an evaluation of just cause and due process. How HR managers address these factors determines whether the courts perceive employers' actions as fair.

FIGURE 9-5 Criteria for Evaluating Just Cause and Due Process

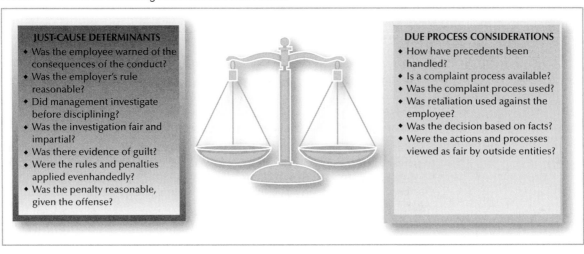

JUST-CAUSE DETERMINANTS
- Was the employee warned of the consequences of the conduct?
- Was the employer's rule reasonable?
- Did management investigate before disciplining?
- Was the investigation fair and impartial?
- Was there evidence of guilt?
- Were the rules and penalties applied evenhandedly?
- Was the penalty reasonable, given the offense?

DUE PROCESS CONSIDERATIONS
- How have precedents been handled?
- Is a complaint process available?
- Was the complaint process used?
- Was retaliation used against the employee?
- Was the decision based on facts?
- Were the actions and processes viewed as fair by outside entities?

Work-Related Alternative Dispute Resolution

Disputes between management and employees over different work issues are normal and inevitable, but how the parties resolve their disputes can become important. Formal grievance procedures and lawsuits provide two resolution methods. However, more and more companies are looking to alternative means of ensuring that due process occurs in cases involving employee rights. Dissatisfaction with the expenses and delays that are common in the court system when lawsuits are filed explains the growth in alternative dispute resolution (ADR) methods such as arbitration, peer review panels, and ombuds.

Arbitration is a process that uses a neutral third party to make a decision, thereby eliminating the necessity of using the court system. Some firms use *compulsory arbitration*, which requires employees to sign a preemployment agreement stating that all disputes will be submitted to arbitration, and that employees waive their rights to pursue legal action until the completion of the arbitration process. Requiring arbitration as a condition of employment is legal. However, in some situations, exceptions have been noted, so a legal check of compulsory arbitration as part of ADR should be done before adopting the practice.

Some employers allow their employees to appeal disciplinary actions to an internal committee of employees. This panel reviews the actions and makes recommendations or decisions. **Peer review panels** use fellow employees and a few managers to resolve employment disputes. Panel members are specially trained volunteers who sign confidentiality agreements, after which the company empowers them to hear appeals.

Some organizations ensure process fairness through **ombuds**—individuals outside the normal chain of command who act as independent problem solvers for both management and employees. Ombuds address employees' complaints and operate with a high degree of confidentiality.

MANAGING INDIVIDUAL EMPLOYEE AND EMPLOYER RIGHTS ISSUES

Employees who join organizations in the United States bring with them certain rights, including *freedom of speech, due process*, and *protection against unreasonable search and seizure*. Although the U.S. Constitution grants these and other rights to citizens, over the years, laws and court decisions have identified limits on them in the workplace.

Employers have legitimate rights and needs to ensure that employees are doing their jobs and working in a secure environment, while employees expect their rights, both at work and away from work, to be protected. The **right to privacy** is defined in legal terms as an individual's freedom from unauthorized and unreasonable intrusion into personal affairs.

The dramatic increase in Internet communications, twitters, specialized computers, and telecommunications systems is transforming many workplaces. The use of technology items by employers to monitor employee actions is amplifying concerns that the privacy rights of employees are being threatened.

Privacy Rights and Employee Records

As a result of concerns about protecting individual privacy rights in the United States, the Privacy Act of 1974 was passed. It includes provisions affecting HR recordkeeping systems.

Employee Medical Records.   Recordkeeping and retention practices have been affected by the Americans with Disabilities Act (ADA). As interpreted by attorneys and HR practitioners, the Act requires that all medical-related information be maintained separately from all other confidential files.

Additionally, it is important that specific access restrictions and security procedures for employee records be established. These restrictions and procedures are designed to protect the privacy of employees and to protect employers from potential liability for improper disclosure of personal information. For instance, security breaches can occur through employer records regarding an employee's Social Security data, home address, and family details, especially by electronic means.[8]

A legal regulation called the Data Protection Act requires employers to keep personnel records up-to-date and to keep only the details that are needed. Personnel files and records usually should be maintained for three years. However, different types of records should be maintained for shorter or longer periods of time based on various legal and regulatory standards.

Electronic Records.   Another concern is how electronic records are maintained and secured, given the changes in software, e-mail, and other technology. Employers should establish electronic records policies to ensure legal compliance and to avoid violating individuals' personal rights.

Employees' Free Speech Rights

The right of individuals to freedom of speech is protected by the U.S. Constitution. However, that freedom is *not* an unrestricted one in the workplace. Three areas in which employees' freedom of speech has collided with employers' restrictions are controversial views, whistle blowing, and use of the Internet and other technology.

Questions of free speech arise over the right of employees to advocate controversial viewpoints at work. Employers must follow due process procedures and demonstrate that disciplinary actions taken against employees can be justified by job-related reasons.

Individuals who report real or perceived wrongs committed by their employers are called **whistle blowers.** The reasons why people report actions that they question vary and often are individual in nature. However, whistle blowers are less likely to lose their jobs in public employment than in private employment because most civil service systems follow rules protecting whistle blowers. A 2009 U.S. federal amendment said that for private employers to receive federal stimulus funding, they must have the same whistle-blowing regulations as the federal government.[9] However, no comprehensive whistle-blowing law fully protects the right to free speech of both public and private employees.

Technology and Employer/Employee Issues

The growth of technology use by employers and employees is constantly creating new issues to be addressed. Such technology usages as twitters, wikis, social networking, and blogs require attention by employers. Employers have a right to monitor what is said and transmitted through their network and voicemail systems, despite employees' concerns about free speech. Advances in information and telecommunications technology have become a major employer issue regarding employee and workplace privacy. There are recommended actions for employers to take when monitoring technology. Employers should monitor only for business purposes and strictly enforce the policy.

Given all the time and effort spent on technology through both work and personal actions, it is important for HR professionals to provide guidance to executives, managers, and employees. Some areas in which HR policies need to be made can include the following:

- Establishing security for voicemail system
- Communicating that the employer will attempt to monitor security, but it may not be totally guaranteed
- Restricting the use of employee records to a few individuals

Many employers have developed and disseminated electronic communications policies. Figure 9-6 depicts recommended employer actions, beginning with the development of these policies.

FIGURE 9-6 Recommended Employer Actions Regarding Electronic Communications

Employee Rights and Personal Behavior Issues

Another area to which employers must give attention is employee personal behavior. Personal behavior on or off the job could be an issue. For example, if an employer investigates off-the-job charges of illegal behavior, an invasion-of-privacy claim might result. On the other hand, failure to do due diligence could jeopardize disciplinary actions that should be taken by employers.

Employers may decide to review unusual behavior by employees both on and off the job. Organizations and HR also must deal with actions such as employees or managers being inappropriately angry, insulting, or extremely rude to customers, suppliers, or employees at different levels. Employers have put limits on employees' dress and appearance in some situations, including items such as visible tattoos, certain clothing and accessories, and body piercings.

BALANCING EMPLOYER SECURITY AND EMPLOYEE RIGHTS

Balancing employer and employee rights is difficult. On one side, employers have a legitimate need to ensure that employees are performing their jobs properly in a secure environment. On the other side, employees expect the rights that they have both at work and away from work to be protected.

Workplace Monitoring

In the United States, the right of protection from unreasonable search and seizure protects an individual against activities of the government only. Thus, employees of private-sector employers can be monitored, observed, and searched at work by representatives of the employer. Several court decisions have reaffirmed the principle that both private-sector and government employers may search desks, files, lockers, and computer files without search warrants if they believe that work rules have been violated.

Numerous employers have installed video surveillance systems in workplaces. Some employers use these systems to ensure employee security, such as in parking lots, garages, and dimly lit exterior areas. Other employers have installed them on retail sales floors and in production areas, parts and inventory rooms, and lobbies.

Employee activity may be monitored to measure performance, ensure performance quality and customer service, check for theft, or enforce company rules or laws. The common concerns in a monitored workplace usually center not on whether monitoring should be used, but on how it should be conducted, how the information should be used, and how feedback should be communicated to employees.

Employer Investigations

Another area of concern regarding employee rights involves workplace investigations. The U.S. Constitution protects public-sector employees in the areas of due process, search and seizure, and privacy at work, but private-sector employees are not protected. Whether on or off the job, unethical or illegal employee behavior can be a serious problem for organizations. Employee misconduct may include illegal drug use, falsification of documents, misuse of company funds, disclosure of organizational secrets, workplace violence, employee harassment, and theft.

Substance Abuse and Drug Testing

Employee substance abuse and drug testing have received a great deal of attention. Concern about substance abuse at work is appropriate, given that absenteeism, accident/damage rates, and theft/fraud are higher for workers using illegal substances or misusing legal substances such as drugs and alcohol.

The U.S. Supreme Court has ruled that certain drug-testing plans do not violate the Constitution. Private-employer programs are governed mainly by state laws, which can be a confusing hodgepodge. The Drug-Free Workplace Act of 1988 requires government contractors to take steps to eliminate employee drug use.

Drug Testing and Employee Rights.   Unless federal, state, or local law prohibits testing, employers have a right to require applicants or employees to submit to a drug test. Preemployment drug testing is widely used. When employers conduct drug testing of current employees, they generally use one of three policies: (1) random testing of everyone at periodic intervals, (2) testing only in cases of probable cause, or (3) testing after accidents.

From a policy standpoint, it is most appropriate to test for drugs when the following conditions exist:

- Job-related consequences of the abuse are severe enough that they outweigh privacy concerns.
- Accurate test procedures are available.
- Written consent of the employee is obtained.
- Results are treated confidentially, as are any medical records.
- Employer offers a complete drug program, including an employee assistance program.

HR POLICIES, PROCEDURES, AND RULES

HR policies, procedures, and rules greatly affect employee rights (just discussed) and discipline (discussed next). Where there is a choice among actions, policies act as general guidelines that help focus those organizational actions. **Policies** are general in nature, whereas procedures and rules are specific to the situation. The important role of all three requires that they be reviewed regularly.

Procedures provide customary methods of handling activities and are more specific than policies. For example, a policy may state that employees will be given vacations according to years of service, and a procedure establishes a specific method for authorizing vacation time without disrupting work.

Rules are specific guidelines that regulate and restrict the behavior of individuals. They are similar to procedures in that they guide action and typically allow no discretion in their application. Rules reflect a management decision that action be taken—or not taken—in a given situation, and they provide more specific behavioral guidelines than do policies.[10]

Employee Handbooks.   An employee handbook can be an essential tool for communicating information about workplace culture, benefits, attendance, pay practices, safety issues, and discipline. The handbooks are sometimes written in a formal legalistic fashion, but need not be. Handbooks may contain many different areas, but some policies commonly covered in them include:

- At-will prerogatives
- Harassment
- Electronic communication
- Pay and benefits
- Discipline
- Hours worked

To communicate and discuss HR information, a growing number of firms are distributing employee handbooks electronically using an intranet, which enables employees to access policies in employee handbooks at any time. It also allows changes in policies to be made electronically rather than distributed as paper copies.

EMPLOYEE ABSENTEEISM

One major application of HR policies and practices by employers relates to employees who are absent from their work and job responsibilities. **Absenteeism** is any failure by an employee to report for work as scheduled or to stay at work when scheduled. Being absent from work may seem like a normal matter to an employee. But if a manager needs 12 people in a unit to get the work done, and 4 of the 12 are absent much of the time, the work of the unit will decrease or additional workers will have to be hired to provide results.

Types of Absenteeism

Employees can be absent from work or tardy for several reasons. Clearly, some absenteeism is inevitable because of illness, death in the family, and other personal reasons. Though absences such as those that are health related are unavoidable and understandable, they can be very costly. Many employers have sick leave policies that allow employees a certain number of paid days each year for those types of *involuntary* absences. However, much absenteeism is avoidable, or *voluntary*.

One problem is that a number of employees see no real concern about being absent or late to work because they feel that they are "entitled" to some absenteeism. In many firms, a relatively small number of individuals are responsible for a large share of the total absenteeism in the organization. Sometimes work-related stress and strain can lead to absenteeism.[11]

Regardless of the reason, employers need to know if someone is going to be absent. Various organizations have developed different means for employees to report their absences. Regardless of the method used, employers need to have a clear policy on how the employee should notify the employer when an absence occurs.

Controlling Absenteeism

Voluntary absenteeism is better controlled if managers understand its causes clearly. Once they do, they can use a variety of approaches to reduce it. Organizational policies on absenteeism should be stated clearly in an employee handbook and emphasized by supervisors and managers.

There are a number of methods that employers can use to address absenteeism. The disciplinary approach is the most widely used. Other methods include positive reinforcement and paid-time-off programs.

HR Metrics: Measuring Absenteeism.   A major step in reducing the expense of absenteeism is to decide how the organization is going to record absences and what calculations are necessary to maintain and benchmark their rates. Controlling or reducing absenteeism must begin with continuous monitoring of the absenteeism statistics in work units. Such monitoring helps managers pinpoint employees who are frequently absent and departments that have excessive absenteeism. Various methods of measuring or computing absenteeism exist. One formula suggested by the U.S. Department of Labor is as follows:

$$\frac{\text{Number of person-days lost through job absence during period}}{(\text{Average number of employees}) \times (\text{Number of workdays})} \times 100$$

The absenteeism rate also can be based on number of hours instead of number of days.

One set of metrics that can be calculated is the rate of absenteeism, which can be based on annual, monthly, quarterly, or other periods of time. Other useful measures of absenteeism might include:

- *Incidence rate*: The number of absences per 100 employees each day
- *Inactivity rate*: The percentage of time lost to absenteeism
- *Severity rate*: The average time lost per absent employee during a specified period of time (a month or a year)

EMPLOYEE DISCIPLINE

The earlier discussion about employee rights provides an appropriate introduction to the topic of employee discipline, because employee rights often are a key issue in disciplinary cases. **Discipline** is a form of training that enforces organizational rules. Those most often affected by the discipline systems are problem employees. Common disciplinary issues caused by problem employees include absenteeism, tardiness, productivity deficiencies, alcoholism, and insubordination.

Training supervisors and managers on when and how discipline should be used is crucial. Employees see disciplinary action as more fair when given by trained supervisors who base their responses on procedural justice than when discipline is done by untrained supervisors.[12]

Approaches to Discipline

The disciplinary system can be viewed as an application of behavior modification to a problem or unproductive employee. The best discipline is clearly self-discipline. Most people can be counted on to do their jobs effectively when they understand what is required at work. But for some people, the prospect of external discipline helps their self-discipline. One approach is positive discipline.

Positive Discipline Approach.   The positive discipline approach builds on the philosophy that violations are actions that usually can be corrected constructively without penalty. In this approach, managers focus on using fact finding and guidance to encourage desirable behaviors, rather than using penalties to discourage undesirable behaviors.

Progressive Discipline Approach.   Progressive discipline incorporates steps that become progressively more stringent and are designed to change the employee's inappropriate behavior. Figure 9-7 shows a typical progressive

FIGURE 9-7 Progressive Discipline Process

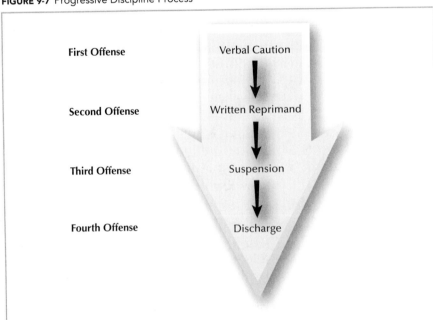

discipline process; most progressive discipline procedures use verbal and written reprimands and suspension before resorting to dismissal.

Discharge: The Final Disciplinary Step. The final stage in the disciplinary process may be called *discharge, firing, dismissal,* or *termination,* among other terms. Regardless of the word used, **discharge** is when an employee is removed from a job at an employer. Both the positive and the progressive approaches to discipline clearly provide employees with warnings about the seriousness of their performance problems before dismissal occurs.

From a legal standpoint, terminating workers because they do not keep their own promises is likely to appear equitable and defensible in many courts, but nevertheless, it is important for the employer to consistently document reasons for termination and to follow appropriate HR processes discussed earlier.

NOTES

1. G. Leters, et al., "Towards a Balanced Approach in Risk Identification," *Engineering Management Journal,* Winter 2007, 3–9.
2. David Nevmark, et al., "The Impact of Provider Choice on Worker's Compensation Costs and Outcomes," *Industrial and Labor Relations Review,* 60 (2007), 121–141.
3. Bill Leonard, "OSHA Issues Final Rule on Personal Protective Equipment," *HR News,* November 19, 2007, *www.shrm.org, 1.*
4. *Marshall v. Barlow's, Inc.,* 98 S. Ct. 1816 (1978).
5. Nancy Delogv, "Essential Elements of a Drug-Free Workplace Program," *Professional Safety,* November 2007, 48–51.
6. Dian-Yan Liou and Chin-Huang Lin, "Human Resources Planning on Terrorism and Crises in the Asia Pacific Region," *Human Resource Management,* Spring 2008, 49–72.
7. Edward C. Tomlinson and William N. Bockanic, "Avoiding Liability for Wrongful Termination," *Employee Responsibilities and Rights Journal,* 21 (2009), 77–88.
8. Jared Shelly, "Hazardous Leaks," *Human Resource Executive,* September 2, 2009, 34–36.
9. Jessica Marquez, "Firms Getting Stimulus Face Tougher Whistle-Blower Law," *Workforce Management,* April 6, 2009, 4.
10. David W. Lehmon and Rangaraj Ramanujam, "Selectivity in Organizational Rule Violations," *Academy of Management Review,* 34 (2009), 643–657.
11. W. Darr and G. Johns, "Work Strain, Health, and Absenteeism," *Journal of Occupational Health Psychology* 13 (2008), 292–318.
12. Leanne E. Atwater, et al., "The Delivery of Workplace Discipline: Lessons Learned," *Organizational Dynamics,* 36 (2007), 392–403.

INTERNET RESOURCES

WorkersCompensation.com—This is a national website providing workers' compensation news and information for employers, employees, insurers, and medical providers. Visit the site at *www.workerscompensation.com.*

Occupational Safety & Health Administration— Access to OHSA regulations for compliance, newsroom, and much more can be found at the OSHA home page by visiting the website at *www.osha.gov.*

Human Resources Law Cases—This website provides information on workplace issues such as employment contracts and other issues. Visit the site at *www.hrlawindex.com.*

SHRM Policy Handbooks—This website contains sample policies, procedures, and handbooks collected by the Society for Human Resource Management. Visit the website at *www.shrm.org,* and click on Templates and Tools.

SUGGESTED READINGS

Donna Scimia, "A Common Sense Approach to Reducing Liability in Today's Workplace," *Employee Relations Law Journal,* Autumn 2007, 23–29.

Michael Burke, et al., "Relative Effectiveness of Worker Safety and Health Training Methods," *American Journal of Public Health,* 96, (2006) 315–325.

Lawrence P. Postol, "Drafting Noncompete Agreements for All 50 States," *Employee Relations Law Journal,* 33 (2007), 65–73.

Barry A. Friedman and Lisa J. Reed, "Workplace Privacy: Employee Relations and Legal Implications of Monitoring E-mail Use," *Employee Responsibilities Rights Journal,* 19 (2007), 75–83.

Union/Management Relations

HR—MEETING MANAGEMENT CHALLENGES

Even though union membership has been changing in the United States, labor relations must be considered an important part of HR. The future of employer-union relations may be evolving as political and work environments change. Key issues are:

- Why the state of unions in the United States has been changing
- How a number of legal requirements affect employer HR policies and practices
- When to resolve employee complaints and grievances

The changing nature of unions and unionization efforts will be interesting to observe during the next decade. Even though fewer workers have chosen to be union members than in the past, employers and HR professionals still need to have an understanding of the system of laws, regulations, court decisions, and administrative rulings related to unions. This is important because unions remain an alternative for employees in the event of poor HR management.

UNIONS: EMPLOYEE AND MANAGEMENT PERSPECTIVES

A **union** is a formal association of workers that promotes the interests of its members through collective action. The very existence of unions depends upon laws and legal action. An economic look at labor unions reveals "two faces." The "good face" emphasizes the fact that unions give members a "voice" to express dissatisfactions to management that likely would not be expressed otherwise. Some increases in productivity and an increase in earnings for members are typically associated with unionizing. The "bad face" emphasizes the negative effects that union wages have on allocation of resources, profitability, and productivity when the substantial compensation gains are considered.[1] But unions clearly have a place in the scheme of things, as they provide a balance to the unchallenged decision-making power of management where needed.

Exactly how economic and workforce changes affect employers and unions will be factors in the future of the labor/management relationship. Even though fewer workers have chosen to be union members in recent years than in the past, employers and HR professionals still need to understand the system of laws, regulations, court decisions, and administrative rulings related to. With this legal foundation, unions remain a strong alternative for employees in the event of poor HR management.

Unions did not seem to have a bright future in the 1930s when the National Labor Relations Act (NLRA) was passed, giving unions a legal right to exist. But they grew to represent about 36% of the workforce in the 1950s, only to see their strength in the private sector drop to less than 8% recently. However, in the public sector, union strength grew until recently.

In the United States, unions follow the goals of increasing compensation, improving working conditions, and influencing workplace rules. When a union is present, working conditions, pay, and work rules are determined through collective bargaining and designated in formal contracts. Part of understanding the current state of unionization in the United States is knowing why employees join unions and why employers resist unionization.

Why Employees Unionize

Whether a union targets a group of employees or the employees request union assistance, the union must win support from the employees to become their legal representative. Over the years employees have joined unions for two general reasons: (1) they are dissatisfied with how they are treated by their employers, and (2) they believe that unions can improve their work situations. If employees do not receive what they perceive as fair treatment from their employers, they may turn to unions for help in obtaining what they believe is equitable.[2] As Figure 10-1 shows, the major factors that can trigger unionization are issues of compensation, working conditions, management style, and employee treatment.

Why Employers Resist Unions

Employers usually would rather not have to deal with unions because doing so constrains what managers can and cannot do in a number of areas. Further, union workers receive higher wages and benefits than do nonunion workers. In turn, unions sometimes can be associated with higher productivity, although management must find labor-saving ways of doing work to offset the higher labor costs. Some employers pursue a strategy of good relations with unions, while others choose an aggressive, adversarial approach.

HR Responsibilities and Unionization.   To prevent unionization, as well as to work effectively with unions already representing employees, both HR professionals and operating managers must be attentive and responsive to employees. The pattern of dealing with unionization varies among organizations. In some organizations, operating management handles labor relations and HR has limited involvement. In other organizations, the HR unit takes primary responsibility for resisting unionization or dealing with unionized employees.

FIGURE 10-1 Factors Leading to Employee Unionization

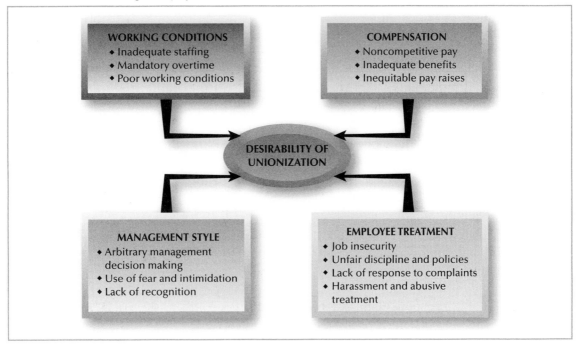

Unions Globally

Globalization, which causes economic competition among workers, companies, and nations around the world, is here to stay. The ability of a country to create jobs and attract investments can be affected by the favorability of union arrangements and labor laws. Changes in information technology have also decreased union bargaining power relative to management bargaining power. However, labor unions and labor movements have not been weakened in all cases, despite such pressures. Different laws and traditions have produced very different arrangements in different countries.

Laws that make it easier and cheaper to hire and fire employees may reduce unemployment. But in many countries, such laws cause discomfort because of the great inequality they create in the balance of power in the employer–employee relationship. As the world economy becomes more integrated, unions worldwide are facing changes from the pressures.

UNION MEMBERSHIP IN THE UNITED STATES

The statistics on union membership tell a disheartening story for organized labor in the United States during the past several decades. As shown in Figure 10-2, unions represented more than 30% of the workforce from 1945

FIGURE 10-2 Union Membership as a Percentage of the U.S. Civilian Workforce

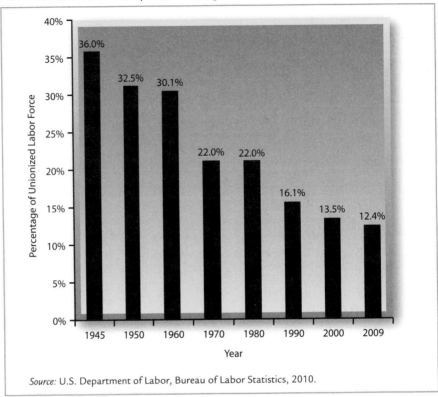

Source: U.S. Department of Labor, Bureau of Labor Statistics, 2010.

to 1960. But by 2009, unions in the United States represented only 12.4% of all civilian workers and 7.4% of the private-sector workforce. In fact, for the first time, the number of union workers employed by the government outnumbered union members in the private sector. Local, state, and federal union workers made up 51.5% (7.9 million) of all union members while private-sector union members dropped to 7.4 million.[3] The actual number of members has declined in most years even though more people are employed than previously.

But within those averages, some unions have prospered. In the past several years, certain unions have organized thousands of janitors, health care workers, cleaners, and other low-paid workers using publicity, pickets, boycotts, and strikes.

Reasons for U.S. Union Membership Decline

Several general trends have contributed to the decline of U.S. union membership, including deregulation, foreign competition, a larger number of people looking for jobs, and a general perception by firms that dealing with unions is expensive compared with nonunion alternatives. Management at many employers has taken a much more activist stance against unions than during the previous years of union growth, and economic downturns also have had negative impacts. Therefore, unions may no longer be seen as necessary for many workers, even though those workers enjoy the results of past union efforts to influence legislation that has been a benefit to them.

During the past decade, job growth in the United States has been the greatest in states located in the South, the Southwest, and the Rocky Mountains. Most of these states have little tradition of unions, more "employer-friendly" laws, and relatively small percentages of unionized workers. Much of the decline of union membership can be attributed to the shift in U.S. jobs from industries such as manufacturing, construction, and mining to service industries. There is a small percentage of union members in wholesale/retail industries and financial services, the sectors in which many new jobs have been added, whereas the number of industrial jobs continues to shrink.

One area that has led to union membership decline is the retirement of many union members in older manufacturing firms. Extremely high retiree pensions and health benefits costs have led some employers to face demands for cuts in benefits for both current and retired union employees. They also have led to employers reducing the number of current plants and workers, and unions attempting to maintain benefits costs and job security for remaining workers. In summary, private-sector union membership is primarily concentrated in the shrinking part of the economy, and unions are not making significant inroads into the fastest-growing segments in the U.S. economy.

Workforce Changes. Many of the workforce changes discussed in earlier chapters have contributed to the decrease in union representation of the labor force. The decline in many blue-collar jobs in manufacturing has been especially significant. Many white-collar workers see unions as resistant to change and not in touch with the concerns of the more educated workers in technical and professional jobs. In addition, many white-collar workers exhibit attitudes and preferences quite different from those held by blue-collar union members, and they tend to view unions as primarily blue-collar oriented.

Public-Sector Unionism

Unions have had significant success with public-sector employees. The government sector (federal, state, and local) is the most highly unionized part of the U.S. workforce, with more than 40% of government workers represented by unions. Local government workers have the highest unionization percentage of any group in the U.S. workforce. Although unions in the federal government hold the same basic philosophy as unions in the private sector, they do differ somewhat. Previous laws and executive orders have established methods of labor/management relations that consider the special circumstances present in the federal government.

Union Targets for Membership Growth

The continuing losses have led to disagreements among unions about how to fight the decline. Rather than remaining a part of the traditional AFL-CIO labor organization, seven unions split into a new group in 2005. Calling itself Change to Win (CtW), this association has a goal of taking a more aggressive approach to adding union members and affecting U.S. political legislation.

To attempt to counteract the overall decline in membership, unions are focusing on a number of industries and types of workers. One reason why Change to Win split off from the AFL-CIO was to target more effectively the addition of members in the retail, hospitality, home health care, and other service industries.

Historical Evolution of U.S. Unions

The union movement in the United States has existed in one form or another for more than two centuries. During this time, the nature of unions has evolved because of legal and political changes. The union movement in the United States began with early collective efforts by workers to address job concerns and counteract management power. As early as 1794, shoemakers organized a union, picketed, and conducted strikes. In those days, unions in the United States received very little support from the courts. In 1806, when the shoemakers' union struck for higher wages, a Philadelphia court found union members guilty of engaging in a "criminal conspiracy" to raise wages.

The *American Federation of Labor (AFL)* united a number of independent national unions in 1886. Its aims were to organize skilled craft workers and to emphasize economic issues and working conditions. As industrialization increased in the United States, many factories used semiskilled and unskilled workers. However, it was not until the *Congress of Industrial Organizations (CIO)* was founded in 1938 that a labor union organization focused on semiskilled and unskilled workers. Years later, the AFL and the CIO merged to become the AFL-CIO. That federation is the major organization coordinating union efforts in the United States today despite the split described previously.

Union Structure

Labor in the United States is represented by many different unions. Regardless of size and geographic scope, two basic types of unions have developed over time. In a **craft union,** members do one type of work, often using specialized skills and training. Examples are the International Association of Bridge, Structural, Ornamental and Reinforcing Iron Workers, and the American Federation of Television and Radio Artists. An **industrial union** includes many persons working in the same industry or company, regardless of jobs held. The United Food and Commercial Workers, the United Auto Workers, and the American Federation of State, County, and Municipal Employees are examples of industrial unions.

AFL-CIO Federation.   Labor organizations have developed complex organizational structures with multiple levels. The broadest level is the **federation,**

which is a group of autonomous unions. A federation allows individual unions to work together and present a more unified front to the public, legislators, and members. The most prominent federation in the United States is the AFL-CIO, which is a confederation of unions currently representing about 10 million workers.

Change to Win. The establishment of Change to Win (CtW) in 2005 meant that seven unions with about 6 million members left the AFL-CIO. The primary reason for the split was a division between different unions about how to stop the decline in union membership, as well as some internal organizational leadership and political issues.[4] Prominent unions in the CtW are the Teamsters, the Service Employees International Union, and the United Food and Commercial Workers.

National and International Unions. National and international unions are not governed by a federation even if they are affiliated with it. They collect dues and have their own boards, specialized publications, and separate constitutions and bylaws.

Like companies, unions find strength in size. In the past several years, about 40 mergers of unions have occurred, and a number of other unions have considered merging. For smaller unions, these mergers provide financial and union-organizing resources, and larger unions can add new members to cover managerial and administrative costs without spending funds to organize nonunion workers to become members.

Local Unions. Local unions typically have business agents and union stewards. A **business agent** is a full-time union official who operates the union office and assists union members. The agent runs the local headquarters, helps negotiate contracts with management, and becomes involved in attempts to unionize employees in other organizations. A **union steward** is an employee who is elected to serve as the first-line representative of unionized workers. Stewards address grievances with supervisors and generally represent employees at the worksite.

U.S. LABOR LAWS

The right to organize workers and engage in collective bargaining offers little value if workers cannot freely exercise it. Management has consistently developed practices to prevent unions from organizing employees. Over a period of many years, the federal government has taken action both to hamper unions and to protect them. Beginning in the late 1800s, federal and state legislation related to unionization was passed. The two most prominent acts are discussed next.

The Railway Labor Act (RLA) of 1926 represented a shift in government regulation of unions. The result of a joint effort between railroad management and unions to reduce transportation strikes, this act gave railroad employees "the right to organize and bargain collectively through representatives of their own choosing." In 1936, airlines and their employees were added to those covered by the RLA. In 1932, Congress passed the Norris-LaGuardia Act, which guaranteed workers some rights to organize and restricted the issuance of court injunctions in labor disputes.

The economic crises of the early 1930s and the continuing restrictions on workers' ability to organize into unions led to the passage of landmark labor legislation, the Wagner Act, in 1935. Later acts reflected other pressures and issues that required legislative attention. Three acts passed over a period of almost 25 years constitute the U.S. labor law foundation: (1) the Wagner Act, (2) the Taft-Hartley Act, and (3) the Landrum-Griffin Act. Each act was passed to focus on some facet of the relations between unions and management. Figure 10-3 indicates the primary focus of each act. Two other pieces of legislation, the Civil Service Reform Act and the Postal Reorganization Act, have affected union/management relations in the federal government.

Wagner Act (National Labor Relations Act)

The National Labor Relations Act, more commonly referred to as the Wagner Act, was an outgrowth of the Great Depression. With employers having to close or cut back their operations, workers were left with little job security. Unions stepped in to provide a feeling of solidarity and strength for many workers. The Wagner Act declared, in effect, that the official policy of the U.S. government was to encourage collective bargaining. Specifically, it established the right of workers to organize unhampered by management interference through unfair labor practices.

Unfair Labor Practices.   To protect union rights, the Wagner Act prohibited employers from using unfair labor practices. Five of those practices were identified as follows:

- Interfering with, restraining, or coercing employees in the exercise of their right to organize or to bargain collectively

FIGURE 10-3 Major National Labor Laws

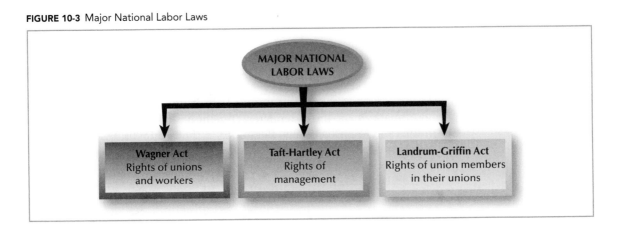

- Dominating or interfering with the formation or administration of any labor organization
- Encouraging or discouraging membership in any labor organization by discriminating with regard to hiring, tenure, or conditions of employment
- Discharging or otherwise discriminating against an employee because the employee filed charges or gave testimony under the act
- Refusing to bargain collectively with representatives of the employees

National Labor Relations Board. The Wagner Act established the National Labor Relations Board as an independent entity to enforce the provisions of the act. The NLRB administers all provisions of the Wagner Act and of subsequent labor relations acts. The primary functions of the NLRB include conducting unionization elections, investigating complaints by employers or unions through its fact-finding process, issuing opinions on its findings, and prosecuting violations in court. The five members of the NLRB are appointed by the President of the United States and confirmed by the U.S. Senate.

Taft-Hartley Act (Labor Management Relations Act)

The passage in 1947 of the Labor Management Relations Act, better known as the Taft-Hartley Act, was accomplished as a means to offset the pro-union Wagner Act by limiting union abuses. It was considered to be pro-management and became the second of the major labor laws.

The new law amended or qualified in some respect all the major provisions of the Wagner Act and established an entirely new code of conduct for unions. The Taft-Hartley Act allows the President of the United States to declare that a strike presents a national emergency. A national emergency strike is one that would impact an industry or a major part of it in such a way that the national economy would be significantly affected. The act allows the U.S. President to declare an 80-day "cooling off" period during which union and management continue negotiations. Only after that period can a strike occur if settlements have not been reached.

Right-to-Work Provision. One specific provision of the Taft-Hartley Act, section 14(b), deserves special explanation. This section allows states to pass laws that restrict compulsory union membership. Accordingly, several states have passed **right-to-work laws,** which prohibit requiring employees to join unions as a condition of obtaining or continuing employment. The laws were so named because they allow a person the right to work without having to join a union. The states that have enacted these laws are shown in Figure 10-4.

Landrum-Griffin Act (Labor Management Reporting and Disclosure Act)

The third of the major labor laws in the United States, the Landrum-Griffin Act, was passed in 1959. Because a union is supposed to be a democratic

FIGURE 10-4 Right-to-Work States

institution in which union members freely vote on and elect officers and approve labor contracts, the Landrum-Griffin Act was passed in part to ensure that the federal government protects the democratic rights of the members. Under the Landrum-Griffin Act, unions are required to establish bylaws, make financial reports, and provide union members with a bill of rights. The law appointed the U.S. Secretary of Labor to act as a watchdog of union conduct.

In a few instances, union officers have attempted to maintain their jobs by physically harassing or attacking individuals who have tried to oust them from office. In other cases, union officials have "milked" pension fund monies for their own use. Such instances are not typical of most unions, but illustrate the need for legislative oversight to protect individual union members.[5]

Civil Service Reform and Postal Reorganization Acts

Passed as part of the Civil Service Reform Act of 1978, the Federal Service Labor Management Relations statute made major changes in how the federal government deals with unions. The act also identified areas subject to bargaining and established the Federal Labor Relations Authority (FLRA) as an independent agency similar to the NLRB. The FLRA, a three-member body, was given the authority to oversee and administer union/management relations in the federal government and to investigate unfair practices in union organizing efforts.

In a somewhat related area, the Postal Reorganization Act of 1970 established the U.S. Postal Service as an independent entity. Part of the 1970 act prohibited postal workers from striking and established a dispute resolution process for them to follow.

Proposed Legislation

Other laws have been proposed, but at this writing none of them has been passed. One such law would bar companies from replacing workers who go on strike, which means that a union could in effect close a business down because strikers could not be replaced. Replacement workers or "scabs" have allowed companies to defeat union strikes in some cases in the past.

Another proposed law, the "Employee Free Choice Act," would allow unions to sign up workers and become recognized without an election. This approach goes against the U.S. tradition in which negotiated contracts must be agreed to by both parties. The proposed legislation has spawned considerable concern among businesses. Several large employers have resorted to direct actions in opposition to the EFCA.[6]

THE UNIONIZATON PROCESS

The typical union organizing process may begin in one of two primary ways: (1) a union targeting an industry or a company, or (2) employees requesting union representation. In the first case, the local or national union identifies a firm or an industry in which it believes unionization can succeed. The logic for targeting is that if the union succeeds in one firm or a portion of the industry, then many other workers in the industry will be more willing to consider unionizing. In the second case, the impetus for union organizing occurs when individual workers at an employer contact a union and express a desire to unionize. The employees themselves—or the union—may then begin to campaign to win support among the other employees.

Organizing Campaign

Like other entities seeking members, a union usually mounts an organized campaign to persuade individuals to join. As would be expected, employers respond to unionization efforts by taking various types of opposing actions.

Employers' Union Prevention Efforts. Management representatives may use various tactics to defeat a unionization effort. Such tactics often begin when union publicity appears or during the distribution of authorization cards. Some employers such as Con Agra, Coca-Cola, and Wal-Mart hire consultants who specialize in combating unionization efforts. Using these "union busters," as they are called by unions, appears to enhance employers' chances of winning the representation election. Union prevention efforts that may be conducted by consultants or done by management and outside labor attorneys include:[7]

- Holding mandatory employee meetings
- Distributing antiunion leaflets at work and mailing antiunion letters to employees' homes
- Providing and using antiunion videos, e-mails, and other electronic communications

Employers may make strategic decisions and take aggressive steps to remain nonunion. Such a choice is perfectly rational, but may require some specific HR policies and philosophies.

Unions' Organizing Efforts.   The organizing and negotiating successes of unions are tied to the economy and economic trends. The persuasion efforts by unions can take many forms, including personally contacting employees outside work, mailing materials to employees' homes, inviting employees to attend special meetings away from the company, and publicizing the advantages of union membership. Brochures and leaflets can be given to employees as they leave work, mailed to their homes, or even attached to their vehicles, as long as the union complies with the rules established by laws and the NLRB. The purpose of all this publicity is to encourage employees to sign authorization cards. To encourage individuals to become involved in unionization efforts, unions have adopted electronic means, such as establishing websites where interested workers can read about benefits of unionization. However, an employer can prohibit workers from using its e-mail system for union business.[8]

Authorization Cards

A **union authorization card** is signed by employees to designate a union as their collective bargaining agent. At least 30% of the employees in the targeted group must sign authorization cards before an election can be called.

Union advocates have lobbied for changing laws so that elections are not needed if more than 50% of the eligible employees sign authorization cards. As mentioned earlier, the proposed Employee Free Choice Act would eliminate the secret ballot for electing union representation and make it so that the union would automatically represent all workers if more than 50% of the employees signed authorization cards.

However, the fact that an employee signs an authorization card does not necessarily mean that the employee is in favor of a union. It means only that the employee is willing to put the union question to a vote. Employees who do not want a union might sign authorization cards because they want management to know they are disgruntled or because they want to avoid upsetting coworkers who are advocating unionization.

Representation Election

An election to determine if a union will represent the employees is supervised by the NLRB for private-sector organizations and by other legal bodies for public-sector organizations. If two unions are attempting to represent employees, the employees will have three choices: union A, union B, and no union.

Bargaining Unit. Before any election, the appropriate bargaining unit must be determined. A **bargaining unit** is composed of all employees eligible to select a single union to represent and bargain collectively for them. If management and the union do not agree on who is and who is not included in the unit, the regional office of the NLRB must make the determination. Employees who constitute a bargaining unit have mutual interests in the following areas:

- Wages, hours, and working conditions
- Traditional industry groupings for bargaining purposes
- Physical location and amount of interaction and working relationships between employee groups
- Supervision by similar levels of management

Supervisors and Union Ineligibility. Provisions of the National Labor Relations Act exclude supervisors from voting for or joining unions. As a result, supervisors cannot be included in bargaining units for unionization purposes, except in industries covered by the Railway Labor Act. A major case decided by the U.S. Supreme Court found that charge nurses with RN degrees were supervisors because they exercised independent judgment. This case and others have provided employers and unions with some guidance about who should be considered supervisors and thus excluded from bargaining units.[9]

Election Unfair Labor Practices. Employers and unions engage in a number of activities before an election. Both the Wagner Act and the Taft-Hartley Act place restrictions on these activities. Once unionizing efforts begin, all activities must conform to the requirements established by applicable labor laws. Both management and the union must adhere to those requirements, or the results of the effort can be appealed to the NLRB and overturned.

Election Process. If an election is held, the union needs to receive only a majority of the votes. For example, if a group of 200 employees is the identified bargaining unit, and only 50 people vote, only 26 (50% of those voting plus 1) need to vote yes for the union to be named as the representative of all 200 employees. Typically, the smaller the number of employees in the bargaining unit, the higher the likelihood that the union will win.

If either side believes that the other side used unfair labor practices, the election results can be appealed to the NLRB. If the NLRB finds evidence of unfair practices, it can order a new election. If no unfair practices were used and the union obtains a majority in the election, the union then petitions the NLRB for certification.

Certification and Decertification

Official certification of a union as the legal representative for designated private-sector employees is given by the NLRB, or for public-sector employees by an equivalent body. Once certified, the union attempts to negotiate a contract with the employer. The employer *must* bargain; refusing to bargain with a certified union constitutes an unfair labor practice.

When employees no longer wish to be represented by the union, they can use **decertification,** which is a process whereby a union is removed as the representative of a group of employees. Employees attempting to oust a union must obtain decertification authorization cards signed by at least 30% of the employees in the bargaining unit before an election may be called. If a majority of those voting in the election want to remove the union, the decertification effort succeeds.

Contract Negotiation (Collective Bargaining)

Collective bargaining, the last step in unionization, is the process whereby representatives of management and workers negotiate over wages, hours, and other terms and conditions of employment. This give-and-take process between representatives of the two organizations attempts to establish conditions beneficial to both. It is also a relationship based on relative power.

COLLECTIVE BARGAINING ISSUES

A number of issues can be addressed during collective bargaining. Although not often listed as such in the contract, management rights and union security are two important issues subject to collective bargaining. These leave issues common to collective bargaining.

Management Rights

Virtually all labor contracts include **management rights,** which are rights reserved so that the employer can manage, direct, and control its business. By including such a provision, management attempts to preserve its unilateral right to make changes in areas not identified in a labor contract. A typical provision might read as follows:

> *The employer retains all rights to manage, direct, and control its business in all particulars, except as such rights are expressly and specifically modified by the terms of this or any subsequent agreement.*

Union Security

A major concern of union representatives when bargaining is the negotiation of **union security provisions,** which are contract clauses to help the union obtain and retain members. One type of union security clause in labor contracts is the *no-layoff policy*, or *job security guarantee*. Such a provision is especially important to many union workers because of all the mergers, downsizings, and job reductions taking place in many industrial, textile, and manufacturing firms. However, for these very reasons, management is often unwilling to consider this type of provision.

Union Dues Issues.   A common union security provision is the *dues checkoff* clause, which provides for the automatic deduction of union dues from the payroll checks of union members. The dues checkoff provision makes it much easier for the union to collect its funds, and without it, the union must collect dues by billing each member separately.

However, federal court cases have been filed that restrict unions from using such checkoff clauses for contributions to political and congressional candidates. A U.S. Supreme Court case supported the constitutionality of state laws that require labor unions to get written consent before using nonmember fees for political purposes. The Court noted that Washington, like many other states, allows public-sector unions to levy fees on nonmember employees, as well as "agency shop" agreements. But it held that under such arrangements, the union must obtain express authorization from the nonmembers to use their agency fees for election-related purposes.[10]

Types of Required Union Membership.   Another form of union security provision is *requiring union membership* of all employees, subject to state right-to-work laws. Closed shops require union membership to get a job, and are illegal except in limited situations within the construction industry. But other types of arrangements can be developed.

Classification of Bargaining Issues

The NLRB has defined collective bargaining issues in three ways. The categories it has used are mandatory, permissive, and illegal.

Issues identified specifically by labor laws or court decisions as subject to bargaining are **mandatory issues.** If either party demands that issues in this category be subject to bargaining, then that must occur. Generally, mandatory issues relate to wages, benefits, nature of jobs, and other work-related subjects. Mandatory subjects for bargaining include the following:

- Discharge of employees
- Grievances
- Work schedules
- Union security and dues checkoff
- Retirement and pension coverage
- Vacations and time off
- Rest and lunch break rules
- Safety rules
- Profit-sharing plans
- Required physical exam

Issues that are not mandatory and that relate to certain jobs are **permissive issues.** For example, the following issues can be bargained over if both parties agree: benefits for retired employees, product prices for employees, and performance bonds.

A final category, **illegal issues,** includes those issues that would require either party to take illegal action. Examples would be giving preference to union members when hiring employees or demanding a closed-shop provision in the contract. If one side wants to bargain over an illegal issue, the other side can refuse.

COLLECTIVE BARGAINING PROCESS

The collective bargaining process involved in negotiating a contract consists of a number of stages: preparation and initial demands, negotiations, settlement or impasse, and strikes and lockouts. Throughout the process, management and labor deal with the specifics of their relationship.

Preparation and Initial Demands

Both labor and management representatives spend considerable time preparing for negotiations. Employer and industry data concerning wages, benefits, working conditions, management and union rights, productivity, and absenteeism are gathered. If the organization argues that it cannot afford to pay what the union is asking, the employer's financial situation and accompanying data become relevant to the process. However, the union must request such information before the employer is obligated to provide it. Typical bargaining includes initial proposals of expectations by both sides. The amount of rancor or calmness exhibited may set the tone for future negotiations between the parties.

Core Bargaining Issues. The primary focus of bargaining for both union and management is on the core areas of wages, benefits, and working hours and conditions. The importance of this emphasis is seen in several ways.

Union wages and benefits generally are higher in unionized firms than in nonunionized firms. In a recent year, median earnings for union members were $908/week compared with the nonunion amount of $710/week. The additional $198/week represents almost $10,000/year more for each union members' wages over nonunion wages. This labor cost difference is one reason management resists unions.

Continuing Negotiations

After taking initial positions, each side attempts to determine what the other side values highly so that the best bargain can be struck. Provisions in federal law require that both employers and union bargaining representatives negotiate in good faith. In good-faith negotiations, the parties agree to send negotiators who can bargain and make decisions, rather than people who do not have the authority to commit either group to a decision. To be more effective, meetings between the parties should be conducted professionally and address issues, rather than being confrontational. Refusing to bargain, scheduling meetings at absurdly inconvenient hours, and using other conflicting tactics may lead to employers or unions filing complaints with the NLRB.

Settlement and Contract Agreement

After reaching an initial agreement, the bargaining parties usually return to their respective constituencies to determine if the informal agreement is acceptable. A particularly crucial stage is **ratification** of the labor agreement, which occurs when union members vote to accept the terms of a negotiated labor agreement. Before ratification, the union negotiating team explains the agreement to the union members and presents it for a vote. If the members approve the agreement, it is then formalized into a contract. Figure 10-5 lists the typical items in a labor agreement.

Bargaining Impasse

Regardless of the structure of the bargaining process, labor and management do not always reach agreement on the issues. If they reach an impasse, then the disputes can be taken to conciliation, mediation, or arbitration.

Conciliation and Mediation. When an impasse occurs, an outside party such as the Federal Mediation and Conciliation Service may help the two deadlocked parties to continue negotiations and arrive at a solution. In **conciliation,** the third party assists union and management negotiators to reach a voluntary settlement, but makes no proposals for solutions. In **mediation,** the third party may suggest ideas for solutions to help the negotiators reach a settlement.

FIGURE 10-5 Typical Items in a Labor Agreement

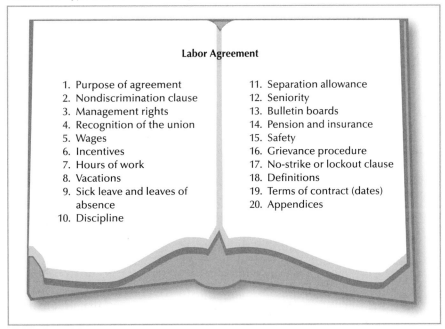

Labor Agreement

1. Purpose of agreement
2. Nondiscrimination clause
3. Management rights
4. Recognition of the union
5. Wages
6. Incentives
7. Hours of work
8. Vacations
9. Sick leave and leaves of absence
10. Discipline
11. Separation allowance
12. Seniority
13. Bulletin boards
14. Pension and insurance
15. Safety
16. Grievance procedure
17. No-strike or lockout clause
18. Definitions
19. Terms of contract (dates)
20. Appendices

In conciliation and mediation, the third party does not attempt to impose a solution. Sometimes fact finding helps to clarify the issues of disagreement as an intermediate step between mediation and arbitration.

Arbitration. In **arbitration,** a neutral third party makes a decision. Arbitration can be conducted by an individual or a panel of individuals. "Interest" arbitration attempts to solve bargaining impasses, primarily in the public sector. This type of arbitration is not frequently used in the private sector because companies generally do not want an outside party making decisions about their rights, wages, benefits, and other issues. However, grievance or "rights" arbitration is used extensively in the private sector. Fortunately, in many situations, agreements are reached through negotiations without the need for arbitration. When disagreements continue, strikes or lockouts may occur.

Strikes and Lockouts

If a deadlock cannot be resolved, an employer may revert to a lockout—or a union may revert to a strike. During a **strike,** union members refuse to work in order to put pressure on an employer. Often, the striking union members picket or demonstrate against the employer outside the place of business by carrying placards and signs.

In a **lockout,** management shuts down company operations to prevent union members from working. This action may avert possible damage or sabotage to company facilities or injury to employees who continue to work. It also gives management leverage in negotiations. As a result of the decline in union power, work stoppages due to strikes and lockouts are relatively rare. In a recent year, a limited number of strikes or lockouts occurred nationally, and they were all settled quickly.

UNION/MANAGEMENT COOPERATION

The adversarial relationship that naturally exists between unions and management may lead to strikes and lockouts. However, as noted, such conflicts currently are relatively rare. Even more encouraging is the recognition on the part of some union leaders and employer representatives that cooperation between management and labor unions offers a useful route if organizations are to compete effectively in a global economy.

During the past decade, numerous firms have engaged in organizational and workplace restructuring in response to competitive pressures in their industries. Restructurings have had significant effects, such as lost jobs, changed work rules, and altered job responsibilities. When restructurings occur, unions can take different approaches, ranging from resistance to cooperation.

Employee Involvement Programs

It seems somewhat illogical to suggest that union/management cooperation or involving employees in making suggestions and decisions could be bad, and yet some decisions by the NLRB appear to have done just that. Some historical perspective is required to understand the issues that surrounded the decisions.

In the 1930s, when the Wagner Act was written, certain employers would form sham "company unions," coercing workers into joining them to keep legitimate unions from organizing the employees. As a result, the Wagner Act contained prohibitions against employer-dominated labor organizations. These prohibitions were enforced, and company unions disappeared. But the use of employee involvement programs in organizations today has raised new concerns along these lines.

Because of the Wagner Act, some employee involvement programs may be illegal, according to an NLRB decision dealing with Electromation, an Elkhart, Indiana, firm. Electromation used teams of employees to solicit other employees' views about such issues as wages and working conditions. The NLRB labeled these teams "labor organizations," in line with requirements of the Wagner Act. It further found that the teams were "dominated" by management, which had formed them, set their goals, and decided how they would operate. The results of this and other decisions have forced many employers to rethink and restructure their employee involvement efforts.

Federal court decisions have upheld the NLRB position in some cases and reversed it in others. One key to decisions allowing employee involvement committees and programs seems to be that these entities should not deal directly with traditional collective bargaining issues such as wages, hours, and working conditions. Other keys are that the committees should be composed primarily of workers and that they have broad authority to make operational suggestions and decisions.

Unions and Employee Ownership

Unions in some situations have encouraged workers to become partial or complete owners of the companies that employ them. These efforts were spurred by concerns that firms were preparing to shut down, merge, or be bought out. Such results were likely to cut the number of union jobs and workers.

Unions have been active in helping members put together employee stock ownership plans to purchase all or part of some firms.[11] Such programs have been successful in some situations but have caused problems in others. Some in the labor movement fear that such programs may undermine union support by creating a closer identification with the concerns and goals of employers, instead of "union solidarity."

GRIEVANCE MANAGEMENT

Unions know that employee dissatisfaction is a potential source of trouble for employers, whether it is expressed or not. Hidden dissatisfaction grows and creates reactions that may be completely out of proportion to the original concerns. Therefore, it is important that dissatisfaction be given an outlet. A **complaint,** which is merely an indication of employee dissatisfaction, is one outlet. If an employee is represented by a union, and the employee says, "I should have received the job transfer because I have more seniority, which is what the union contract states," and she submits it in writing, then that complaint becomes a grievance. A **grievance** is a complaint formally stated in writing.

Management should be concerned with both complaints and grievances, because both indicate potential problems within the workforce. Without a grievance procedure, management may be unable to respond to employee concerns because managers are unaware of them. Therefore, a formal grievance procedure provides a valuable communication tool for organizations, whether a union is present or not.

The typical division of responsibilities between the HR unit and operating managers for handling grievances is shown in Figure 10-6. These responsibilities vary considerably from one organization to another, even between unionized firms.

Grievance Procedures

Grievance procedures are formal channels of communication designed to resolve grievances as soon as possible after problems arise. First-line supervisors are usually closest to a problem. However, these supervisors are concerned with many other matters besides one employee's grievance, and may even be the subject of an employee's grievance. To receive the appropriate attention, grievances go through a specific process for resolution.[12]

Union Representation in Grievance Procedures.   A unionized employee generally has a right to union representation if the employee is being questioned by management and if discipline may result. If these so-called *Weingarten rights* (named after the court case that established them) are violated and the employee is dismissed, the employee usually will be reinstated with back pay. Employers are not required to allow nonunion workers to have coworkers present in grievance procedure meetings. However, employers may voluntarily allow such presence.

FIGURE 10-6 Typical Division of HR Responsibilities: Grievance Management

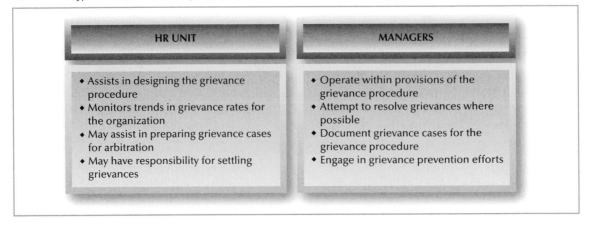

HR UNIT	MANAGERS
• Assists in designing the grievance procedure • Monitors trends in grievance rates for the organization • May assist in preparing grievance cases for arbitration • May have responsibility for settling grievances	• Operate within provisions of the grievance procedure • Attempt to resolve grievances where possible • Document grievance cases for the grievance procedure • Engage in grievance prevention efforts

Steps in a Grievance Procedure

Grievance procedures can vary in the steps included. A typical grievance procedure consists of the following steps:

1. The employee discusses the grievance with the union steward (the representative of the union on the job) and the supervisor.

2. The union steward discusses the grievance with the supervisor's manager and/or the HR manager.

3. A committee of union officers discusses the grievance with appropriate company managers.

4. The representative of the national union discusses the grievance with designated company executives or the corporate industrial relations officer.

5. If the grievance is not solved at this stage, it goes to arbitration. An impartial third party may ultimately dispose of the grievance.

Grievance arbitration is a means by which a third party settles disputes arising from different interpretations of a labor contract. This process should not be confused with contract or issues arbitration, discussed earlier, in which arbitration is used to determine how a contract will be written. The U.S. Supreme Court has ruled that grievance arbitration decisions issued under labor contract provisions are enforceable and generally may not go to court to be changed. Grievance arbitration includes more than 50 topic areas, with discipline and discharge, safety and health, and security issues being most prevalent.

NOTES

1. Barry Hirsh, "Sluggish Institutions in a Dynamic World: Can Unions and Industrial Competition Coexist?" *Journal of Economic Perspectives*, 22 (2008), 153–176.

2. Steven Abraham, et al., "The Relationship Among Union Membership, Facets of Satisfaction and Intent to Leave," *Employee Responsibilities and Rights Journal*, 20 (2008), 1–11.

3. "More Union Workers Now in Government," *The Denver Post*, January 23, 2010, 6B.

4. Gary Chaison, "The AFL-CIO Split: Does It Really Matter?" *Journal of Labor Research*, Spring 2007, 301–311.

5. Bill Leonard, "Court Upholds Union Reporting Requirements," *HR Magazine*, July 2008, 24.

6. Ann Zimmerman and Kris Maher, "Wal-Mart Warns of Democrat Win," *The Wall Street Journal*, August 1, 2008, W1.

7. For example, Jackson Lewis, a law firm with 29 offices nationwide, represents management exclusively; see *www.jacksonlewis.com*.

8. Rita Zeidner, "NLRB: Unions Not Guaranteed Use of Company E-Mail," *HR News*, December 28, 2007, *www.shrm.org*, 1.

9. Leigh Tyson and W. Jonathan Martin, "NLRB Clarifies When an Employee Is a 'Supervisor,'" *Ceridian Abstracts*, *www.hrcompliance.ceridian.com*.

10. Joanne Deschenaux, "High Court Upholds Limits on Use of Non Member's Union Fees," *Workplace Law Library—Labor Relations*, June 15, 2007.

11. Jacquelyn Yates, "Unions and Employee Ownership: A Road to Economic Recovery," *Industrial Relations*, 45 (2006), 709.

12. Annette Cox, et al., "Applying Union Mobilization Theory to Explain Gendered Collective Grievances," *Journal of Industrial Relations*, 49, (2007), 717–738.

INTERNET RESOURCES

Cornell Global Labor Institute—This website provides information and projects on union efforts to strengthen the response to globalization challenges. Visit the site at *www.ilr .cornell.edu/ globallaborinstitute.*

AFL-CIO—The AFL-CIO home page provides union movement information. Visit the website at *www.aflcio.org.*

National Labor Relations Board—For information on workplace rights and other issues, visit the NLRB website at *www.nlrb.gov.*

LaborNet—This website describes unions, news, legislation, and upcoming union events. Visit the site at *www.labornet.org.*

Federal Mediation & Conciliation Service—This service organization provides services and resources to promote stable labor and management relationships. Visit the website at *www.fmcs.gov.*

SUGGESTED READINGS

John Schmitt, et al., "Unions and Upward Mobility for Low Wage Workers," *Journal of Labor and Society,* 11 (2008), 337–348.

Lyle Scruggs and Peter Lange, "Where Have All the Members Gone? Globalization, Institutions and Union Density," *Journal of Politics,* 64 (2008), 126–153.

Lawrence Nurse and Dwayne Devonish, "Grievance Management and Its Links to Workplace Justice," *Employee Relations,* 29, (2007), 89–109.

Matthew Frankiewicz, "How to Win Your Arbitration Case Before It Even Starts," *Labor Law Journal,* 2009, 115–120.

Appendix A

Internet Resources

HR-RELATED INTERNET LINKS

Academy of Management
www.aom.pace.edu

American Arbitration Association
www.adr.org

American Federation of Labor/Congress of Industrial Organizations (AFL-CIO)
www.aflcio.org

American Institute for Managing Diversity
www.aimd.org

American Payroll Association
www.americanpayroll.org

American Psychological Association
www.apa.org

American Society for Industrial Security
www.asisonline.org

American Society for Training and Development
www.astd.org

Australian Human Resource Institute
www.ahri.com.au

Chartered Institute of Personnel and Development (UK)
www.cipd.co.uk

CPR International Institute for Conflict Prevention & Resolution
www.cpradr.org

Employee Benefit Research Institute
www.ebri.org

Foundation for Enterprise Development
www.fed.org

Hong Kong Institute of Human Resource Management
www.hkihrm.org

Human Resource Certification Institute
www.hrci.org

International Association for Human Resource Information Management
www.ihrim.org

International Association of Industrial Accident Boards and Commissions
www.iaiabc.org

International Foundation of Employee Benefit Plans (IFEBP)
www.ifebp.org

International Institute of Human Resource Management
www.iihrm.org

International Personnel Assessment Council
www.ipacweb.org

International Personnel Management Association
www.ipma-hr.org

Labor and Employment Relations Association
www.lera.uiuc.edu

National Center for Employee Ownership
www.nceo.org

National Health Information Resource Center
www.nhirc.org

Social Media Policies
www.socialmediagovernance.com

Society for Human Resource Management
www.shrm.org

Union Resource Network
www.unions.org

World at Work
www.worldatwork.org

SELECTED GOVERNMENT INTERNET LINKS

Bureau of Labor Statistics
www.stats.bls.gov
Census Bureau
www.census.gov
Department of Labor
www.dol.gov
Employment and Training Administration
www.doleta.gov
Equal Employment Opportunity Commission
www.eeoc.gov
FedStats
www.fedstats.gov
National Institute of Environmental Health
Sciences
www.niehs.nih.gov
National Institute for Occupational Safety and
Health (NIOSH)
www.cdc.gov/niosh

National Labor Relations Board
www.nlrb.gov
Occupational Safety and Health Administration
www.osha.gov
Office of Personnel Management
www.opm.gov
Pension and Welfare Benefits Administration
www.dol.gov/ebsa
Pension Benefit Guaranty Corporation
www.pbgc.gov
Small Business Administration
www.sba.gov
Social Security Administration
www.ssa.gov
U.S. House of Representatives
www.house.gov
U.S. Senate
www.senate.gov

Appendix B

Major Federal Equal Employment Opportunity Laws and Regulations

Act	Year	Key Provisions
Broad-Based Discrimination		
Title VII, Civil Rights Act of 1964	1964	Prohibits discrimination in employment on basis of race, color, religion, sex, or national origin
Executive Orders 11246 and 11375	1965 1967	Require federal contractors and subcontractors to eliminate employment discrimination and prior discrimination through affirmative action
Executive Order 11478	1969	Prohibits discrimination in the U.S. Postal Service and in the various government agencies on the basis of race, color, religion, sex, national origin, handicap, or age
Vietnam Era Veterans' Readjustment Assistance Act	1974	Prohibits discriminations against Vietnam-era veterans by federal contractors and the U.S. government and requires affirmative action
Civil Rights Act of 1991	1991	Overturns several past Supreme Court decisions and changes damage claims provisions
Congressional Accountability Act	1995	Extends EEO and Civil Rights Act provisions to U.S. congressional staff
Race/National Origin Discrimination		
Immigration Reform and Control Act	1986 1990 1996	Establishes penalties for employers who knowingly hire illegal aliens; prohibits employment discrimination on the basis of national origin or citizenship
Gender/Sex Discrimination		
Equal Pay Act	1963	Requires equal pay for men and women performing substantially the same work
Pregnancy Discrimination Act	1978	Prohibits discrimination against women affected by pregnancy, childbirth, or related medical conditions; requires that they be treated as all other employees for employment-related purposes, including benefits

(Continued)

Act	Year	Key Provisions
Age Discrimination		
Age Discrimination in Employment Act (as amended in 1978 and 1986)	1967	Prohibits discrimination against persons over age 40 and restricts mandatory retirement requirements, except where age is a bona fide occupational qualification
Older Workers Benefit Protection Act of 1990	1990	Prohibits age-based discrimination in early retirement and other benefits plans
Disability Discrimination		
Vocational Rehabilitation Act and Rehabilitation Act of 1974	1973 1974	Prohibit employers with federal contracts over $2,500 from discriminating against individuals with disabilities
Americans with Disabilities Act	1990	Requires employer accommodations for individuals with disabilities

Sample Application Form

Application for Employment
An Equal Opportunity Employer*

Today's Date _____

PERSONAL INFORMATION

Please Print or Type

Name	(Last)	(First)	(Full middle name)	Social Security number

Current address	City	State	Zip code	Phone number ( )

What position are you applying for?	Date available for employment?	E-mail address

Are you willing to relocate? ☐ Yes ☐ No	Are you willing to travel if required? ☐ Yes ☐ No	Any restrictions on hours, weekends, or overtime? If yes, explain.

Have you ever been employed by this Company or any of its subsidiaries before? ☐ Yes ☐ No	Indicate location and dates

Can you, after employment, submit verification of your legal right to work in the United States? ☐ Yes ☐ No	Have you ever been convicted of a felony? ☐ Yes ☐ No	*Convictions will not automatically disqualify job candidates. The seriousness of the crime and the date of conviction will be considered.*

PERFORMANCE OF JOB FUNCTIONS

Are you able to perform all the functions of the job for which you are applying, with or without accommodation?

☐ Yes, without accommodation   ☐ Yes, with accommodation   ☐ No

If you indicated you can perform all the functions with an accommodation, please explain how you would perform the tasks and with what accommodation.

EDUCATION

School level	School name and address	No. of years attended	Did you graduate?	Course of study
High school				
Vo-tech, business, or trade school				
College				
Graduate school				

PERSONAL DRIVING RECORD

This section is to be completed ONLY if the operation of a motor vehicle will be required in the course of the applicant's employment.

How long have you been a licensed driver?	Driver's license number	Expiration date	Issuing State

List any other state(s) in which you have had a driver's license(s) in the past:

Within the past five years, have you had a vehicle accident? ☐ Yes ☐ No	Been convicted of reckless or drunken driving? ☐ Yes ☐ No If yes, give dates:	Been cited for moving violations? If yes, give dates: ☐ Yes ☐ No

Has your driver's license ever been revoked or suspended? If yes, explain: ☐ Yes ☐ No	Is your driver's license restricted? If yes, explain: ☐ Yes ☐ No

*We are an Equal Opportunity Employer. We do not discriminate on the basis of race, religion, color, gender, age, national origin, or disability.

Guidelines to Lawful and Unlawful Preemployment Inquiries

Subject of Inquiry	It May Not Be Discriminatory to Inquire about . . .	It May Be Discriminatory to Inquire about . . .
1. **Name**	a. Whether applicant has ever worked under a different name	a. The original name of applicant whose name has been legally changed b. The ethnic association of applicant's name
2. **Age**	a. If applicant is over the age of 18 b. If applicant is under the age of 18 or 21 if that information is job related (e.g., for selling liquor in a retail store)	a. Date of birth b. Date of high school graduation
3. **Residence**	a. Applicant's place of residence b. Alternative contact information	a. Previous addresses b. Birthplace of applicant or applicant's parents c. Length lived at current and previous addresses
4. **Race or Color**		a. Applicant's race or color of applicant's skin
5. **National Origin and Ancestry**		a. Applicant's lineage, ancestry, national origin, parentage, or nationality b. Nationality of applicant's parents or spouse
6. **Sex and Family Composition**		a. Sex of applicant b. Marital status of applicant c. Dependents of applicants or child-care arrangements d. Whom to contact in case of emergency
7. **Creed or Religion**		a. Applicant's religious affiliation b. Applicant's church, parish, mosque, or synagogue c. Holidays observed by applicant
8. **Citizenship**	a. Whether the applicant is a U.S. citizen or has a current permit/visa to work in the United States	a. Whether applicant is a citizen of a country other than the United States b. Date of citizenship

(*Continued*)

Subject of Inquiry	It May Not Be Discriminatory to Inquire about . . .	It May Be Discriminatory to Inquire about . . .
9. **Language**	a. Language applicant speaks and/or writes fluently, if job related	a. Applicant's native tongue b. Language used at home
10. **References**	a. Names of persons willing to provide professional and/or character references for applicant b. Previous work contacts	a. Name of applicant's religious leader b. Political affiliation and contacts
11. **Relatives**	a. Names of relatives already employed by the employer	a. Name and/or address of any relative of applicant b. Whom to contact in case of emergency
12. **Organizations**	a. Applicant's membership in any professional, service, or trade organization	a. All clubs or social organizations to which applicant belongs
13. **Arrest Record and Convictions**	a. Convictions, if related to job performance (disclaimer should accompany)	a. Number and kinds of arrests b. Convictions, unless related to job requirements and performance
14. **Photographs**		a. Photographs with application, with résumé, or before hiring
15. **Height and Weight**		a. Any inquiry into height and weight of applicant, except where a BFOQ exists
16. **Physical Limitations**	a. Whether applicant has the ability to perform job-related functions with or without accommodation	a. The nature or severity of an illness or physical condition b. Whether applicant has ever filed a workers' compensation claim c. Any recent or past operations, treatments, or surgeries and dates
17. **Education**	a. Training applicant has received, if related to the job b. Highest level of education applicant has attained, if validated that having certain educational background (e.g., high school diploma or college degree) is needed to perform the specific job	a. Date of high school graduation
18. **Military**	a. Branch of the military applicant served in and ranks attained b. Type of education or training received in military	a. Military discharge details b. Military service records
19. **Financial Status**		a. Applicant's debts or assets b. Garnishments

Appendix E

Questions Commonly Asked in Selection Interviews

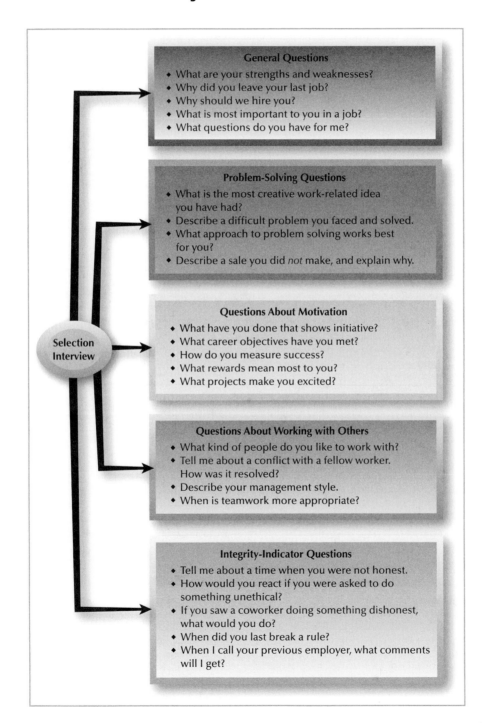

Selection Interview

General Questions
- What are your strengths and weaknesses?
- Why did you leave your last job?
- Why should we hire you?
- What is most important to you in a job?
- What questions do you have for me?

Problem-Solving Questions
- What is the most creative work-related idea you have had?
- Describe a difficult problem you faced and solved.
- What approach to problem solving works best for you?
- Describe a sale you did *not* make, and explain why.

Questions About Motivation
- What have you done that shows initiative?
- What career objectives have you met?
- How do you measure success?
- What rewards mean most to you?
- What projects make you excited?

Questions About Working with Others
- What kind of people do you like to work with?
- Tell me about a conflict with a fellow worker. How was it resolved?
- Describe your management style.
- When is teamwork more appropriate?

Integrity-Indicator Questions
- Tell me about a time when you were not honest.
- How would you react if you were asked to do something unethical?
- If you saw a coworker doing something dishonest, what would you do?
- When did you last break a rule?
- When I call your previous employer, what comments will I get?

Glossary

A

absenteeism Any failure by an employee to report for work as scheduled or to stay at work when scheduled.

active practice Performance of job-related tasks and duties by trainees during training.

adverse selection Situation in which *only* higher-risk employees select and use certain benefits.

affirmative action The hiring of groups of people based on their race, age, gender, or national origin.

affirmative action plan (AAP) A document reporting on the composition of an employer's workforce, required for federal contractors.

alternate work arrangements Nontraditional schedules that provide flexibility to employees.

arbitration Process that uses a neutral third party to make a decision.

assessment centers Collections of instruments and exercises designed to diagnose individuals' development needs.

attitude survey A survey that focuses on employees' feelings and beliefs about their jobs and the organization.

availability analysis Identifies the number of protected-class members available to work in the appropriate labor markets for given jobs.

B

balanced scorecard A framework used to report a diverse set of performance measures.

bargaining unit Employees eligible to select a single union to represent and bargain collectively for them.

base pay Basic compensation that an employee receives, usually as a wage or salary.

behavior modeling Copying someone else's behavior.

benchmark jobs Jobs found in many organizations that can be used for the purposes of comparison.

benchmarking Comparing the business results to industry standards.

benefit An indirect reward given to an employee or group of employees as part of membership in the organization.

bona fide occupational qualification (BFOQ) Characteristic providing a legitimate reason why an employer can exclude persons on otherwise illegal bases of consideration.

bonus One-time payment that does not become part of the employee's base pay.

broadbanding Practice of using fewer pay grades with much broader ranges than in traditional compensation systems.

burden of proof What individuals who file suit against employers must prove in order to establish that illegal discrimination has occurred.

business agent A full-time union official who operates the union office and assists union members.

business necessity A practice necessary for safe and efficient organizational operations.

C

career Series of work-related positions a person occupies throughout life.

career paths Represent employees' movements through opportunities over time.

cash balance plan Retirement program in which benefits are based on an accumulation of annual company contributions plus interest credited each year.

central tendency error Occurs when a rater gives all employees a score within a narrow range in the middle of the scale.

churn Hiring new workers while laying off others.

cognitive ability tests Tests that measure an individual's thinking, memory, reasoning, verbal, and mathematical abilities.

collective bargaining Process whereby representatives of management and workers negotiate over wages, hours, and other terms and conditions of employment.

commission Compensation computed as a percentage of sales in units or dollars.

compa-ratio Pay level divided by the midpoint of the pay range.

compensable factor Job value commonly present throughout a group of jobs within an organization.

competencies Individual capabilities that can be linked to enhanced performance by individuals or teams.

competency-based pay Rewards individuals for the capabilities they demonstrate and acquire.

complaint Indication of employee dissatisfaction.

compressed workweek A workweek in which a full week's work is accomplished in fewer than five 8-hour days.

conciliation Process by which a third party assists union and management negotiators to reach a voluntary settlement.

constructive discharge Process of deliberately making conditions intolerable to get an employee to quit.

consumer-driven health (CDH) plan Health plan that provides employer financial contributions to employees to help cover their own health-related expenses.

contingent worker Someone who is not an employee, but a temporary or part-time worker for a specific period of time and type of work.

contrast error Tendency to rate people relative to others rather than against performance standards.

contributory plan Pension plan in which the money for pension benefits is paid by both employees and the employer.

copayment Strategy of requiring employees to pay a portion of the cost of insurance premiums, medical care, and prescription drugs.

core competency A unique capability that creates high value and differentiates an organization from its competition.

cost-benefit analysis Comparison of costs and benefits associated with training.

craft union Union whose members do one type of work, often using specialized skills and training.

critical incident method The manager keeps a written record of both highly favorable and unfavorable actions performed by an employee during the entire rating period.

cross training Training people to do more than one job.

cumulative trauma disorders (CTDs) Muscle and skeletal injuries that occur when workers repetitively use the same muscles to perform tasks.

D

decertification Process whereby a union is removed as the representative of a group of employees.

defined-benefit plan Retirement program in which employees are promised a pension amount based on age and service.

defined-contribution pension plan Retirement program in which the employer makes an annual payment to an employee's pension account.

development Efforts to improve employees' abilities to handle a variety of assignments and to cultivate employees' capabilities beyond those required by the current job.

disabled person Someone who has a physical or mental impairment that substantially limits life activities, who has a record of such an impairment, or who is regarded as having such an impairment.

discharge When an employee is removed from a job at an employer.

discipline Form of training that enforces organizational rules.

disparate impact Occurs when members of a protected category are substantially underrepresented as a result of employment decisions that work to their disadvantage.

disparate treatment Occurs when members of a group are treated differently from others.

diversity Differences in human characteristics and composition in an organization.

draw Amount advanced against, and repaid from, future commissions earned by the employee.

dual-career ladder System that allows a person to advance up either a management or a technical/professional ladder.

due diligence A comprehensive assessment of all aspects of the business being acquired.

due process Requirement that the employer use a fair process to determine employee wrongdoing and that the employee have an opportunity to explain and defend his or her actions.

duty Work segment composed of several tasks that are performed by an individual.

E

electronic human resource management systems (e-HRM) The planning, implementation, and application of information technology to perform HR activities.

employee assistance program (EAP) Program that provides counseling and other help to employees having emotional, physical, or other personal problems.

employee stock ownership plan (ESOP) Plan designed to give employees significant stock ownership in their employers.

employment-at-will (EAW) Common-law doctrine stating that employers have the right to hire, fire, demote, or promote whomever they choose, unless there is a law or contract to the contrary.

employment contract Formal agreement that outlines the details of employment.

entitlement philosophy Assumes that individuals who have worked another year are entitled to pay increases, with little regard for performance differences.

environmental scanning The assessment of internal and external environmental conditions that affect the organization.

equity Perceived fairness between what a person does and what the person receives.

ergonomics Study and design of the work environment to address physical demands placed on individuals.

essay method The manager writes a short essay describing each employee's performance during the rating period.

exempt employees Employees who are not paid overtime.

expatriate A citizen of one country who is working in a second country and employed by an organization headquartered in the first country.

F

401(k) plan Agreement in which a percentage of an employee's pay is withheld and invested in a tax-deferred account.

federation Group of autonomous unions.

flexible benefits plan Program that allows employees to select the benefits they prefer from groups of benefits established by the employer.

flexible spending accounts Benefits plans that allow employees to contribute pretax dollars to fund certain additional benefits.

flextime Scheduling arrangement in which employees work a set number of hours a day but vary starting and ending times.

forced distribution Performance appraisal method in which ratings of employees' performance levels are distributed along a bell-shaped curve.

forecasting Using information from the past and the present to identify expected future conditions.

G

gainsharing System of sharing with employees greater-than-expected gains in profits and/or productivity.

graphic rating scale Scale that allows the rater to mark an employee's performance on a continuum.

green-circled employee Incumbent who is paid below the range set for a job.

grievance Complaint formally stated in writing.

grievance arbitration Means by which a third party settles disputes arising from different interpretations of a labor contract.

grievance procedures Formal channels of communication used to resolve grievances.

H

Halo effect Occurs when a rater scores an employee high on all job criteria because of performance in one area.

health General state of physical, mental, and emotional well-being.

health maintenance organization (HMO) Plan that provides services for a fixed period on a prepaid basis.

health promotion Supportive approach of facilitating and encouraging healthy actions and lifestyles among employees.

health reimbursement arrangement (HRA) Health plan in which the employer sets aside money in a health reimbursement account to help employees pay for qualified medical expenses.

health savings accounts (HSAs) High-deductible health plans with federal tax advantages.

host-country national A citizen of one country who is working in that country and employed by an organization headquartered in a second country.

hostile environment Sexual harassment in which an individual's work performance or psychological well-being is unreasonably affected by intimidating or offensive working conditions.

HR audit A formal research effort to assess the current state of HR practices.

HR metrics Specific measures tied to HR performance indicators.

human capital return on investment (HCROI) Directly shows the operating profit derived from investments in human capital.

human capital value added (HCVA) Calculated by subtracting all operating expenses *except* for labor expenses from revenue and dividing by the total full-time head count.

human economic value added (HEVA) Wealth created per employee.

human resource (HR) management Designing management systems to ensure that human talent is used effectively and efficiently to accomplish organizational goals.

human resource planning Process of analyzing and identifying the need for and availability of human resources so that the organization can meet its objectives.

I

illegal issues Collective bargaining issues that would require either party to take illegal action.

immediate confirmation Based on the idea that people learn best if reinforcement and feedback are given as soon as possible after training.

individual-centered career planning Career planning that focuses on an individual's responsibility for a career rather than on organizational needs.

industrial union Union that includes many persons working in the same industry or company, regardless of jobs held.

informal training Training that occurs through interactions and feedback among employees.

J

job analysis Systematic way of gathering and analyzing information about the content, context, and human requirements of jobs.

job description Identification of the tasks, duties, and responsibilities of a job.

job design Organizing tasks, duties, responsibilities, and other elements into a productive unit of work.

job duties Important elements in a given job.

job enlargement Broadening the scope of a job by expanding the number of different tasks to be performed.

job enrichment Increasing the depth of a job by adding responsibility for planning, organizing, controlling, or evaluating the job.

job evaluation Formal, systematic means to identify the relative worth of jobs within an organization.

job family Group of jobs having common organizational characteristics.

job rotation Process of shifting a person from job to job.

job satisfaction A positive emotional state resulting from evaluating one's job experiences.

job sharing Scheduling arrangement in which two employees perform the work of one full-time job.

job specifications The knowledge, skills, and abilities (KSAs) an individual needs to perform a job satisfactorily.

L

labor markets External supply pool from which organizations attract employees.

leniency error Occurs when ratings of all employees fall at the high end of the scale.

living wage Earnings that are supposed to meet the basic needs of an individual working for an organization.

lockout Shutdown of company operations undertaken by management to prevent union members from working.

lump-sum increase (LSI) One-time payment of all or part of a yearly pay increase.

M

managed care Approaches that monitor and reduce medical costs through restrictions and market system alternatives.

management by objectives (MBO) Performance appraisal method that specifies the performance goals that an individual and manager identify together.

management rights Rights reserved so that the employer can manage, direct, and control its business.

mandatory issues Collective bargaining issues identified specifically by labor laws or court decisions as subject to bargaining.

market banding Grouping jobs into pay grades based on similar market survey amounts.

market line Graph line that shows the relationship between job value as determined by job evaluation points and job value as determined by pay survey rates.

market pricing Use of market pay data to identify the relative value of jobs based on what other employers pay for similar jobs.

mediation Process by which a third party helps the negotiators reach a settlement.

motivation The desire within a person causing that person to act.

multinational corporation (MNC) A corporation that has facilities and other assets in at least one country other than its home country.

N

negligent hiring Occurs when an employer fails to check an employee's background and the employee injures someone on the job.

negligent retention Occurs when an employer becomes aware that an employee may be unfit for work but continues to employ the person, and the person injures someone.

nepotism Practice of allowing relatives to work for the same employer.

noncompete agreements Agreements that prohibit individuals who leave an organization from working with an employer in the same line of business for a specified period of time.

noncontributory plan Pension plan in which all the funds for pension benefits are provided by the employer.

nonexempt employees Employees who must be paid overtime.

O

offshoring The relocation by a company of a business process or operation from one country to another.

ombuds Individuals outside the normal chain of command who act as problem solvers for both management and employees.

open shop Firm in which workers are not required to join or pay dues to a union.

organizational commitment The degree to which employees believe in and accept organizational goals and desire to remain with the organization.

organizational culture The shared values and beliefs in an organization.

organizational mission The core reason for the existence of the organization and what makes it unique.

organization-centered career planning Career planning that focuses on identifying career paths that provide for the logical progression of people between jobs in an organization.

orientation Planned introduction of new employees to their jobs, coworkers, and the organization.

outsourcing Transferring the management and performance of a business function to an external service provider.

P

paid-time-off (PTO) plan Plan that combines all sick leave, vacation time, and holidays into a total number of hours or days that employees can take off with pay.

panel interview Interview in which several interviewers meet with candidate at the same time.

pay compression Occurs when the pay differences among individuals with different levels of experience and performance become small.

pay grades Groupings of individual jobs having approximately the same job worth.

pay survey Collection of data on compensation rates for workers performing similar jobs in other organizations.

pay-for-performance philosophy Requires that compensation changes reflect performance differences.

Peer review panels A committee of employees and managers whole resolve employment disputes when employees appeal disciplinary actions.

pension plan Retirement program established and funded by the employer and employees.

performance appraisal Process of determining how well employees do their jobs relative to a standard and communicating that information to them.

performance management Series of activities designed to ensure that the organization gets the performance it needs from its employees.

performance standards Indicators of what the job accomplishes and how performance is measured in key areas of the job description.

permissive issues Collective bargaining issues that are not mandatory and that relate to certain jobs.

perquisites (perks) Special benefits—usually noncash items—for executives.

person/job fit Matching the KSAs of individuals with the characteristics of jobs.

phased retirement Approach in which employees gradually reduce their workloads and pay levels.

physical ability tests Tests that measure an individual's abilities such as strength, endurance, and muscular movement.

placement Fitting a person to the right job.

policies General guidelines that focus organizational actions.

portability A pension plan feature that allows employees to move their pension benefits from one employer to another.

predictors of selection criteria Measurable or visible indicators of selection criteria.

preferred provider organization (PPO) A health care provider that contracts with an employer or an employer group to supply health care services to employees at a competitive rate.

primacy effect Occurs when a rater gives greater weight to information received first when appraising an individual's performance.

procedures Customary methods of handling activities.

productivity Measure of the quantity and quality of work done, considering the cost of the resources used.

profit sharing System to distribute a portion of the profits of an organization to employees.

protected category A group identified for protection under EEO laws and regulations.

psychological contract The unwritten expectations employees and employers have about the nature of their work relationships.

psychomotor tests Tests that measure dexterity, hand—eye coordination, arm—hand steadiness, and other factors.

Q

quid pro quo Sexual harassment in which employment outcomes are linked to the individual granting sexual favors.

R

ranking Performance appraisal method in which all employees are listed from highest to lowest in performance.

rater bias Occurs when a rater's values or prejudices distort the rating.

ratification Process by which union members vote to accept the terms of a negotiated labor agreement.

reasonable accommodation A modification to a job or work environment that gives a qualified individual an equal employment opportunity to perform.

recency effect Occurs when a rater gives greater weight to recent events when appraising an individual's performance.

recruiting Process of generating a pool of qualified applicants for organizational jobs.

red-circled employee Incumbent who is paid above the range set for a job.

reinforcement Based on the idea that people tend to repeat responses that give them some type of positive reward and avoid actions associated with negative consequences.

responsibilities Obligations to perform certain tasks and duties.

retaliation Punitive actions taken by employers against individuals who exercise their legal rights.

return on investment (ROI) Calculation showing the value of an investment.

right to privacy An individual's freedom from unauthorized and unreasonable intrusion into personal affairs.

rights Powers, privileges, or interests that belong to a person by law, nature, or tradition.

right-to-work laws State laws that prohibit requiring employees to join unions as a condition of obtaining or continuing employment.

risk management Involves responsibilities to consider physical, human, and financial factors to protect organizational and individual interests.

rules Specific guidelines that regulate and restrict the behavior of individuals.

S

sabbatical Time off the job to develop and rejuvenate oneself.

safety Condition in which the physical well-being of people is protected.

salaries Consistent payments made each period regardless of the number of hours worked.

salting Practice in which unions hire and pay people to apply for jobs at certain companies to begin organizing efforts.

security Protection of employees and organizational facilities.

security audit Comprehensive review of organizational security.

selection The process of choosing individuals with the correct qualifications needed to fill jobs in an organization.

selection criterion Characteristic that a person must possess to successfully perform work.

self-efficacy People's belief that they can successfully learn the training program content.

seniority Time spent in an organization or on a particular job.

serious health condition Health condition requiring in-patient, hospital, hospice, or residential medical care or continuing physician care.

severance pay Security benefit voluntarily offered by employers to individuals whose jobs are eliminated or who leave by mutual agreement with their employers.

sexual harassment Actions that are sexually directed, are unwanted, and subject the worker to adverse employment conditions or create a hostile work environment.

situational judgment tests Tests that measure a person's judgment in work settings.

statutory rights Rights based on laws or statutes passed by federal, state, or local governments.

stock option plan Plan that gives employees the right to purchase a fixed number of shares of company stock at a specified price for a limited period of time.

straight piece-rate system Pay system in which wages are determined by multiplying the number of units produced by the piece rate for one unit.

strategic planning The process of defining organizational strategy and allocating resources toward its achievement.

strategy An organization's proposition for how to compete successfully and thereby survive and grow.

stress interview Interview designed to create anxiety and put pressure on applicants to see how they respond.

strictness error Occurs when ratings of all employees fall at the low end of the scale.

strike Work stoppage in which union members refuse to work in order to put pressure on an employer.

structured interview Interview that uses a set of standardized questions asked of all applicants.

substance abuse Use of illicit substances or misuse of controlled substances, alcohol, or other drugs.

succession planning The process of identifying a plan for the orderly replacement of key employees.

T

task Distinct, identifiable work activity composed of motions.

team interview Interview in which applicants are interviewed by the team members with whom they will work.

telework Employees work with technology via electronic, telecommunications, and Internet means.

third-country national A citizen of one country who is working in a second country and employed by an organization headquartered in a third country.

total rewards Monetary and nonmonetary rewards provided by companies to attract, motivate, and retain employees.

training Process whereby people acquire capabilities to perform jobs.

turnover The process in which employees leave an organization and have to be replaced.

U

undue hardship Significant difficulty or expense imposed on an employer in making an accommodation for individuals with disabilities.

union Formal association of workers that promotes the interests of its members through collective action.

union authorization card Card signed by employees to designate a union as their collective bargaining agent.

union security provisions Contract clauses to help the union obtain and retain members.

union steward Employee elected to serve as the first-line representative of unionized workers.

unit labor cost Computed by dividing the average cost of workers by their average levels of output.

utilization analysis Identifies the number of protected-class members employed in the organization and the types of jobs they hold.

utilization review Audit of services and costs billed by health care providers.

V

variable pay Compensation linked to individual, group/team, and/or organizational performance.

vesting Right of employees to receive certain benefits from their pension plans.

W

wages Payments calculated directly from the amount of time worked by employees.

well pay Extra pay for not taking sick leave.

wellness programs Programs designed to maintain or improve employee health before problems arise.

whistle blowers Individuals who report real or perceived wrongs committed by their employers.

work sample tests Tests that require an applicant to perform a simulated task that is a specified part of the target job.

workers' compensation Security benefits provided to persons injured on the job.

wrongful discharge Termination of an individual's employment for reasons that are illegal or improper.

Index